THE
BLACK
HEAVENS

THE
BLACK
HEAVENS

Abraham Lincoln and Death

BRIAN R. DIRCK

Southern Illinois University Press • Carbondale

Southern Illinois University Press
www.siupress.com

22 21 20 19   4 3 2 1

Jacket illustration: *Mystery* (cropped), by Chris Heisey

LIBRARY OF CONGRESS CATALOGING-IN-
PUBLICATION DATA
Names: MacDonald, David, 1943– author. | Waters,
    Raine, author.
Title: Kaskaskia : the lost capital of Illinois / David
    MacDonald and Raine Waters.
Description: Carbondale : Southern Illinois
    University Press, 2019. | Series: Shawnee books |
    Includes bibliographical references and index.
Identifiers: LCCN 2018041357 | ISBN 9780809337316
    (paperback) | ISBN 9780809337323 (e-book)
Subjects: LCSH: Kaskaskia (Ill.)—History. | BISAC:
    history / United States / State & Local / Midwest
    (IA, IL, IN, KS, MI, MN, MO, ND, NE, OH, SD,
    WI). | social science / Regional Studies. | history
    / Social History. | architecture / Regional.
Classification: LCC F549.K3 M28 2019 |
    DDC 977.3/92—dc23 LC record available at
    https://lccn.loc.gov/2018041357

Printed on recycled paper. ♻

This paper meets the requirements of ANSI/NISO
Z39.48-1992 (Permanence of Paper) ∞

In memory of my mother, Dolores Ann Dirck (1944–2015)

CONTENTS

Gallery of illustrations beginning on page 107

ACKNOWLEDGMENTS

A book about death and mourning must necessarily bring to mind the loss of Phil Paludan, my mentor, advisor, and friend, an outstanding Lincoln and Civil War historian whom I still miss a great deal. How he carried himself as a scholar exercises a tremendous ongoing influence on me, and I hope I have been at least somewhat worthy of his example.

I must also profusely thank my editor at Southern Illinois University Press, Sylvia Frank Rodrigue. This was not an easy book to write or (I'm sure) edit, and Sylvia displayed her usual sense of humor, extraordinary patience, and care in helping me see it through to fruition. Both Sylvia and the rest of the very able staff at the press did heroic work in editing and preparing this project for publication. I would also like to express my deep gratitude to the anonymous peer reviewers who offered their excellent observations and saved me from numerous pitfalls and errors. I of course am solely responsible for any errors that remain.

I have been blessed with a congenial professional environment at Anderson University, where I have had the honor to teach for the last twenty years. My colleagues Dan Allen, Michael Frank, David Murphy, Abigail Post, Jaye Rogers, and Joel Shrock are actually more than that; they are valued friends. Our department secretary, Jan Bell, has also been of tremendous help, both in preparing this manuscript and in other professional matters. And I thank all my students, who have enriched my life in uncountable ways. I learn from them at least as much as they learn from me.

My father and my children have been, as always, forthcoming with their love and support, listening with admirable patience to my ramblings about my latest book project. This has probably been a more taxing matter than usual, given the dark subject matter contained in what they dubbed "the death book." I am grateful for their forbearance. I want to thank Lavada for her support, as well as the occasional "little push." I would also like to thank my friend and colleague Kris McCusker, professor of history at Middle Tennessee State University, who read early portions of the manuscript and offered valuable input.

In October 2013, we received the news that my mother had been diagnosed with stage 4 breast cancer. Her prospects were dim from the outset, and her suffering was painful for me and my family to watch. Yet for over a year she fought the disease with a forthrightness and bravery that impressed all who knew her. She passed away in February 2015, while I was in the process of writing this book. As a rule, historians are unwilling to admit that personal circumstances play a role in their research and writing: "the past for the past's sake," or so goes the saying. Yet honesty compels me to admit that my mother's lengthy illness and passing away played a role in how I approached the subject of Lincoln and death, though just how is not altogether clear, even to me. But I am certain that the experience of watching her difficult final months is in these pages. How could it be otherwise? I would like to think that in the end, this has not been a bad thing. My experience with my mother's death helped me better understand Lincoln's various experiences in this regard; or at least I hope so.

THE
BLACK
HEAVENS

INTRODUCTION: PHILADELPHIA, JUNE 16, 1864

"I suppose that this toast was intended to open the way for me to say something." People laughed. They would not have been altogether surprised that President Lincoln opened his speech with a little joke. By now, during what would be the war's last summer, they knew what to expect.

Accounts differ regarding who delivered the toast, either John Welsh, a prominent member of Philadelphia's charitable community, or Thomas H. Webster, a businessman and philanthropist who had founded a school for the education and training of African American soldiers. The banquet attracted many such dignitaries, including Edward Everett, the distinguished former governor of Massachusetts and president of Harvard, who eight months previously, along with Lincoln, had spoken at the dedication of Gettysburg's new cemetery. Many others were prominent members of the Sanitary Commission, the North's leading civilian private relief organization. The Sanitary Commission had organized the banquet as part of a fair that stretched through buildings covering all of Logan Square in downtown Philadelphia, mixing fund-raising, patriotic ceremonies, and laudatory pronouncements on the commission's good works.[1]

One newspaperman thought the fair offered a respite from the war's gloom. It was "some compensation for the dreadful scenes of our conflict," he wrote. "The war . . . has not, to us Philadelphians, seemed so palpably present, nor its horrors so lurid, since the Fair opened." The flag-bedecked buildings, the expressions of support for the army and the cause, and above all, the fact that the Sanitary Commission was dedicated not to violence and death, but rather to alleviation of the war's sufferings—providing comfort and medical care to the soldiers at the front—made it seem as if the commission had "smoothed down the sharper points of 'grim visage war,' and taught us that even where battle rages, there the kind and far-reaching charity of our Fair are felt."

Perhaps. Yet reminders of that deadly time persisted. In the vast main hall, where Lincoln stood to respond to his banquet toast, muskets, swords, pistols, bayonets, and other weaponry mixed with the festive sea of red, white, and blue flags, streamers, and bunting. The correspondent found the overall effect "charming," but however benevolent the fair's purpose, everyone knew that a war lurked behind the festivities.[2]

Lincoln knew. Men were dying, and he was squarely in the middle of it all. The day Lincoln arrived in Philadelphia, George Cutter, a Union soldier from Lawrence, Massachusetts, was killed in the trenches before Petersburg, Virginia. A sniper's bullet or cannon shot? The available records do not say. A Pennsylvania private named F. Roudenbush (the rolls do not give his full first name) also died that day, from wounds he had received nearly two weeks earlier at the Battle of Cold Harbor. Another private, Newton Dutcher from New Jersey, was mortally wounded at a little firefight in Pine Knob, Georgia; he would expire three weeks later. The death rolls were now so long.[3]

The laughter from Lincoln's little opening joke faded away. It is not hard to imagine a pause, as Lincoln looked at the many faces turned toward him. He did not know Dutcher, or Roudenbush, or Cutter. And yet he did. His smile—if he had one—dwindled. He looked old, with stooped shoulders, a weary, prematurely aged man.

"War, at the best, is terrible," he said, "and this war of ours, in its magnitude and in its duration, is one of the most terrible." He briefly cataloged the war's many material costs. "It has deranged business, totally in many localities, and partially in all localities," he noted. "It has destroyed property, and ruined homes; it has produced a national debt and taxation unprecedented, at least in this country."

The death toll came to mind: the graves by which he and Everett stood at Gettysburg, the windows and doors of countless American homes hung in black crepe, the wives and mothers and sisters clad in mourning dress, the strips of black cloth on the arms of bereaved fathers, brothers, and sons. A bit of black cloth adorned Lincoln's own stovepipe hat, in memory of his dead son, Willie, gone now for over two years. Black cloth, black crepe were everywhere; the White House itself was draped in black for Willie. Mary Lincoln wore nothing but black for at least a year after their child died; she may still have been clad in black when she and their youngest son, Tad, accompanied the president to Philadelphia. The war "has carried mourning to almost every home," he told the audience at the Sanitary Fair banquet, "until it can almost be said that the 'heavens are hung in black.'"[4]

He was borrowing from Shakespeare, quoting the opening lines of *Henry VI*'s funeral scene at Westminster Abbey, where the duke of Bedford spoke for the English nation at the mourning of their deceased and beloved king, Henry V, dead before his time at the relatively young age of thirty-six:

> Hung be the heavens with black, yield day to night!
> Comets, importing change of times and states,
> Brandish your crystal tresses in the sky,
> And with them scourge the bad revolting stars
> That have consented unto Henry's death![5]

Lincoln always appreciated a poetic turn of phrase. He would have liked Shakespeare's pairing of mourning with the sanguinity of "the heavens," of brightness bedimmed with a nationwide misery so profound that almost—just almost—the timeless stars themselves seemed faded and worn. The combination of death's darkness and starlit hope would have appealed to this man, at once so oddly sad yet optimistic, leading his nation through the worst bloodletting in its history but also toward a "new birth of freedom," a future liberated from the human bondage that had stained the United States since the days of its founding. America was, as he famously put it, the "last best hope of earth." Yet that hope was scarred with graves.

He had seen many a grave long before the war. He knew death and dying from an early age, having experienced as a boy the painful deaths of his mother, sister, and a young woman named Ann Rutledge and later the passing of two of his four boys and the Civil War's ungodly carnage. Along the way, Lincoln interpreted and reinterpreted dying in ways that were at once both typical of other Americans of his time and unique to his own singular personality.

It is a curiously unexplored story, curious because death might easily vie with emancipation and restoration of the Union as one of the great central truths of Lincoln's life. Death frequently appears in the vast Lincoln literature, but rarely as a subject of study in its own right. Even the growing historical literature on the experience of death during the Civil War era has left Abraham Lincoln's own personal encounters with death largely unexplored.

Or perhaps it is not so curious, for whereas Lincoln spoke at length about emancipation and the Union, leaving a large cache of his own words on those subjects for historians to mine for clues, he spoke less directly about his understanding of death and its attendant meanings. Death seeps around the edges of some of his famous wartime speeches and letters, with occasional references to the black heavens and the like but little else, and he was still more reticent about the ways in which he processed internally the deaths of his children, loved ones, and friends. Exploring Lincoln's understanding of death admittedly requires a fair amount of conjecture and educated guesswork.

Moreover, there is a mystical, overwrought quality to the depictions of Lincoln and death in American popular culture. Scholars, novelists, and artists have long been fascinated with what we might term the haunted Lincoln—Lincoln the tragic figure, weighed down by the spiritual burdens of death, reacting always with extraordinary pathos to the dying that surrounds him. He walks the hallways of the White House sleepless in the night, he picks his way carefully among the bodies as he tours a Civil War battlefield, he is always (to borrow from the title of a recent novel) Lincoln in the Bardo, communing with the ghosts of the dead.

Lincoln would probably have been perplexed by all this. While he was mildly superstitious, his dominant intellectual trait was fidelity to what he called the need for ideas "hewn from the solid quarry of sober reason." He was far more given to rationalism than superstition, rarely spoke of ghosts or other manifestations of the spirit world, and in general confronted the problems of death and dying with the same pragmatism that guided other aspects of his life. Certainly he underwent emotional distress and anguish at the losses he suffered, both privately and as the leader of the nation during a horrendous civil war. But his private anguish was just one aspect of a larger, more complicated picture, one composed not only of suffering but also of the ostensibly more mundane matters of social and cultural norms, and even what might be called the politics of death.

What we see when we map the entirety of Lincoln's encounters with death is not a steady immersion into pathos and ghostly haunting, but rather much the opposite. From the time when, as a child, he watched his mother undergo a painful ordeal of suffering and dying in the Indiana wilderness, Lincoln learned to approach death and mourning from a detached and rational perspective. He of course felt pangs of emotion when he buried his loved ones and during the early days of the war, when he mourned the deaths in battle of close friends and acquaintances. He also increasingly turned to God and religion as the war's casualty lists lengthened. He never downplayed the war's terrible human cost.

But he learned ways to separate himself emotionally from death while president. He learned to accept death as a necessary price to pay for the Union and for the freedom that he always believed the Union, properly understood, embodied and exemplified. And this acceptance entailed a gradual shift away from any sentimental or hyperemotional engagement with dying and mourning.

How could it have been otherwise? How else could he have sent Dutcher, Cutter, Roudebush, and many thousands of other young men to their death? To have lost himself in the sea of death that was the Civil War, to have dwelt overlong on that war's nearly unfathomable human cost, would have been to risk drowning, to risk his ability to make decisions and lead a war-ravaged nation, possibly even to risk his very sanity.

How he avoided this, how he handled death—as a son, father, and husband, and as a politician and president—is a story worth examining in its own right. When we watch Lincoln negotiate his black heavens, we learn more about him, his character, and the grim times in which he lived.

1. GOOD DEATH

Nancy was tired, suffering from a deep, bone-weary sort of fatigue. This in itself was not unusual. She knew weariness, knew it all too well. But this was something deeper and different. Nancy's death began with this particular tiredness.

She was thirty-four in the fall of 1818, having lived to that point an unremarkable and weather-beaten life. She grew up in Virginia and later Kentucky, getting by as a seamstress and living with various relatives and employers. Rumors later circulated that she was of a "low character," but these seem to have been baseless. Most people who knew her were struck by her stoicism, a sort of gentle and persistent doggedness. She was by all accounts unassuming and intelligent, "amiable and kind," and not someone who complained much.[1]

She was living in Elizabethtown, Kentucky, when she met and married Thomas Lincoln, a man of equally humble origins and means. Thomas lost his father to a Shawnee bullet during a raid on the family farm in western Virginia when he was eight years old. He narrowly escaped capture himself; a Shawnee warrior grabbed Thomas and ran, only to be shot and mortally wounded by Thomas's older brother Mordecai. The Shawnee dropped the terrified little boy (who was screaming, "Don't kill me! Take me prisoner!") and staggered away into the woods. He was tracked by his blood trail to a tree, within which was tangled his lifeless body, where perhaps he had been trying to scramble to hide from pursuers.[2]

Thomas thereafter struggled mightily to get by. He lived with his widowed mother in Kentucky in "very narrow circumstances," according to his son, and made do with farm labor, odd jobs, and carpentry skills he learned from a relative. He was almost entirely illiterate, somewhat hapless, and although industrious, he was not one who could ever be described as "successful"—a "piddler," remembered a neighbor, someone who was "always doing but doing nothing great."[3]

They lived a hard life in a hard world, did Thomas and Nancy Lincoln. Physically, they were quite different—Thomas was stout and rock-ribbed, Nancy thin and delicately framed—but on a more subtle level, they were much the same. They were like a couple of tough trees, barely noticed by most of the people around them, their chief accomplishment in life simply remaining upright.[4]

Worried about shaky land titles—Kentucky was notorious for its bad record keeping—and Thomas not being enamored of slavery, they left the state in the fall of 1816 with their two children, Sarah and Abraham, and cousin Dennis Hanks; piled their belongings aboard a ferry; and made their way across the Ohio River into Indiana. They found a likely spot to settle a few miles north of the river, in Spencer County, and if Kentucky was undeveloped and rural, Indiana was utterly primitive—a "wild region," Abraham later wrote.[5]

Indiana's early settlers ran the constant risk of attack by the area's teeming wildlife: bears, wild boar, various types of wildcats, panthers, and the like. A boar could weigh more than two hundred pounds and possessed razor-sharp teeth. They would "attack people when hard pressed," noted an observer, and were capable of inflicting severe injuries. Panthers were the most terrifying of all. Stories made the rounds in early Indiana about people caught suddenly unarmed or unawares by one of these sleek, deadly predators. Not long before the Lincolns' arrival, the young child of a new emigrant family from Tennessee unwisely wandered away from her family's settlement. A search party went looking for her in the thick underbrush. They "had gone nearly a quarter of a mile before they heard the most terrible scream of a panther mingled with the outcry of the unfortunate girl. . . . [And] coming to an open space, they saw several animals which were biting and scratching at the body of the girl they killed." These animals were a panther mother and her two young kittens. "After she had killed the girl, [the mother panther] was teaching the young ones how to attack their prey, and she would bound onto the prostrate form and bite and scratch it. The kittens would go through the same motions, and thus had torn [the little girl] to pieces."[6]

This sort of death, of the flesh-rending, pitiless variety, surrounded the Lincolns from the moment they arrived in Spencer County. It is not difficult to imagine a wide-eyed Abraham Lincoln, only seven years old when he and his family arrived, overhearing tales of ugly deaths visited upon people, even children his age, by bears, panthers, "Indians," and the very landscape itself, all blended together in the early American mind as the "frontier" and the "wilderness." Later in life, when as an adult he tried his hand at poetry, Lincoln referenced this very thing, writing in "The Bear Hunt":

> When first my father settled here,
> 'Twas then the frontier line:
> The panther's scream, filled night with fear
> And bears preyed on the swine.[7]

People brushed elbows with deadly things on the "frontier line," and Abraham Lincoln did not forget it. He never romanticized his boyhood experiences in the Indiana wilderness, never pretended that Indiana did not have razor-sharp edges of all kinds, edges that maimed and killed.[8]

Food was an ongoing challenge. Thomas and his family relied on hunting, a common enough approach in a place like Indiana. "We all hunted pretty much all the time," Dennis remembered. "The country was full of wild game, dense with vegetation [and] swampy. We could track a bear, deer, [or] wolf . . . for miles through the matted pea vines. . . . We more or less depended on it for a living."[9]

The hunting that Dennis so matter-of-factly described was a messy and dangerous affair. Once shot, a wild animal—say, a bear or a deer—might well require tracking as it lurched off through Indiana's thick underbrush, leaving a blood trail for the hunter to follow, sometimes with gory results. A hunter in Morgan County, Indiana, set his dog to following the blood drops of a deer he had wounded with his musket. Following along behind, the hunter came to an open area in the woods that was "torn to pieces and beaten flat," according to the story's chronicler, "and near the center lay the wounded deer, dead, and terribly torn, and near it was the old dog, covered with blood and bruised, and torn almost in pieces by the sharp hoofs and antlers of the desperate deer."[10]

Bears were particularly risky prey. Two young boys stalking bear and deer in the area around Newburgh, Indiana, encountered a mother bear with her two cubs; they shot and badly wounded one of the cubs and chased off the other cub and the mother. When they laid down their muskets and tried to finish the dying cub with their knives, the mother bear reappeared, setting off a mad melee in the brush. One boy reached for his gun and shot the bear as it mauled his brother, breaking his brother's arm, but the shot only enraged the mother bear still further, and it then turned on the shooter and chewed up his legs. "The boy with the broken arm stabbed the bear many times with his hunting knife and finally hurt it fatally." Even so, the mother tried to follow after the cubs "but had only gone about a hundred yards when it laid down and died."[11]

Anyone who hunted in the Little Pigeon Creek area—including Lincoln's father (who loved hunting), Dennis himself, neighbors, and friends—was immersed in a violent, blood-soaked exercise. Freshly slain animals exuded copious amounts of blood and other bodily fluids, as well as strong and unpleasant smells. It is not difficult to imagine Thomas or Dennis toiling away over the bloody remains of a slain animal, partially immersed in the animal's blood, grunting and sweating as they tried to push a knife through tough gristle or muscle or saw their way through a stubborn hunk of bone, the animal's entrails lying in a heap nearby, steam rising from the rapidly cooling corpse of what had until recently been a living, breathing animal.

Abraham surely accompanied his father and cousin on some of these hunting excursions during their early days in Indiana. In "The Bear Hunt," he described the killing of a bear by hunters with a vividness that suggests he was an eyewitness to such scenes:

> Bang,—bang—the rifles go.
> And furious now, the dogs he tears,
> And crushes in his ire.
> Wheels right and left, and upward rears,
> With eyes of burning fire.
> But leaden death is at his heart,

9

Vain all the strength he plies.
And, spouting blood from every part,
He reels, and sinks, and dies.[12]

Right after they arrived at Little Pigeon Creek, Abraham spotted a flock of turkeys nearby. Thomas and Dennis were away from camp at the time, and Abraham was too little to load and prime a gun himself, so Nancy had to do it. "Abe poked the gun through the crack of the camp and accidentally killed one," Dennis recalled.[13]

But that was the extent of his direct involvement in slaying an animal for food. He later wrote that he had "never since pulled a trigger on any larger game."[14] He disliked hunting, which was an unusual trait, especially among young boys of his time and place. More generally, he did not much like killing in the boyish sense of torturing and slaying the animals that were everywhere in the Indiana woods. One neighbor recalled him writing essays "on bein cind to animals and crawling insects." When his stepbrother captured a turtle and crushed it against a tree, Abraham "preached against cruelty to animals, contending that an ant's life was to it as sweet as ours to us."[15]

Friends and neighbors called this "tender-heartedness," which was accurate enough. But one wonders if there was more to this than an unusual squeamishness. As a young boy, the most common way Abraham Lincoln encountered death was in this manner: the pain and death of animals, large and small, in the Indiana wilderness, something he would have seen and heard and felt on a nearly daily basis. These were forms of death that his Hoosier neighbors took as ordinary living, the white noise background of frontier life. His cousin Dennis and his father seem never to have given a second thought to putting a bullet into a deer or a bear, plunging a hunting knife into the quivering belly of a mortally wounded animal, or tearing open its innards to field dress and prepare it for a future meal. But the young Abraham Lincoln did give it a second thought. He recoiled at the idea of inflicting pain and death, and he seems to have felt the need to put it all at arm's length.

Sometime in the early fall of 1818, his mother, Nancy, walked the short distance from the family's little cabin to another, even smaller structure: what Dennis called a "half-face camp"—really just a glorified lean-to—which had served as the family's first home until they constructed a better cabin nearby. But the little half-face camp had not stood empty for long; soon after the Lincolns moved, it was reoccupied by Nancy's aunt Elizabeth and her husband, Thomas Sparrow, two important people in Nancy's early life. She had lived with the Sparrows for a period of time while younger, and by some accounts, she felt close enough to refer to them as "mother" and "father." They were probably following in Nancy and Thomas's footsteps, living in the half-face camp until they could acquire a place and land of their own.[16]

Cows wandered about freely in the Little Pigeon Creek area, eating what they could, and at some point a cow owned by someone in the area ate a particular species of plant called by locals "snakeroot" for its propensity to grow in shaded areas where snakes lurked. It had other names as well: "deerwort," "Indian weed," and "squaw weed." Usually around three feet tall, snakeroot sprouted clusters of small white flowers in the late summer or fall, releasing fluffy spores that blew into the breeze and propagated the species.[17]

Snakeroot did not grow in the East, so while it was familiar to the Shawnee and other Native Americans in the area—as suggested by some of its names—it was a new type of plant to most Indiana settlers, and they knew little of its properties. Nor did the science of the time afford much help; it did not tell Hoosiers that snakeroot contains the toxic compound tremetol. Tasteless and odorless, when ingested by humans, it was usually fatal.[18]

A cow in the Little Pigeon Creek area ate some snakeroot, attracted by its bright green and white coloring at a time of the year when most of the surrounding foliage was fading into dull brown. Soon thereafter, the tremetol began churning away inside the cow, creating in its milk an undetectable toxin. Possibly the animal was owned by the Sparrows, but it might also have been owned by Peter and Nancy Brooner, a German couple that lived nearby with their children, or by any of a number of other settlers in the Little Pigeon Creek area.[19]

Both the Sparrows and Nancy Brooner fell ill with what was called the "milk sickness." Symptoms varied from person to person, but milk sickness generally caused victims to lose their energy and drive, feel a soreness and stiffness in their muscles and limbs, and suffer intense abdominal cramps. Soon the Sparrows and Nancy Brooner would have begun to vomit repeatedly, accompanied by painful constipation as the tremetol ate its way into the fatty deposits in their livers and kidneys. Visitors to their cabins would have noticed a foul smell coming from their breath.[20]

No one in 1818 understood disease pathology; they knew people fell ill from drinking milk, but they did not understand that the cause of their suffering was not so much the milk itself, but rather a plant and a cow's digestive habits. Nor did they understand that dairy products derived from tainted milk, such as butter and cheese, could also prove fatal, as could the meat of animals that had consumed tremetol-laced substances. The victims who took ill from the "milk sickness" may not have actually drunk milk, and they may not have owned the cow from which the poison originated; trading food products was a common practice in an Indiana frontier community. One observer later remembered that "the Milk Sick was very prevalent among the Setlers this year (1818), nearly all that were attacked with it deid," suggesting that the Brooners and Nancy Sparrow were part of a larger outbreak.[21]

On learning of her neighbors' and her family's misfortune, Nancy Lincoln did what she could to ease their suffering. This was no small undertaking. Nancy was busy raising two young children on a fledgling backwoods farm; she would have possessed little spare time, still less so as she trekked back and forth among her cabin, the half-face camp, and the Brooners' place.

Maybe she was administering water-thinned milk (a recommended treatment at the time) and drank some herself. Or perhaps she ate a tainted dairy or meat product. She might have reached for a bit of bread and butter while tending to Mrs. Brooner in her cabin or eaten beef from freshly slaughtered (and tainted) cattle. If the disease followed its usual path, she would have felt tired and sore at first—nothing altogether alarming, an expected consequence of working so hard. But soon thereafter, the stomach cramps, the intestinal problems, and vomiting would have begun, along with the growing terrible realization that she would now share in the Sparrows and Nancy Brooner's suffering—and their eventual fate.

"She struggled on day by day," Dennis later recalled. No one who witnessed this would subsequently record any hint of emotional distress on Nancy's part. Possibly she was visibly and openly traumatized by her impending doom, and her friends and loved ones chose for reasons of decorum and respect to avoid noting the fact. But it seems more likely that Nancy Lincoln coped with her death as she had always coped with her life: quietly and with a resigned acceptance of her lot.[22]

Eventually she was bedridden and laid up in the little Lincoln cabin, no longer able to help the Sparrows, Mrs. Brooner, or anyone else. At least one neighbor, a man named William Wood, remembered sitting up with Nancy all night as she lay dying. No doubt others came to her aid as well.[23]

"She knew she was going to die," Dennis said, and she "called up the children to her dying side and told them to be good and kind to their father, to one another and to the world." She then "express[ed] a hope that they might live as they had been taught by her, to love men, and [to] love, reverence and worship God." Thus passed away, Dennis remarked, "one of the very best women of the whole race."[24]

Dennis was an old man when he recalled these events. His memory of Nancy's death was not necessarily inaccurate, but it would have been filtered by the passage of time and by the accepted cultural norms of what historian Drew Gilpin Faust termed the "Good Death," the fixation of nineteenth-century Americans on the need to die well. This meant either expressing repentance for a wicked life as it neared its end or imparting final advice and exhortation to loved ones to follow the dying person's example for a life well lived. "Sometimes a bad life may be attended with a good death," wrote one clergyman, "but where a godly and gracious life hath gone before, there a good death must of necessity follow."[25]

There were commonly accepted forms of the Good Death: a domestic setting (it was important that a person died at home), pious recognition of the supremacy of God's will, and appropriate last words. The Good Death was an act of cleansing, a sanitizing of death's more foul and revolting aspects. It was acceptance: people dying a Good Death did not rave, rant, or scream; they did not even seem to be in much pain. Perhaps most of all, the Good Death created a moral to one's life story; it suffused death with a sense of purpose and a logic that ordered and gave grace to something as seemingly random as milk sickness.[26]

Dennis's little vignette contained all the hallmarks of the Good Death: the saintly, rapidly expiring mother, exhorting the children whom she would never see again to follow the precepts she had set forth for Christian kindness, piety, and filial duty. Anyone hearing Dennis's tale would have quickly recognized his story's basic features, for it was a common narrative, applied as a balm to the emotional wounds of grieving family members.

Nancy's passing could not have been the peaceful and clean death she might have wished for herself or Dennis would have us believe. Even assuming everything he said was true, the fact remains that she was lying in a "rude cabin" (Dennis's words) only slightly removed from the "wilderness" and its entirely unromantic muck and violence and filth, where wild animals killed and died, where death was a nasty, natural fact of life. A Good Death was a rare thing in Little Pigeon Creek.[27]

Abraham probably saw the first symptoms in his mother only a day or so after she began trekking back and forth to the half-face camp and the Brooners' cabin. Exactly what he felt and experienced as a nine-year-old boy, watching his mother exhibit the symptoms that everyone around him must have noted with growing alarm signaled her imminent death, is unknown and unknowable, but children in similar circumstances share characteristics from which we can generalize. Children who lose a parent at an early age often wrestle with conflicting emotions they are ill equipped to control. An impotent sort of anger at what seems an unfair loss is common, as is a general sense of helplessness and foreboding about the future. Most of all, children of a dying parent experience a loss of security and comfort. Parents typically offer their young children a sense of permanence—in Lincoln's case, a mother who was always present and supplied his daily needs as he grew up in Kentucky and Indiana—that death would now sever. The presence of a healthy remaining parent (like Thomas Lincoln) matters a great deal, for bereaved children require guidance from the adults in their lives to help lessen the shock and provide reassurance.[28]

The historical record regarding Lincoln's childhood is so barren that we have no way of knowing how Abraham reacted to his mother's fatal illness. No reliable contemporary descriptions exist of Abraham Lincoln as a boy; reminiscences from older people like Dennis Hanks, recorded long after the fact, are all we have, and these are often little more than bromides describing Abraham as a nearly perfect boy. No one recorded how he reacted to his mother's illness and death, whether he lashed out in frustration, kept his turmoil buried deep inside, or exhibited some other form of behavior.

From what we do know regarding his later personality traits, it seems likely that Abraham tended more to bury his emotions rather than openly act on any inner feelings of rage, helplessness, or despair. This is merely an educated guess, and we should be careful in extrapolating from Lincoln the adult too many assumptions regarding Lincoln the child. But people who knew him later in life agreed that he was generally an undemonstrative sort, not given to revealing his emotions: "shut pan," as Lincoln described himself.[29]

Nor can we know whether Thomas or any of the other adults around Abraham helped him cope with his mother's situation. He and his father were not close, so it seems unlikely that Thomas offered his young son much in the way of guidance or emotional support. His sister, Sarah, was a child of eleven, and Dennis was only nineteen and likely undergoing his own inner turmoil at the deaths of not only his aunt Nancy but also the Sparrows, with whom he had been living when they became ill. Adult neighbors might have been of some comfort to Abraham—the aforementioned William Wood, who sat up with Nancy and to whom Abraham felt close enough to call him "Uncle," although they weren't related—but many of these people had sick friends and relatives of their own to care for, with the widespread outbreak of milk sickness in the area.[30]

Abraham probably endured a sort of quiet, inner desolation as he watched his mother, the woman from whom "Abe got his mind and his fixed morals," according to Wood, grow steadily weaker. The very silence of the historical record suggests as much; friends and relatives who later recalled in some detail the circumstances surrounding Nancy's illness and death had nothing to say, good or bad, about her young son's reaction. Dennis remembered that at the time, both Abraham and his sister, Sarah, "did some work, little jobs, errand[s] and light work." But neither Dennis nor anyone else recorded how exactly Abraham reacted emotionally to the ordeal. Very possibly he faded into the background, nursing a private grief while his father and other family members and friends were preoccupied with easing Nancy's final days. Lincoln later remembered this time as an exceedingly lonely episode in his life, and some historians have theorized that Lincoln's adult bouts of melancholy and depression stemmed from this experience.[31]

If Thomas Lincoln tried to help his son, he would have done so via the Bible and his faith. He was a religious man and had been at least since Abraham's birth in Kentucky. Thomas and Nancy adhered to a particular strain of Baptist thought, whose followers were variously called "Separate" or "Hardshell" Baptists. This group emphasized predestination, the Calvinist idea that one's fate is predetermined at birth. This fatalism could serve many purposes, including a ready explanation for a sudden, tragic death such as that which was befalling Nancy. It was God's inscrutable will, part of a grand divine plan. There was solace in such an idea, and maybe Thomas or some other adult tried to explain what was happening to Abraham in such terms.[32]

Whatever the theological leanings of his faith, Thomas could count on little in the way of a church social network, for the Little Pigeon Creek community was too new and too small. The local Baptists numbered around forty people, and they did not yet have a regular minister or a church building.

The Little Pigeon Creek Baptist Church would not be completed until several years after Nancy's death; Thomas would loan his carpentry skills to the project.[33]

It is therefore not surprising that Nancy's funeral was a perfunctory affair, stripped bare of all but the most basic trappings. Given the pall of death from the milk sickness that claimed several victims in the area, no one seems to have possessed much energy for conducting anything more than a rudimentary service. "There was scarcely enough will in the neighborhood that fall to Bury those that deid," recalled a neighbor. Thomas fashioned a simple coffin of green wood, which he and his neighbors loaded onto a makeshift sled and dragged up a small knoll to a grove of persimmon trees. A Kentucky minister named David Elkin conducted the funeral service; he was a friend of the Lincoln family and happened to be visiting the Little Pigeon Creek area at the time. No one thought to record what he said or whether anything else occurred—the singing of a hymn, for example. After shoveling dirt on the coffins, Nancy Brooner's husband, Peter, who had buried his wife a week earlier, shook Thomas Lincoln's hand, remarking, "We are brothers now."[34]

That was it: a small gathering around a gravesite dug atop an isolated hill in the southern Indiana woods, some fitting words spoken by the local minister, and a handshake with a fellow bereaved farmer. Abraham was surely present—he probably helped push the sled carrying his mother's body up to the gravesite—but exactly what he did or how he behaved that day is unknown.[35]

Unlike Dennis, he never sentimentalized his mother's passing, never pasted over the affair with a Good Death tale. If he saw any meaning in Nancy's passing or its circumstances, he never recorded the fact. Referring briefly in a letter many years later to his mother's final resting place, he observed that it was "as unpoetical as any spot of the earth." Otherwise, he barely mentioned Nancy's death at all, just a brief, dry reference in one campaign autobiography he wrote (in the third person): "In the autumn of 1818 his mother died."[36]

Nor did he comment much on the other major family loss he endured while growing up in Indiana: the death of his older sister, Sarah, in 1828 from complications related to childbirth. Variously described as "good humored," "industrious," and "quick minded," Sarah was thickset (like her father) with dark hair and complexion (like her mother). She was eleven years old—two years older than her little brother—when their mother died.[37]

Eight years later, she married a neighbor named Aaron Grigsby, part of the large Grigsby clan that lived nearby. They settled into the farming life, and Sarah soon became pregnant. She went into labor one cold wintry night in early January 1828, in the cabin she shared with her husband, not far from the Lincoln family home.

What happened next was a dreadful ordeal. The delivery went badly awry, with some unidentified complication sinking Sarah into the depths of nearly unendurable pain. A neighbor woman later remembered her calling in agony for her father, who heard her screams and woke Abraham and Dennis, saying "something is the matter." Thomas then went after a doctor, but he was too late. "They let her lay too long," thought the neighbor. Sarah gave birth to a stillborn son and then died herself, either during the birth or shortly afterward.[38]

As with so much else surrounding Abraham Lincoln's early life, we have little information regarding precisely what happened to Sarah and her baby. There seems to have been a midwife present (the aforementioned neighbor's aunt), and Aaron was nearby, though typically fathers did not attend childbirths. While one account has Thomas sending for a doctor, another has Aaron growing alarmed at his wife's labor pains, hitching a team of oxen to a sleigh, and driving her to his father's house three-quarters of a mile away, a panicky decision that did his suffering wife no good, as the rig careened "over snags and rough ground, with every jolt sharpening Sarah's labor pains." When he reached his family's house, Aaron then sent for a doctor, but the doctor was so drunk they were forced to find a second doctor, who lived far away and did not arrive before it was too late.[39]

Which story is accurate and what exactly went wrong is impossible to determine. A stillbirth could result from a number of possible causes: one of various congenital birth defects that fatally distressed the baby prior to labor, an issue with the umbilical cord being wrapped around the baby's neck or exiting before the baby, or possibly a blockage in the baby's oxygen supply causing it to suffocate. Letting Sarah "lay too long" suggests there was an issue with extracting the baby that eventually proved fatal, though again we do not know exactly what letting her "lay too long" meant.[40]

Sarah experienced even less of a Good Death than her mother—a painful and probably gory ordeal on a hard winter's night, leavened by no sentimental scenes of last rituals or soft words. She and her child were buried together in the Little Pigeon Creek Baptist Church's cemetery, the son's body wrapped in the mother's arms. According to several accounts, Abraham grieved for the death of his sister. He "sat down on a log and hid his face in his hands while the tears rolled down," remembered one observer. Local tradition had it that Abraham felt not only grief but anger toward Aaron and his family, holding them responsible for allowing Sarah to suffer too long. There may well be some truth to this, for Abraham did nurture a grudge toward the Grigsbys, fed according to one neighbor by Aaron's "cruel treatment of his wife."[41]

"Cruel" is also an apt word to describe Lincoln's Indiana childhood. In later years, he occasionally referenced his frontier roots by way of illustrating that he was no stranger to either hard work or manual labor, but he did not sugarcoat those years with the traditional American rags-to-riches story of the poor boy who made good. Indiana was instead for Lincoln more about perseverance in the face of the capricious deaths of his mother and sister. It was not so much about success as survival—his survival, when others close to him perished.

He was nineteen when his sister died, a big, gangling, and restless young man who by now wanted badly to leave Little Pigeon Creek. He finally made his escape in 1831, after the entire family had relocated to equally primitive circumstances on a farm in eastern Illinois. He wandered into the village of New Salem, where he settled into a life pursuing odd jobs—manual laborer, postman, store clerk, surveyor—which at best "procured bread, and kept soul and body together," as Lincoln later put it.[42]

Sometime soon after he arrived, Lincoln met Ann Rutledge, the teenage daughter of a New Salem innkeeper with whom Lincoln boarded. Ann was "amiable," "a good looking, smart, lively girl," according to neighbors, with fair hair and eyes and a lively disposition. She was also "a good housekeeper, with a moderate education," having had a bit of schooling in nearby Jacksonville.[43]

At some point, Abraham and Ann apparently struck up a romantic relationship. The entire affair is shrouded in mystery and a lack of solid primary source evidence. According to the best available accounts, Ann was engaged to marry another man named John McNamar, but he had left the New Salem area, and after a prolonged absence, Ann was uncertain whether he would return. She seems to have subsequently agreed to marry Lincoln. But before they could do so, typhoid fever swept through the area. It killed Ann's father, and she died on August 25, 1835.[44]

Some people later claimed that Abraham went nearly insane with grief. "The effect upon Mr. Lincoln's mind was terrible," recalled Ann's brother Robert. "He became plunged in despair, and many of his friends feared that reason would desert him." Others noted that he became "temporarily deranged," to the point that his friends felt compelled to remove sharp objects from his presence. One neighbor remembered that "Lincoln was locked up by his friends . . . to prevent derangement or suicide."[45]

Some thought that Lincoln was ever after "changed and sad." These stories of Lincoln's lifelong grief extended even into his later years as president. According to Isaac Cogdal, a New Salem friend who later visited the White House, Lincoln still mourned his lost love, even during the war. "'Abe is it true that you fell in love with and courted Ann Rutledge?'" Cogdal recalled the conversation. "'It is true, true indeed I did,'" Lincoln is supposed to have replied. "'I have loved the name of Rutledge to this day. . . . I did honestly and truly love the girl and think often, often of her now.'"[46]

But aside from such reminiscences, recorded after Lincoln's death and many years after he left New Salem, there is no direct record of Lincoln's reaction to Ann Rutledge's death. He never mentioned or alluded to her, or even hinted at any relationship with her in any extant letter or speech. This absence of direct evidence, along with the various biases and idiosyncrasies of William Herndon—Lincoln's former law partner, who gathered nearly all the available information regarding Ann and who first broached the idea of a romance between her and Abraham—has led some historians to doubt whether any such romance existed.[47]

Given the multiple eyewitness accounts, it seems a stretch to suggest that Abraham and Ann were not romantically involved at all, and thus it is reasonable to conclude that when she died, Lincoln was distraught with grief. But those two simple, hard nuggets of truth, the romance and the grief, have long been heavily swathed in multiple layers of syrupy sentimentality. Tales of Ann's flawless character and beauty ("she was beloved by everybody and everybody respected and loved her, so sweet and angelic was she") and Lincoln's bottomless sorrow have been piled upon still more tales, to the point that friends, fawning biographers, and even Hollywood added in later years improbable details that beggar belief: that the real cause of Ann's death was her conflicted heart over Lincoln and his rival, John McNamar; that Lincoln never carried a pocketknife after her death for fear of the sudden impulse to injure himself on recollection of her tragic demise; that his grieving was suddenly triggered by violent weather ("we watched during storms, fogs [and] damp gloomy weather Mr. Lincoln for fear of an accident").[48]

In its way, this Ann Rutledge myth is yet another iteration of the Good Death. Where Nancy was the pious Christian mother imparting last words of wisdom to her children, Ann was the star-crossed lover, the flower cut short before its full bloom, robbing her beau of his chance at eternal marital bliss and ever after giving him thoughts of gloom and worse, triggered by the gothic detail of a thunderstorm. "I can never be reconcile[d] to have the snow, rains and storms to beat on her grave," he is supposed to have declared. Another friend believed that he avoided using the word *love* after Ann died, his heart "sad and broken."[49]

In fact, Ann's passing could not have been such a Good Death, any more than was Nancy Lincoln's endless puking in that smoke-filled cabin, or Sarah Lincoln Grigsby's grisly stillbirth on a miserable winter night. Typhoid was a terrible way to die, its symptoms not all that different from those of milk sickness. Caused by a bacterial infection resulting from the contamination of drinking water with human feces, typhoid subjected its victims to ever more debilitating bouts of diarrhea, stomach cramps, and above all head-aches and a crushing fever—one reason why it was often referred to as "brain fever" in Lincoln's day.[50]

Lincoln saw Ann suffer the throes of "brain fever," much as he surely saw his mother's paroxysms of pain and suffering from the milk sickness years earlier. She lingered for four or five days, and he visited her at least once before she died. "It was very evident that he was much distressed," remembered a friend who saw him after the visit.[51]

But what is telling here is not so much the secondhand accounts of Lincoln's "distress" or supposedly suicidal behavior, but rather his silence, his failure to ever even once mention his relationship with Ann or his reaction to her death. A year after she died, he began a brief courtship with another young woman, named Mary Owens. Mary later wrote, "I do not now recollect of ever hearing him mention [Ann's] name." Others also recalled that Lincoln was more or less business as usual soon after Ann died.[52]

It is a curious matter on its face, but then again, perhaps not, for it would be entirely in keeping with Lincoln's reactions to the deaths of his mother and sister. Ann died much as Nancy and Sarah: in a sudden, ugly way, cut short before their time by yet another form of death that stalked the primitive areas in which he lived. Some people believed that the deaths of Nancy, Sarah, and Ann fostered in him a lifelong tendency toward melancholy and a certain deep-seated loneliness that dated from those dark days.[53]

Perhaps. But on a more direct, observable level, the deaths of these three women were raw, ugly, unfiltered things, cruel contrasts with the genteel Good Death that respectable Americans of his day thought they deserved and strove to attain. Their deaths occurred in environments that discouraged romantic ideas about the nature of living and dying. Had Lincoln been born and raised in different circumstances in early nineteenth-century America— say, a comfortable middle-class home in a more settled area—he might well have learned to thickly coat death in the layers of sentiment and unctuous emotionalism that characterized the era's idea of the best way to die.

But Lincoln never seems to have thought much about a Good Death. Instead, he learned very early in his life that death could be and often was raw and unforgiving, from the screams of his dying sister to the wretched wasting away from disease evident in his mother and fiancée to the almost daily feral encounters common in the Indiana wilderness. "I am not a very sentimental man," Lincoln once remarked, and this was certainly true where death and dying was concerned.[54]

Years later, when Lincoln the lawyer and politician had made a successful transition into respectable middle-class society, he would again encounter a death that was sadly and uncomfortably close. By this time, he had learned the customs of mourning. And if he still did not overly sentimentalize death's truths, he did at least know how to play by the rules.

2. EDDY

Eddy's death began in early December 1849, with a cough. It was slight at first but persistent, a little thing in Abraham Lincoln's little three-year-old son. Lincoln might not have thought much of it, at least not right away.

He was now far removed from the "wilderness" of his youth. Panthers and bears did not stalk the streets of Springfield, Illinois (though dogs, chickens and the occasional pig were not uncommon), and the log cabins had given way to a sturdy clapboard cottage, a single story with a large loft that he later expanded into a full second story, on Eighth and Jackson Streets near the town's central square—a respectable dwelling for a respectable man and his family.[1]

Nor was Lincoln any longer a penniless jack-of-all-trades, scraping by on whatever he could find. Rumor had it that he and Ann Rutledge had delayed their marriage until "certain studies" could be completed—law studies, with Lincoln burying himself in borrowed law books to pass an Illinois bar exam. This he accomplished in 1836, and soon thereafter he left New Salem for the bustling burg of Springfield.[2]

As he grew into middle age, Lincoln was steadily becoming a proper lawyer with solid prospects, and he had a proper wife in Mary Todd Lincoln.

More than proper, she hailed from a wealthy Kentucky family, had attended a Lexington finishing school, and knew French, music, and manners. Theirs was a difficult courtship, but the marriage worked well enough to have produced two children by 1849, Robert and Eddy.[3]

They had been married for seven years in 1849. They were not poor by any means, but Mary was frugal; a neighbor remembered six-year-old Robert in patched pants and his mother being "very plain in her ways . . . [going] to church wearing a cheap calico dress and a sunbonnet." Their house was a tight fit, but it was serviceable, "sweet and fresh," and situated in a solid neighborhood. Robert was a strong, bright young boy; Mary was in the prime of her life, having just celebrated her thirty-first birthday; and Abraham, soon to turn forty-one, was entering a vigorous maturity with no serious health problems.[4]

But illness dogged their younger son. In one of the few surviving letters to her husband, Mary referred to Eddy's having "recovered from his little spell of sickness," but she offered no details. The previous summer, Mary and the children had accompanied Abraham on a speaking tour of upstate New England, where Eddy had also fallen ill, compelling Mary to devote much of her time and energy to nursing him.[5]

Now he had this cough, which grew steadily worse. If his parents were initially inclined to downplay its significance, believing it to be just one more unfortunate but manageable trial for their little boy, they were soon disabused of that notion. The coughing became ferocious, with Eddy experiencing ever greater trouble catching his breath. They might also have noticed spots of blood on his lips and chin or in a greenish-yellow phlegm he had begun to expel. They would have seen the problem growing ever more severe: at the kitchen table when Eddy dropped his fork from a coughing fit, perhaps, or as they tucked him into bed at night and listened to him gag and wheeze as he fell into an exhausted, rasping slumber. The sound would have reverberated throughout the little house, probably keeping his parents and brother awake on more than one night.

Mary may have at first tried to treat Eddy herself. Mothers in that day and age were expected to solve such problems on their own before consulting a doctor, and there was an extensive literature available to help them do so. Perhaps she possessed a copy of *Gunn's Domestic Medicine, or The Poor Man's Friend*, the most popular home medical guide of the day, written by a Tennessee doctor named John C. Gunn, who offered ready advice on everything from midwifery to heartburn. His recommendation for treating

a cough was "antimonial wine," or garlic juice made palatable with a little honey. Laudanum was useful, he also suggested, for severe coughing at
night. Mary might have tried thickening egg whites in vinegar to create a
homemade cough syrup. Commercial remedies were also available, such as
"Hough and Halton's cough candy," sold at Snow, Hill and Company's store
on the west side of the Springfield town square.[6]

Not that Mary (or anyone else) understood what she was treating. This
particular sickness had killed people for centuries, but no one knew why.
Some people thought it wasn't so much a communicable disease as a "constitutional" condition; it happened to those who were born physically weak.[7]
Others realized it was an affliction that had little to do with physical stamina
or willpower. In 1720, an English physician named Benjamin Marten theorized that the terrible lung disease, "so endemick to this nation and generally fatal to those it seizes on," was characterized chiefly by "ulcers" on the
lungs and transmitted by "creatures" through the air. The result, as Marten
described it, was "a wearing away or consuming of all the muscular or fleshy
parts of the body." Marten and those living in the Lincolns' time called it
"consumption." This was a catchall phrase in those scientifically imprecise
times, connoting any disease causing a consuming or a "wasting of the body."
Scientific classification was so vague that some historians have since wondered what exactly caused Eddy's illness. Odds are that it was tuberculosis.[8]

Accompanying the coughing, the blood, and the mucus was fatigue, serious and prolonged, as Eddy's never robust frame shuddered under the
strain of fighting the deadly bacteria that was now devouring his lungs.
The flow of blood and mucus would have continued, along with a general
soreness accompanying the incessant coughing and labored breathing. He
also would have developed a fever as the bacteria wrought havoc with his
immune system—again, never a very strong system under the best of circumstances. Mary might, with an increasing sense of desperation, have applied
cold compresses to Eddy's forehead and face, paging through Dr. Gunn's
manual and other books for some type of fever treatment or scanning advertisements in the newspapers for potentially useful products such as John
Sappington's Fever and Ague Pills or Wallace and Diller's Western Tonic,
guaranteed to work in advertisements in the *Sangamo Journal.* Nothing
would have helped much.[9]

Abraham and Mary consulted a doctor, though it is unknown exactly
when and whom.[10] They surely called on their family physician, William S.

Wallace, who ran his practice and a drugstore in a space beneath Lincoln's law office. A graduate of Jefferson Medical College in Philadelphia, Wallace was competent enough by the day's standards. He was also motivated by a close personal tie to the patient: Eddy was his nephew, Wallace's wife being Mary's sister. Either he or another doctor did prescribe medication of some kind. Older remedies once included doses of mercury and various opiates, but these treatments had fallen out of favor. Consumptive patients were instead encouraged to seek climates where the atmosphere was supposedly conducive to less labored breathing—Colorado or someplace else out west with drier air, options that Eddy's parents could not realistically pursue.[11]

By the end of January, everyone knew Eddy's condition was grave. The wasting aspect of the disease would now have been evident. His skin would have had a whitish pallor (hence the name "white plague" attached by some to the disease), and his muscle tone would have been diminished, both from the blood's decreased oxygen content and from what was likely by this point a prolonged period of time spent in bed. The difficult breathing and coughing spells continued, punctuated by hoarseness and a diminishing ability to speak. Night sweats were another common symptom, and some late-stage tuberculosis patients suffered bouts of diarrhea, adding yet a further dimension of misery.[12]

This merciless obliteration of a child was not an easy thing to watch. No written record survives of Eddy's daily suffering, so we can only guess what life must have been like in the Lincoln home. Mary was doubtless busy, dealing with not only Eddy's needs but those of Abraham and Robert as well, and she seems to have shouldered the load without domestic help. The Lincolns periodically employed servants, as did many other Springfield households, and two years previously they had hired a young girl named Ruth Burns Stanton as a live-in servant. But they let her go sometime in 1849, possibly to economize. "The Lincolns were poor then," Stanton recalled. "After I left, Mrs. Lincoln had to do all of her own housework, for she could not afford to get another servant." They do not seem to have hired anyone else until Abraham approached an African American woman named Mariah Vance about a job two months after Eddy died, apparently having scraped together enough money at that point.[13]

If Eddy had lived in a later age, he might have been taken to one of the tuberculosis sanatoriums with other consumptive patients, places that segregated the dying process with their own institutionalized rules and routines.

Instead, he spent his last days at home.[14] The neighbors would have known about his condition. They might have heard his coughs as they walked by the house or asked after him when they encountered Abraham or Mary on the streets. Perhaps they occasionally helped with the household chores or brought a meal after a particularly tough day. There was James Gourley, a shoemaker whose yard bordered the Lincolns and who became a good friend to the entire Lincoln family, joining Abraham on occasion for a game of handball and even sometimes staying the night at the Lincoln home when Abraham was away on the legal circuit and Mary felt insecure. It is hard to imagine Gourley remaining uninvolved in Eddy's ordeal. There was also Mary Remann, a German immigrant whose husband, Henry, had died from tuberculosis not long before Eddy became ill. After Eddy died, his mother gave some of his clothes to Mrs. Remann, who had a little boy about the same age. Mary Remann's sister-in-law, Elizabeth Black, lived for a while with her, and during her stay she gave birth to a baby boy who died shortly thereafter, of unknown causes. Mary Lincoln, by this point also grieving for Eddy's loss, visited and prayed with Elizabeth, the two mothers commiserating over the loss of their sons.[15]

Mary also had family in Springfield: her cousin John Todd Stuart (Lincoln's first law partner) and his wife and Mary's sisters, Elizabeth, Frances, and Ann. Her eldest sister, Elizabeth, was a particularly important figure in Mary's life. Mary moved to Springfield at her urging, Abraham courted Mary in Elizabeth's parlor, and the sisters remained close thereafter (aside from a few difficult spots). As the eldest Todd living in Springfield and the wife of Ninian Edwards, a wealthy and successful Illinois politician, Elizabeth often assumed the role of quasi-matriarch and advisor; "you have . . . such an influence over Mary," Abraham once told her. Surely she was involved in Eddy's care, along with the other Todd sisters.[16]

But Mary was Eddy's primary caregiver, and as the days took their toll, she must have been exhausted and nearly overwhelmed. "My wife is not well," Lincoln remarked at the time, and he tied this directly to Eddy's illness. However, there is no evidence that Mary was unequal to the task or that she suffered any kind of breakdown. She did what was necessary.[17]

Abraham was there to help. Throughout their married life, he performed various chores around the house: chopping wood, doing a bit of gardening, or attending to the family cow that was pastured near the house—"a domestic man by nature," thought one friend. Gourley remembered him sometimes milking away in his slippers and an old pair of pants held aloft by only one suspender. He was accustomed to such work since his earliest days at Little Pigeon Creek, more so than Mary, who was raised in a wealthy slaveholding home.[18]

Yet he was also professionally a busy man. Ruth Stanton recalled that while she worked in the Lincoln home, she hardly saw him at all, so preoccupied was he with his law practice. No one in 1850 would have expected Lincoln, however attentive a husband and father, to significantly curtail his work schedule to care for a sick child at home, even a dying child such as Eddy. So on most mornings, Lincoln would have headed out the back door to work (he hardly ever used the more formal front entrance), the sound of his son's endless coughing slowly fading away as he walked down Eighth Street, stooping a bit in the frigid weather and wrapped in a faded gray shawl.[19]

He did reduce his workload somewhat. From early December 1849 to the end of January 1850, he and his partner William Herndon litigated only five cases, and he engaged in no serious political or civic activities. By comparison, a year later during that same period, the firm of Lincoln and Herndon litigated twenty cases, and Lincoln closely monitored various activities related to both the Illinois Whig Party and bills pending in the state legislature. The year after that, he and Herndon were involved in only ten cases, but he was busy serving on two subcommittees at the state Whig convention and aiding a local Springfield organization that expressed sympathies for Hungarian revolutionary Louis Kossuth. December and January were typically hectic months for Lincoln, but during the winter of 1849–50, he took on relatively few additional responsibilities.[20]

Still, while he made an effort to cut back and stay closer to home, he also sustained a more or less normal routine. He went to work, argued cases, and wrote letters—all mundane tasks during the performance of which Lincoln betrayed no hint of anything unusual in his family life. He tried to bear his son's ordeal as a "strong man," remembered a friend, one "who had resolved to keep his feelings under firm sway," a description reminiscent of his quiet reaction to his mother's and his sister's deaths.[21]

Sometime toward the end of January, he would have undertaken the practical preparations for the funeral he and everyone else knew was imminent. Springfield was not Little Pigeon Creek or New Salem, where dying was a primitive affair. Arranging for Eddy's funeral would have involved a great deal more, and since these were primarily business transactions, and Mary was no doubt fully occupied with the day-to-day struggles in caring for Eddy, Abraham probably dealt with these matters himself.

Springfield had no funeral directors or homes at that time; the modern funeral service industry did not yet exist. There were people known as "undertakers." The Springfield Steam Power Furniture Manufactory, on the south side of the town square, advertised its willingness to provide "undertaking, in all its branches." The city directory also listed as an "undertaker" a man named Henry Brinkman.[22] But undertaking was not a profession, exactly; it was a vague term attached to craftsmen who built coffins or transferred the body of the deceased from the site of the funeral to the grave. Some undertakers possessed an unsavory reputation as death's mechanics, callous men who nailed boards together into a box or trundled away a corpse for burial and did so for a fee rather than with proper Christian sentiment.[23]

There were also ministers, of course. Lincoln had long since fallen away from his "Hardshell" Baptist upbringing, and he was not a regular church-going man (though Mary did occasionally attend Springfield's Episcopal church). If he did ask a minister for advice concerning how to properly conduct Eddy's funeral, it was most likely Dr. James Smith of Springfield's First Presbyterian Church. An unidentified "lady friend" suggested that Smith call on the Lincolns at some point during Eddy's final days to provide the family with spiritual comfort. Since the Episcopal minister who had performed the Lincolns' marriage was out of town, they called on Smith to conduct Eddy's funeral. They would have discussed with him at some point the order in which the events of funeral and burial should unfold, the proper methods of adornment, and other details.[24]

Lincoln also needed to buy a coffin, and for this he had numerous options. A cabinetmaker named J. Francis advertised his willingness to make "coffins at reduced prices," as did fellow woodworkers D. E. Reickel and J. A. Hough. The Springfield Steam Power Furniture Manufactory advertised among its other products—"mahogany centre tables," "fancy divans," "plain and tufted sofas," and the like—an entire "ware room" that was "devoted exclusively to ready-made coffins, of every quality, and all sizes." One can imagine Lincoln slowly walking through a "ware room" on some winter day in late January, engaged in the melancholy task of finding a coffin small enough for his dying son. He probably chose a simple one constructed of plain wood, metallic coffins falling more within the province of wealthy families. A child's coffin was sometimes adorned with special hardware: a lamb representing Christ's love for innocence or a cut rose representing a life of potential suddenly and prematurely ended. It is not known whether Lincoln chose such an option for Eddy.[25]

Where would his child be buried? This was another grim but necessary decision, entailing more than placing the body on a sled and hauling it to a hilltop, as had been the case with Lincoln's mother. At that time, Springfield possessed two cemeteries: a public cemetery on Adams Street at the western edge of town and the nearby Hutchison cemetery, owned by yet another cabinetmaker, named John Hutchison. Like Francis, Reickel, Hough, and the Steam Power Furniture Manufactory, Hutchison supplemented his furniture business by constructing coffins, but he went further, purchasing land near his house for a private burial ground and advertising that he could supply customers with a hearse and carriage and "all Funeral arrangements."[26]

Neither cemetery was a terribly attractive place. Both were becoming crowded with the dead, even as Springfield became crowded with the living; Hutchison's cemetery alone hosted several hundred graves by 1850. Modern ideas regarding cemeteries as idyllic and carefully planned garden spots were still some years in the future, and while Hutchison may have tried to keep his grounds reasonably weed free and clean, the place was probably a jumble of headstones of various sizes and shapes, with at best minimal landscaping. Organization would have been minimal as well, with general groupings of graves by family and kinship but nothing much more elaborate. This was all Springfield had to offer for Eddy's burial.[27]

Eddy would also need a stone to mark his final resting place. When Lincoln discussed a tombstone with Hutchison or some other craftsman (perhaps a Springfield man named Patrick Flood who worked as a stonecutter), he arranged for a stone bearing what was considered an epitaph suitable for a child: an image of a dove, inscribed with Eddy's name and the phrase "of such is the Kingdom of Heaven" from Matthew 19:14: "Suffer little children, and forbid them not, to come unto me: for of such is the kingdom of heaven."[28]

Doves, Bible verses . . . these were terribly important, invested with an entire community's collective sense of the sacred and the appropriate, the "civilized." Lincoln's community cared a great deal about the rites of dying and mourning because in that day, it often seemed as if the bustling and energetic new market and industrial economy was coarsening the everyday fabric of life. Elaborate funeral and mourning rituals were a counterweight, a balancing of the scales; by observing meticulous social rules for death and mourning, Americans in Lincoln's day wanted to preserve a sense of the hallowed and the profound in an indifferent and even hostile modern world.[29]

This was particularly true regarding the fate of deceased children. The ancient belief that a dead child was doomed to spend an eternity in hell if not baptized or born into a particular church had given way by Lincoln's time to the belief, popularized by the Swedish writer Emanuel Swedenborg, that children were inherently innocent and thus any child who passed away would be welcomed into heaven. It is not clear whether Lincoln read Swedenborg, but he was surely aware that the culture around him associated children with purity and innocence, so any mourning of a dead child likely would have reflected this sensibility.[30]

Lincoln could not afford to ignore these considerations. A man from humble farming roots who constantly strove to escape those roots and enter white middle-class respectability, Lincoln wanted and needed acceptance into polite Springfield circles. The memories of Little Pigeon Creek with all its "wilderness" primitiveness—not to mention his mother, sister, and Ann Rutledge in their awful suffering—could not have been pleasant, and Lincoln wanted to get as far away from that life as possible. He was an ambitious man on the make, and he had to do dying as well as living right.

There was a political element here as well, ironically centered on Lincoln's perceived lack of faith. While running for Congress in 1846, he was accused by his opponent of agnosticism or worse—a serious charge in those days. Lincoln felt threatened enough to respond with a handbill reassuring voters that he had "never denied the truth of the Scriptures," nor had he ever "spoken with intentional disrespect of religion in general, or of any denomination of Christians in particular." He understood the immense power Christianity wielded in shaping Americans' moral sensibilities, and he knew better than to challenge that power. "I do not think I could myself, be brought to support a man for office, whom I knew to be an open enemy of, and scoffer at, religion," he declared. "Leaving the higher matter of eternal consequences, between him and his Maker, I still do not think any man has the right thus to insult the feelings, and injure the morals, of the community in which he may live." Few events touched on the feelings and morals of the community more than death, especially the death of a child. People in those highly religious days noticed that Lincoln did not regularly attend church, and they would have noticed with disapproval had he shown an inclination to ignore the customs surrounding funerals and the mourning process.[31]

Eddy died at six in the morning on Friday, February 1, 1850, just four weeks shy of his fourth birthday. "We lost our little boy," Lincoln wrote to his stepbrother. "He was sick fifty two days." The funeral plans were already in place and ready to go, for they were able to hold Eddy's service the very next morning at eleven o'clock. The body would not have been left alone during the night; someone—likely a family member—would have kept an overnight vigil.[32]

As was the custom of the day, the funeral occurred in the Lincoln home. Eddy's body would have been prepared for viewing in the formal front parlor. He was probably not embalmed, an expensive process not yet widespread in America. He was washed and dressed, tasks usually performed by the deceased's mother, with help from other women. In some communities, ladies advertised their services as "laying-out women," but in all likelihood Mary was assisted by one or more of her sisters and perhaps a neighborhood woman like Mrs. Remann.

Mary also may have cut and preserved a lock of Eddy's hair, a common act steeped in symbolism and intimacy. Americans saw locks of hair as tiny bridges to their deceased loved ones, curiously tangible and potent in their evocation of the dead. "How full thou art of memories, severed tress!" went a sentimental poem of the day.[33] Some grieving mothers incorporated the deceased's hair into brooches and other jewelry—usually fashioned from ebony—or elaborate funeral wreaths.[34]

Whether Mary was present at the service is unknown. Some writers have affirmed that she was definitely not present—there is no direct evidence one way or the other—and have used her absence as proof of her supposed mental and emotional instability. We do not know her exact state of mind that day, and in any event, her absence was expected. Women normally did not attend funerals in that era, since it was believed they could not properly control their emotions.[35]

The service was conducted by Reverend Smith, who likely spoke of Eddy's essential innocence as a child called to God—possibly invoking the quotation from Matthew inscribed on Eddy's headstone—and of the hope of salvation and resurrection in the hereafter. He might also have spoken of Eddy's death as a relief from the child's prolonged suffering. A Presbyterian guide to funeral services of the time instructed ministers to remind listeners of "the frailty of life, and importance of being prepared for death and eternity." Smith possessed a strong Calvinist bent, and with this tendency toward fatalism, he may have intimated in his sermon that God shaped all ends and that his purposes, however inscrutable, were ultimately divine.[36]

Those present would afterward have been served food, a nearly universal practice at any funeral service. Traditionally, varieties of cold meats were common on such occasions—turkey, boiled ham, and roast beef—as well as whatever fruits were available in the winter season. Perhaps they also were given a bit of alcohol and some tobacco, though Lincoln customarily indulged in neither.[37]

This sharing of food was a way of incorporating the neighborhood into the grieving process, and there were other ways, which were (as always) bracketed by social mores and rules. Casual acquaintances of the Lincoln family were not expected to attend the service, but they were expected to visit the family within one week of the funeral, if possible wearing black silk or clothing that was plain and unadorned. Respectable families would also leave mourning cards with black edges, expressing their condolences, displayed on a table in the deceased's home.[38]

After the service, the coffin was carried to a waiting hearse, probably provided by Hutchison. It would have been a simple affair, a black carriage drawn by two or four horses, possibly possessing the glass sides ordinarily associated with such vehicles—though this would become more common later in the century—and almost certainly sporting plumes. Plumes adorned nearly all hearses of the day, a modern outgrowth from the medieval custom of surrounding a dead body with tall candles. White feathered plumage was the accepted symbol for the death of a child.

The hearse drew Eddy away to the gravesite, with Lincoln, Reverend Smith, and the other attendees acting as a small cortege. Both of Springfield's cemeteries were relatively near the Lincoln home, so the procession would not have lasted long or traveled far—a good thing, given the winter season. Immediate family members Abraham and Robert followed in the closest proximity to the casket, with more distant family and friends trailing silently behind, heads bare.[39]

Exactly where Eddy was buried, at least initially, is something of a mystery. In December 1851—nearly two years after his death—the Lincolns purchased a burial plot for their son in Hutchison's cemetery. Where was Eddy's body in the interim? Perhaps he was buried in Hutchison's cemetery and the Lincolns made some sort of arrangement whereby they paid for the plot at a later date. Or possibly Eddy was first buried in Springfield's city cemetery, a less expensive alternative to Hutchison's privately owned affair, and then reinterred later when the Lincolns could afford Hutchison's fee.[40]

Following the burial, the Lincoln family entered a period of mourning, for which society also stipulated a protocol. This varied according to circumstances. Poorer Americans tended to observe fewer and simpler mourning customs, and widows and widowers were subject to considerably longer and more complex rules than the parents, siblings, or grandchildren of deceased relatives. Location played a role as well; a town like Springfield, sophisticated by Illinois standards but rustic according to people living in, say, New York, probably fell somewhere between rigid and lax in its social rules for mourning.[41]

Men and women were subject to different rules. As the father of a dead child, Lincoln wore black clothing and perhaps a black armband or hat wrap for a while—a few months at most. This wasn't much; men were supposed to suppress their feelings during the process of dying, and so too did they submerge their grief afterward. Had Lincoln worn mourning clothing for what his neighbors and friends considered an inordinately long period of time, he would have risked gossip that he had become excessively "feminized" in his grief. He was expected to maintain the outward appearance of keeping his emotions in firm control.[42]

For the most part, he seems to have done so. The people closest to him noticed a deep-seated sadness in the days following Eddy's burial. "I found him very much depressed and downcast at the death of his son," Reverend Smith later remembered when he visited Lincoln to further console him on his loss. This was hardly surprising. But Lincoln reserved the feelings of depression engendered by Eddy's death for private encounters like Reverend Smith's visit. There is reliable evidence of only one public outburst, when immediately after the funeral he saw a card with Eddy's last medical prescription lying on a table. He picked it up, threw it away, and rushed from the room crying.[43]

Otherwise, Lincoln seems to have firmly maintained the self-control expected of him, and even this slight loss of emotional control occurred within his home. His professional behavior in the office and elsewhere was normal—neither his law partner nor other colleagues remarked otherwise— and his correspondence was entirely businesslike and ordinary. His only mention of Eddy's death came in a brief letter on February 23, responding to earlier correspondence from his stepbrother: "As you make no mention of it, I suppose you had not learned that we lost our little boy," Lincoln wrote. "We miss him very much." Whatever turmoil he felt upon Eddy's death he kept contained within himself and out of the public eye.[44]

For Mary, expectations were different. Women were expected to bear the heaviest burden of mourning lost loved ones, for they were the guardians of the family's emotional and social propriety—keepers of the family "heart," so to speak. Her mourning manifested itself in her dress. In the weeks immediately following Eddy's funeral, Mary would have donned "deep mourning," dresses made of somber, dull black material with crepe at the collar and cuffs, and no other trimming of any kind—no bows, ruffles, or flounces. She would have worn a black veil and bonnet, and black gloves made of silk or cloth—kid gloves were not allowed. She may even have carried black-bordered handkerchiefs. She would have worn no jewelry, and her hair would have been arranged in a "perfectly plain" manner, clasped with a single, plain locket.[45]

She remained in deep mourning anywhere from six months to a year; opinions varied regarding what was most appropriate. She then transitioned to "half mourning": still a primarily black motif with crepe trimmings but now interspersed with gray, white, or muted lavender. Simple black or gold jewelry was now allowed. Other Springfield women who called on her were likewise expected to wear somber fashions; if not black crepe, at least colors of a more subdued, grayish type.[46]

Mary was playing a part here, almost as if she were acting out a play for Springfield's benefit. Her assigned role was the anguished mother, working her way through her loss using the vehicles of fashion and clothing that were a woman's primary means of expression in that era. Her friends and neighbors played roles as well. They were tasked with calling on Mary at an appropriate time and place, dressed appropriately and saying fitting words of condolence. They were also to decide when the time for mourning should come to an end and inform Mary when she should put her black crepe away and move on. They were to do so by gently reminding her of her familial obligations to the living. "The friends around a grief stricken mother [are] to tell her when it is time to make her dress more cheerful," offered an advice column in a nineteenth-century magazine, "which she is bound to do for the sake of the survivors"—her husband and her other children.[47]

Mary's grief was profound. The wife of Lincoln's first law partner (and Mary's cousin), John Todd Stuart, visited the Lincoln home one morning shortly after Eddy's death, though exactly when is unclear. At this point, the Lincolns had hired a servant (probably Mariah Vance), and Mrs. Stuart helped the servant prepare breakfast. Abraham brought the meal to Mary, saying to her, "Mary, you must eat, for we must live." But she refused. Abraham dined that morning alone.[48]

A long-standing tradition has Mary doing far more than refusing a meal. Some describe Mary collapsing in swoons of pain and anguish, shutting herself away in her bedroom, curtains drawn, and crying incessantly for days on end. While she would do such things (and more) later in life when confronted with the deaths of Willie and her husband, there is no reliable evidence that on this occasion she either isolated herself for prolonged periods in her room or cried in a hysterical manner. As deeply wounded and exhausted as Mary must have been, her behavior in mourning Eddy was neither overwrought nor all that worrisome to those around her. Americans expected a certain amount of distress from bereaved mothers. Even Abraham's admonishment—"you must eat, for we must live"—fit the social script he and Mary were expected to follow. When he reminded her that they both had a duty to Robert, their living child, he was saying exactly what he was supposed to say.[49]

Whatever she did or did not do, her grieving took place within the privacy of her home. The silence of the historical record is telling. No friends or neighbors commented on a public misstep during this time from either Mary or Abraham, and none of the ugly rumors that later swirled around the Lincoln family life and marriage—everything from Abraham being driven by marital discord to sleep on his office couch to Mary chasing him out of the house with a knife—touched on Eddy's death. They both behaved with what was at the time considered propriety.

This was no insignificant matter, for the social rituals surrounding dying and its aftermath were among antebellum America's most rigidly proscribed and emotionally sensitive. Abraham and Mary were given a certain set of guidelines, cultural tools with which to navigate the dying process for their son. Those tools were partly designed to help ease personal grief, but they also allowed the community to assess the distressed parents' character. People believed they could tell a lot about their neighbors' values, beliefs, even the state of their very souls by watching how they handled death.

Abraham and Mary Lincoln, each in their own way and for their own reasons, cared about what the rest of Springfield thought of them. They were social creatures, after all, deeply embedded within their community. Their friends, relatives, neighbors, colleagues, and clients expected them to behave a certain way and follow established norms as they confronted their child's death, an occurrence that was tragic and traumatic but not all that unusual. Child mortality rates were high in Lincoln's time. Indeed, dying itself was a common thing. In a time cursed with multiple and lethal diseases—not just "consumption," but repeated outbreaks of cholera, malaria, smallpox, diphtheria, measles, lethal forms of the flu—and crude medical knowledge, death was everywhere.

It was experienced not in specialized, isolated settings but directly at home, in the moment, and as an intimate part of everyday life. Abraham and Mary would have daily seen the death of their son, smelled it, felt it, and heard it—for fifty-one days. Certainly this was so for Mary (and Robert), but it was also true for Abraham, even as he left the place where Eddy was dying and went to work in his law office and the courtroom.

It was also practical as well as emotional, nuts and bolts as well as sentiment. It was about the many steps, large and small, that should be taken to treat an illness, the messy and difficult daily problems of caregiving, the sort of coffin in which Eddy should be buried, what should be on the tombstone, how the family might pay for the burial, and exactly what they might do and say to mourn him afterward. Death for Abraham Lincoln was not always an existential intellectual exercise or a search for a deeper meaning and purpose. Sometimes it was simply a matter of getting through the day, making the ledger balance, and trying hard not to offend anyone's sensibilities by allowing brimming emotions to spill over and make a public mess. Those complicated and meticulous cultural rituals of funerals and mourning could be cumbersome and unforgiving, but all the available evidence suggests that both Abraham and Mary followed the rules with care.

3. THE IDEAS OF DEATH

The passing of Eddy, his mother, his sister, and Ann Rutledge each in their own way exposed Abraham Lincoln to death's messy realities. Eddy's slow, agonizing deterioration was different from Sarah's relatively sudden, brutally sharp end in a childbirth gone badly awry or Nancy's and Ann's racking mortal illnesses. But all shared a common element of raw immediacy. Lincoln knew death as something that could not be entirely muted by layers of ceremony or sentiment.

But death could be separated from the fleshy messiness that is the actual end of a living being. What Lincoln experienced as a son, brother, lover, and father could be described as matters of his heart. But there were also matters of the head—of his mind and intellect. He learned of death in what he read in literature and poetry, in what he saw in the courtroom as a professional lawyer, and he learned how death was relevant (or not relevant) to his political career. These constituted the ideas of death that he encountered before the war.

Whatever ideas most Americans carried in their heads regarding death during Lincoln's time came from the Bible, and Lincoln of course read the Bible. He could and did quote it, at length and from memory. He was "often and much moved by the stories" in the Bible, Dennis Hanks recalled. But the precise nature of Abraham Lincoln's religious beliefs, especially prior to the Civil War, has always been a mystery. Not even his own stepmother was entirely sure what he believed. "Abe had no particular religion," she claimed when she was interviewed after the war; he "didn't think of that question at that time, if he ever did. He never talked about it."[1]

When her husband passed away from a kidney disease in 1851, Abraham was not present. His relationship with his father was strained, dating back to their Indiana days: Thomas thought his son rude and impertinent, while Abraham was embarrassed by his father's lack of education and wanted nothing to do with Thomas's farming life. He rarely saw his father after he left home in 1831, although they lived in relatively close proximity, with Thomas steadily sinking into semi-impoverished elder years on a series of farms in Coles County, Illinois, about ninety miles east of Springfield.[2]

Abraham was not completely indifferent to Thomas's fate. When Thomas fell ill in 1849, Lincoln visited his father. Two years later, however, he did not come when Thomas fell ill again, for the final time. There were practical reasons—Mary was also sick at the time, and the Lincolns had a new baby boy, Willie—but the long-standing strains in the relationship between Abraham and Thomas were at least partly an issue. Writing to his stepbrother, John Johnston, he expressed his opinion that a final meeting with his father would be a bad idea. "Say to him that if we could meet now, it is doubtful whether it would not be more painful than pleasant." He followed this with the exhortation to "tell him to remember to call upon, and confide in, our great, and good, and merciful Maker; who will not turn away from him in any extremity," for God "notes the fall of a sparrow, and numbers the hairs of our heads; and He will not forget the dying man, who puts his trust in Him."

But Lincoln did not have much to say about what his father's trust in the Lord might mean in terms of death's consequences or an afterlife. This was entirely in character, for he rarely spoke of a "soul" in any meaningful sense, nor was he given to speculation about the afterlife. At the end of his letter to Johnston, he wrote of Thomas, "If it be his lot to go now, he will soon have a joyous [meeting] with many loved ones gone before."[3] It was a very rare reference to the afterlife; so rare, in fact, that one is tempted to think Lincoln was here merely reciting a well-worn Christian trope that held no deep meaning for him. Yet what held deep meaning for Abraham Lincoln and what did not is difficult to gauge in this man who was so "shut pan," and whose spiritual beliefs were opaque even to his family and friends. Perhaps it would be best to simply observe that, judging from this one letter to his stepbrother, written while his father lay dying, Lincoln could draw on his biblical knowledge to comfort the dying—and he did not choose to do so very often.

When he pondered the deeper spiritual matters of death and dying, he tended more frequently to express himself in his preferences for literature and poetry. Five days after Eddy's funeral, a poem appeared in the *Illinois Daily Journal* titled "Little Eddie."[4] It was a fairly straightforward poetic lament, of a type common to such verse of the day. It dwelt upon the theme of loss—"The angel death was hovering nigh, / And the lovely boy was called to die"—and the merciful end to a sick child's suffering. It explained Eddy's death in the vague terms of an often inscrutable but ultimately just and compassionate God:

> Pure little bud in kindness given,
>> In mercy taken to bloom in heaven.
> Happier far is the angel child
>> With the harp and the crown of gold,
> Who warbles now at the Saviour's feet
>> The glories to us untold.[5]

For years historians wondered who wrote "Little Eddie," speculating that the author must have been Abraham or Mary, or possibly both. It was neither. Historian Samuel P. Wheeler recently discovered that "Little Eddie" was written by a young woman from Saint Louis named Mary E. Chamberlain, who had no known connection to the Lincolns and who wrote the poem in 1849 under the pseudonym "Ethel Grey." Someone in Springfield had read Chamberlain's poem, which was originally titled simply "Eddie," was perhaps struck by the connection to the Lincolns' recent loss, and had it placed in the *Journal*. Possibly Abraham or Mary themselves did so, or editor Francis, or some family member or friend.[6]

But Lincoln did compose a poem in Eddy's memory, a threnody—from the Greek word *thrēnōidia*, meaning a "wailing ode." He showed it to his law partner William Herndon, but it has since been lost.[7] More generally, Lincoln liked poets who wrote of life's inscrutable and ultimately unknowable meaning. This was true of Lincoln's favorite poem, "Mortality," by William Knox, of which he was so enamored that he committed it to memory. Knox was a dour Scotsman who wrote "Mortality" sometime in the 1820s; it was an extended meditation on the fleeting quality of life and the ultimate point-lessness of posturing by even the richest, most beautiful and accomplished people—all will someday be worms' meat. As Knox put it:

> The leaves of the oak and the willow shall fade,
> Be scattered around, and together be laid;
> And the young and the old, and the low and the high,
> Shall moulder to dust, and together shall lie.

Knox's poem was thickly layered in imagery of death and the grave:

> 'Tis the wink of an eye—'tis the draught of a breath—
> From the blossom of health to the paleness of death,
> From the gilded saloon to the bier and the shroud:—
> Oh! why should the spirit of mortal be proud?[8]

When Lincoln took his own turn at poetry, he found his way to similar themes. Traveling in Indiana on a political tour stumping for Whig candidates in 1844, he visited Little Pigeon Creek and his mother's grave. The experience moved him deeply, and he composed a poem. "My Childhood-Home I See Again" was suffused with a longing for home, the transient nature of memory, and death's gloom:

> Till every sound appears a knell,
> And every spot a grave.
> I range the fields with pensive tread,
> And pace the hollow rooms;
> And feel (companions of the dead)
> I'm living in the tombs.[9]

Like so many other nineteenth-century Americans, Lincoln linked emotion, sentiment, and death. He thought about the deeper spiritual meaning of death, its mysteries, and perhaps most poignantly—given the deaths he had witnessed visited upon innocents like his son and mother by illness or upon his sister (and stillborn nephew) by childbirth—death's unfathomable and almost random cruelty:

> O death! Thou awe-inspiring prince,
> That keepst the world in fear;
> Why dost thou tear more blest ones hence . . . ?[10]

By this point in his life, as a middle-aged adult, he had seen his share of suffering and dying within his own family, and he had arrived at a certain resignation and acceptance of death as an inevitable circumstance of living. "The death scenes of those we love, are surely painful enough," he wrote to his close friend Joshua Speed, "but these we are prepared to, and expect to see. They happen to all, and all know they must happen. Painful as they are, they are not unlooked-for-sorrow."[11]

Unlike so many others of his day, Lincoln was not given to explaining death as some benign and understandable part of God's grand design, nor was he inclined to speculate on God's purposes in allowing the good to die as well as the wicked. Death was to him fundamentally a mystery, and Lincoln did not venture much beyond a simple acknowledgment that dying was part of an unknowable, divine journey. God "shapes our ends, rough-hew them how we will" was a favorite Shakespearean passage, taken from *Hamlet*, act 5, scene 2—the death-drenched closing scene, in which Horatio, taking stock of the corpses of Hamlet and the rest of the royal family lying strewn around him, cries out against death's caprice:

> And let me speak to the yet unknowing world,
> How these things came about: So shall you hear
> Of carnal, bloody and unnatural acts;
> Of accidental judgments, casual slaughters;
> Of deaths put on by cunning and forc'd cause.[12]

Lincoln enjoyed Shakespeare, and *Macbeth* was a favorite. He praised Claudius's speech in act 3, scene 3, a scene in which Claudius writhes painfully as he contemplates the awful consequences of his brother's murder:

> O, my offence is rank it smells to heaven;
> It hath the primal eldest curse upon't,
> A brother's murder. Pray can I not,
> Though inclination be as sharp as will;
> My stronger guilt defeats my strong intent.[13]

THE IDEAS OF DEATH

Lincoln's tastes ran to the darker corners of Shakespeare, plays suffused with murder, intrigue, and the consequences of greed, ambition, and the pursuit of revenge. There is a brooding sort of justice here, as death is deservedly visited upon Shakespeare's fascinating but flawed characters, often in tragic ways. But there is little comfort or consolation: death is the means by which Hamlet, Macbeth, King Lear, and others pay for their avarice and their indiscretions. Claudius prays for forgiveness but doubts it will do much good:

> What if this cursed hand
> Were thicker than itself with brother's blood,
> Is there not rain enough in the sweet heavens
> To wash it white as snow? Whereto serves mercy
> But to confront the visage of offence?
> And what's in prayer but this two-fold force,
> To be forestalled ere we come to fall,
> Or pardon'd being down? Then I'll look up;
> My fault is past.[14]

Lincoln's predilections suggest bleak dimensions to his intellectual understanding of death. Beyond the cold comfort of retributive justice in Shakespeare—Macbeth's murder of Duncan, for example, and the subsequent violence and murders that follow, which are in the end avenged by his own battlefield demise—death does not mean a peaceful resolution, still less going "to a better place." The reaper's scythe sweeps away innocence, wickedness, and pride alike.

While it is true, as historian Mark Schantz argues, that most antebellum Americans found death easier to bear because they constantly spoke of a "heavenly eternity of transcendent beauty [that] awaited them beyond the grave," Lincoln was an exception in this regard. He did not articulate a clear sense of what he thought came after death. With the mix of fatalism and mystery influenced by his Calvinist background and expressed in his Shakespearean tastes and his poetry, he possessed only a powerful but inchoate belief in God's inscrutable will and the idea that when human beings died, they did so as part of some grand, mysterious plan. "Lincoln thought that God predestined things," a friend observed simply, and to that end, death was a function of that Almighty will, which he never pretended to fully comprehend.[15]

This was Lincoln the reader, the lover of books, poetry, and Shakespeare. What of Lincoln the lawyer and politician? What ideas regarding death did he absorb from his professional life?

He was self-taught as a lawyer, not at all unusual in that age of few law schools. His primary text was Sir William Blackstone's *Commentaries on the Laws of England*, a treatise first written in 1765 that offered an exhaustive explanation of the underlying philosophy of the English legal system—and by extension, the American system, which was closely modeled on English principles. Rare was the American attorney who had not mastered the *Commentaries*.[16]

Sir William explored rather arcane avenues and aspects of death in the law. He explained, for example, the legal duties of a coroner ("if the body be not found, he cannot sit; He must also sit at the very place where the death happened"); the differences between a "civil" and a "natural" death in ancient law (the former being banishment or entry into a monastery); capital punishments for treason and other high crimes against the state; and ancient laws concerning punishments for wrongful death by negligence ("among the Athenians, whatever was the cause of a man's death, by falling upon him, was exterminated or cast out of the dominions of the republic").[17]

While the pull of his Calvinist upbringing and his literary turn took him to places of the mysterious and the inexplicable, Blackstone took Lincoln to places where death was simply an event, a problem requiring solutions or sometimes a solution to a problem. There is none of Shakespeare's underlying awe of death's leveling power in the *Commentaries*, no sense of its role in tragedy or the pathos of flawed human beings. Death might complicate marriages or the circumstances of childrearing; "since the parents, on whom this care is primarily incumbent, may be snatched away by death before they have completed their duty, the law has provided [the relation] of guardian and ward." It could create difficulties in business relations, property rights, and commerce. It was a crime, parsed by types of murder, manslaughter, and wrongful death. It was a punishment, meted out by the state for heinous offenses.[18]

There is little room for the spiritual realm here: no Good Deaths or bad deaths. Death is bloodless in the pages of the *Commentaries*. It is all about action and reaction, rendered in spare, precise prose. The *Commentaries*— and by extension, the law itself—showed Lincoln that death was not only a matter of threnodies, God's biblical inscrutability, or the tragedies of a

Shakespearean soliloquy. Nor was it only the horrors of seeing his mother wretch and gag in the throes of the milk sickness or hearing his young son's coughs echoing through the house. Death could also be a mere circumstance, an unfortunate event that created problems, but problems that usually were solvable.

What Blackstone taught him in the abstract played itself out in Lincoln's daily life and experiences as a lawyer. In any given year, his caseload almost always included matters touching on death and its legal consequences, and when it did so, the available evidence suggests that lawyer Lincoln approached death much as the *Commentaries* prepared him to do.[19]

Death's presence in the courtroom could be immediate and obvious. There were the various murder cases he litigated, approximately one per year during his twenty-five years at the bar.[20] A murder trial put a death at the forefront of Lincoln's consciousness, along with everyone else in the courtroom, but the attendant emotions had a different tenor than, say, a funeral or a passage in Shakespeare. Shock, dismay, anger . . . these were feelings engendered by a death that were to be suppressed in the name of finding an equitable solution to a dispute or perhaps manipulated in a jury box in the service of winning a case for a client.

This was true in his most famous murder trial—really, his most famous court case of any kind—the Almanac Trial of 1858. The victim in question, James Metzker of Mason County, Illinois, had died under violent circumstances, having been struck in the face with a homemade weapon called a "slungshot" during a drunken fight on the evening of August 29, 1857. Lincoln's client, William "Duff" Armstrong, was accused of striking the deadly blow.[21]

Lincoln's strategy in defending Armstrong involved steering the jury away from the grisly circumstances of the crime—having his face shattered did not kill him immediately; he rode his horse home and died there two days later—and more toward a detached, less emotional appraisal regarding what they did and did not know regarding Metzker's demise. Since he did not die immediately, Lincoln argued, there was no way to know for certain just what had killed the man. Nor could the jury be certain that it was Armstrong who wielded the slungshot that may or may not have delivered the fatal blow; Lincoln cast doubt on the testimony of an eyewitness who claimed to have seen Armstrong commit the assault by the light of a full moon that an almanac proved was not present on the night of the fight.[22]

To win his case, Lincoln needed to sow doubt in the jury's minds. To sow that doubt, he needed to move them carefully away from the certitude of fixating on Metzker's ugly death and more toward a cool appraisal of its vague circumstances. "He Spoke Slow," remembered a spectator, "and Carefully reviewed the whole testimony, picked it all to pieces, and Showed that the man though kiled had not received his wounds at the place or time named by the witness, but afterwards." Lincoln did evoke an emotional response from the jury, but not toward Metzker; instead, in his summation, Lincoln movingly spoke of the dire consequences a conviction would visit upon Armstrong's elderly mother, Hannah, an old friend from his New Salem days who had actually contacted Lincoln about taking her son's case: "He told of his kind feelings towards the Mother of the Prisoner, a widow, That she had been kind to him when *he* was young, lone and without friends." It worked; Lincoln won an acquittal for his client.[23]

A murder case like the Almanac Trial was the most obvious encounter between Lincoln and death in his law practice, but there were a variety of other, more subtle places in which death intruded. The miscellany of a sprawling practice could press death on Lincoln in all sorts of ways. He represented a man who sued the estate of a deceased acquaintance for a lot in Rochester, Illinois. He helped recover the balance of the sale price for a horse from the estate of a Christian County farmer. He served temporarily as a presiding judge in a case involving an insane mother who strangled her infant child. He represented a railroad trying to recover money from the estate of an agent who died only ten days after being paid to perform grading and masonry work.[24]

Death was incidental here, several degrees removed from the core dispute of the case; Lincoln likely was barely cognizant of the fact that a death was at the center of an estate settlement or a debt collection matter. But that was the point. Death could be muted, defanged to some extent, by a focus on procedures, on rules—on the job at hand. If he had chosen to do so, Lincoln could have dwelled on the grisly realities of Metzker's violent death, the sadness of a child strangled by his own mother, or any of a number of other tragic stories created in his professional life by the intersection of death and the law. But in doing so, he would not have been able to effectively do his job.

That job came to increasingly preoccupy him in the immediate aftermath of Eddy's passing. "From 1849 to 1854, both inclusive, [I] practiced law more assiduously than ever before," he later wrote in a brief autobiographical sketch. "I was losing interest in politics, when the repeal of the Missouri Compromise aroused me again."[25] This was in 1854, a date that usually provides for Lincoln's biographers a tidy place to identify his resumption as a politician. But his return really began with a eulogy to Henry Clay, who passed away in June 1852 at the age of sixty-five.

The eulogy was another dimension of the mourning rituals that obsessed nineteenth-century American society, part and parcel of the same general rulebook that determined the color of the plumes on Eddy's hearse and the length of time Mary should wear her widow's weeds. The exact definition of and rules for a eulogy, however, were a bit vague. The term itself comes from the Greek word *eulogia* and means "praise." Americans in Lincoln's day understood a eulogy to be a spoken or written tribute for a recently deceased person, normally providing a brief biography and lauding that person's achievements and character.

Published eulogies for dead presidents and other prominent politicians were common, along with judges, clergy, and other civic leaders. Edward Everett, for example (he of the Gettysburg cemetery dedication and Philadelphia Sanitary Fair) published in 1859 a eulogy for one Thomas Dowse of Massachusetts, which he had delivered before the Massachusetts Historical Society in December of the previous year. Everett's tribute praised Dowse for his philanthropic contributions, recounted his humble origins as the son of a "leather-dresser," and lauded his "generous feeling toward his natural kindred, and an enlightened regard to the public." Referencing a room that housed Dowse's library contributions, Everett enthused, "There, appropriately arranged in convenient and tasteful cabinets at the expense of his executors, and by their liberality, wisely interpreting and carrying out the munificent intentions of the donor . . . it will remain until the end of time . . . a noble monument, more durable, more significant, than marble or brass—to his pure and honored memory."[26]

Florid, a bit excessive and ornate, these were nevertheless the sort of fitting words that Americans in Lincoln's time believed should constitute a good eulogy for a deserving person. Eulogies normally included a laudatory overview of the subject's life, with a tendency (especially where political figures were concerned) to link those events to larger, prouder themes in the American pantheon of values. Eulogies tended to focus on the idea of a legacy, whether it be a record of public achievement, victories in battle, or some other contribution to the community. An 1830 eulogy of the late John

D. Godman, a physician and professor at Columbian College in Washington, D.C., stressed Godman's lengthy publication record as a bequeathal to the advancement of medical science. "This production will long remain a splendid monument of the genius and industry of its author, and be regarded as a model of composition for works of this description," it read. "It should have a place upon the table of every family, and be put into the hands of all the youths of our country."[27]

The more sophisticated eulogies skillfully wove a dead person's life and achievements with what the both the eulogist and the audience believed were also their most cherished values and principles. The subtext ran something like this: the deceased embodied these values, in character and behavior, and since those values are also *your* values and mine, you, I, and the deceased are made whole and profit from our association. Eulogies of particularly revered national figures—Thomas Jefferson and John Adams, for example, who both died on July 4, 1826, to the wonder of the nation—were in this broad sense political documents, blurring the distinction between religious veneration and civic pride. Shrewd eulogists knew they touched on something more profound to ordinary Americans than a stump speech or editorial when they connected death, a sense of the divine, and America's belief in its own exceptionalism. "A summons of more awful import, the Fiat of the Most high, had sped to call them, with humble faith let us say, to another and a better country," noted one Joseph Tillinghast of Rhode Island upon the deaths of Adams and Jefferson. "It was not for them to be borne with the honours of common greatness, upon the tide of an admiring crowd. But their soaring spirits, almost without a figure it may be said, were wafted to heaven upon the acclimations of a free and mighty nation."[28]

By the time he was an adult, Lincoln had heard and read his share of such sentiments; he knew and understood the ways in which public figures were memorialized. He had signed resolutions to mark the passing of deceased colleagues at the bar or in Springfield at large. He had also been both a spectator and a participant in the death and mourning of one of the most famous public men of his day, former president and then congressman John Quincy Adams. As one of Illinois' representatives, Lincoln may have been a witness on February 21, 1848, when Adams, eighty years of age, collapsed and died of a stroke on the floor of the House congressional chamber. He was a member of the committee tasked with planning Adams's memorial service, and he marched in the funeral procession.[29]

So Lincoln understood how public figures should be mourned, but at the time of Henry Clay's death, his only other direct experiences with eulogies had been a brief address in 1842 for Benjamin Ferguson, president of Springfield's Washington Temperance Society, and a eulogy for President Zachary Taylor when he died suddenly in office in July 1850. In Ferguson's case, Lincoln seems to have been acting on the request of the society's members that he deliver fitting words at one of their meetings after Ferguson—a local businessman identified in various sources only as a carpenter and a "contractor and builder"—died following a brief and unidentified illness. Lincoln's eulogy was perfunctory: "In his intercourse with his fellow men," Lincoln said vaguely, "he possessed that rare uprightness of character, which was evidenced by his having no disputes or bickerings of his own, while he was ever the chosen arbiter to settle those of his neighbors."[30]

Lincoln's eulogy for President Taylor was an essay rather than a speech, printed in the *Daily Journal*, a Chicago newspaper edited by Lincoln's friend and political ally Charles L. Wilson. Wilson probably asked Lincoln to prepare something for his paper once news broke regarding Taylor's death. Lincoln did not have much time; Taylor died on July 9, and Lincoln's eulogy would appear in the July 27 edition of the *Daily Journal*. It subsequently bore the marks of a hastily prepared document, with some minor factual errors regarding dates and Taylor's family history.[31]

Lincoln's eulogy for Henry Clay, written two years later, was different. Clay was a personal hero to Lincoln, his "beau ideal of a statesman" and the founding father of Lincoln's beloved Whig Party. During the week following Clay's death on June 29, the entire nation marked his passing with ceremonies and meetings. In Springfield, prominent citizens and members of local civic organizations gathered in the downtown area, where business was suspended and at eleven o'clock, seventy-six "minute guns" marking Clay's birth in the patriotic year of 1776 were fired. The crowd then proceeded from the Springfield Episcopal church to the representatives' chamber in the capitol building, where, according to the *Sangamon Journal*, the "Honorable A. Lincoln pronounced an impressive eulogy on the character and services of the deceased."[32]

Lincoln used the occasion to draw a symbolic connection between Clay's life and that of the nation. He noted their shared 1776 birthdate and declared that "the infant nation, and the infant child began the race of life together. . . . In all that has concerned the nation the man ever sympathised; and now the nation mourns for the man." His eulogy also contained plenty of the effusive and sometimes mawkish praise common to such circumstances; just as Lincoln knew how to properly mourn his dead son two years earlier, so too did he now understand what his audience wanted to hear. "Alas! Who can realize that Henry Clay is dead!" Lincoln declared, quoting a Democratic newspaper. "Ah, it is at times like these, that the petty distinctions of mere party disappear. We see only the great, the grand, the noble features of the departed statesman; and we do not even beg permission to bow at his feet and mingle our tears with those who have ever been his political adherents. . . . Henry Clay belonged to his country—to the world, mere party cannot claim men like him. His career has been national—his fame has filled the earth—his memory will endure to 'the last syllable of recorded time.'"

He mingled with these showers of praise an overview of Clay's long political career. Lincoln made clear to his listeners that he identified closely with the Great Pacificator's underlying political ideology and moral principles and that those principles were relevant in a time of increasing sectional tensions. "As a politician or statesman, no one was so habitually careful to avoid all sectional ground," Lincoln noted. "Whatever he did, he did for the whole country. . . . Feeling, as he did, and as the truth surely is, that the world's best hope depended on the continued Union of these States, he was ever jealous of, and watchful for, whatever might have the slightest tendency to separate them."

These were Lincoln's values as much as Clay's. At the conclusion, Lincoln offered an extended examination of Clay's antislavery ideas, particularly his embrace of gradual emancipation and colonization—ideas Lincoln also shared. "Cast into life where slavery was already widely spread and deeply seated, he did not perceive, as I think no wise man has perceived, how [slavery] could be at *once* eradicated, without producing a greater evil, even to the cause of human liberty itself," Lincoln declared. Clay's "feeling and his judgment, therefore, ever led him to oppose both extremes of opinion on the subject."

The Clay eulogy also marks the emergence of what would thereafter become a hallmark of Lincoln's own antislavery efforts: his constant invocation and reverence for the Declaration of Independence as a rebuke of proslavery extremists. After briefly disparaging abolition extremists who "would shiver into fragments the Union of these States . . . rather than slavery should continue a single hour," Lincoln then declared, "I would also, if I could, array

[Clay's] name, opinions, and influence against the opposite extreme—against a few, but an increasing number of men, who, for the sake of perpetuating slavery, are beginning to assail and to ridicule the white-man's charter of freedom—the declaration that 'all men are created free and equal.'"[33]

The Clay eulogy was as much a description of the living Abraham Lincoln as it was of the dead Henry Clay. Lincoln here expressed his own nationalist and antislavery principles, rooted those principles in the Declaration of Independence, and fastened all of it to the bier of one of the greatest American politicians of his day. It was, in short, Lincoln the politician making professional use of a death.

This was not a crass or cynical exercise. Lincoln genuinely believed in both what he was saying and his fundamental accord with Henry Clay's legacy. But had Lincoln in 1852, at this point an obscure former one-term congressman and state legislator, expressed in a speech his perspective on slavery and the principles of the Declaration of Independence, he would have garnered less attention than by expressing those views at a time of national mourning for a dead American hero. He surely knew this.

Still, there were limits to how he might use death and mourning to benefit himself politically. He did not make politicized eulogies a habit; the Clay eulogy was in fact the last eulogy he would ever compose. "I am not accustomed to the use of language of eulogy," he said many years later; it was quite true.[34]

Nor did he care much for sentimentalizing death in the political arena. On one occasion, he mocked Stephen Douglas's use of a typical Good Death narrative to advance Douglas's own political interests and that of the Little Giant's pet project, popular sovereignty. In an 1858 speech in Bloomington, Illinois (just before their famous series of debates began), Douglas had described a deathbed scene in which Clay gave his blessings to popular sovereignty. When he made such use of Lincoln's "beau ideal of a statesmen," it struck a nerve. "Last evening, in a sort of weeping tone, he described to us a death bed scene," Lincoln said of Douglas during a speech a few days later. "He had been called to the side of Mr. Clay, in his last moments, in order that the genius of 'popular sovereignty' might duly descend from the dying man and settle upon him, the living and most worthy successor. He could do no less than promise that he would devote the remainder of his life to 'popular sovereignty'; and then the great statesman departs in peace." Sneering at Douglas's pretensions in quoting the Whig Clay in service of a Democratic Party policy ("the Judge has evidently promised himself that tears shall be drawn down the cheeks of all old Whigs, as large as half grown apples"), Lincoln belittled the idea that Douglas and his allies were wrecking the Compromise of 1850 in the name of principles Clay supposedly bequeathed to Americans the way a dying parent imparted advice to children. "It would be amusing, if it were not disgusting, to see how quick these compromise-breakers administer on the political effects of their dead adversaries, trumping up claims never before heard of, and dividing the assets among themselves," Lincoln declared. "If I should be found dead tomorrow morning, nothing but my insignificance could prevent a speech being made on my authority, before the end of next week."[35]

Later in 1858, during a speech in Lewistown, Illinois, he grew impassioned about Douglas's habitual parsing of the Declaration of Independence to exclude Americans who were not white. Speaking with "great earnestness" according to an onlooker, Lincoln told his audience:

> If you have been taught doctrines conflicting with the great landmarks of the Declaration of Independence . . . if you have been inclined to believe that all men are *not* created equal in those inalienable rights enumerated by our chart of liberty, let me entreat you to come back.
> . . . You may do anything with me you choose, if you will but heed these sacred principles. You may not only defeat me for the Senate, but you may take me and put me to death. . . . *But do not destroy that immortal emblem of Humanity—the Declaration of American Independence.*[36]

On the eve of the Civil War, Lincoln spoke in similar terms, this time while standing on the steps of Independence Hall in Philadelphia. After referencing the Founders' legacy in the building behind him, he identified as the nation's "great principle" the idea that "in due time the weights should be lifted from the shoulders of all men, and that *all* should have an equal chance." Warming to the subject, and admitting that the times and the location had filled him with deep emotion, he declared, "If it can't be saved upon that principle, it will be truly awful. But, if this country cannot be saved without giving up that principle—I was about to say I would rather be assassinated on this spot than to surrender it."[37]

Few people aroused Lincoln's ire more than Stephen Douglas, and few subjects caused him to wax more eloquently than the Declaration and the Revolutionary generation, so perhaps it is not surprising that these things sometimes drew him to the hyperemotional subject of death. But they were exceptions to the rule. Normally he did not speak in terms of martyrdom or dying for a higher political cause, and he avoided the sort of rhetoric that might have led him to reference death in this way.

This was particularly noteworthy in his reaction to what was arguably the most politically important martyrdom of his time. On the eve of the Civil War, as Lincoln ascended to a position of respect and importance in the new antislavery Republican Party, there appeared on the American public stage someone who came to personify the idea of dying for a cause, and he did so in a way that was guaranteed to stir the deepest sorts of emotional reactions from his fellow Americans, North and South: "Hanging from the beam, / slowly swaying," Herman Melville later wrote in a poem about John Brown, describing him as "the meteor of the war."[38]

John Brown at times seemed almost steeped in violence and death. A flinty man with a hard countenance who harbored few reservations about enlisting lethal tactics in the name of ending slavery, Brown often quoted Hebrews 9:22 ("without the shedding of blood there is no remission of sin") and other Old Testament passages that linked justice to both inflicting and suffering death. He admired Nat Turner—the slave preacher who led a rebellion in 1831 that resulted in the deaths of over fifty white Virginians and a large number of African Americans—and Toussaint Louverture, the leader of Haiti's bloody slave rebellion in the 1790s. More moderate antislavery Americans were reluctant to openly praise either the Turner or Haiti rebellions, even if they secretly were sympathetic: the body counts were too high. But Brown was unperturbed.[39]

He was also willing to act on his convictions. In 1856, Brown and his sons hacked five proslavery settlers to death with swords along the banks of Pottawatomie Creek in Kansas. Three years later, he led a small band of followers in a sunrise raid on Harpers Ferry, Virginia, with the avowed purpose of inciting a bloody slave uprising. "We have reached a point," he told fellow abolitionist William Phillips, "where nothing but war can settle the question."[40]

The entire Harpers Ferry affair was badly botched; the first person to die was an African American railroad employee, caught a fusillade of bullets loosed by Brown's trigger-happy men at a train passing through town. Eventually the raiders barricaded themselves in a small engine house near the arsenal, surrounded by angry townspeople and members of the Virginia militia. Under the command of U.S. Army colonel Robert E. Lee—home on leave in nearby Alexandria—the militiamen rushed the building in a melee of gunfire that killed two of Brown's sons and eight other members of his little band. Brown was wounded from several sword thrusts by an onrushing militia officer, though none of the wounds were fatal. He was taken into custody and ensconced in a Virginia jail.[41]

Some people wondered if Brown had a death wish. When offered the chance to surrender, he shouted from inside the building, "No, I prefer to die here!" Following his arrest, he was resigned to his fate. When the governor of Virginia in an interview with Brown urged him to "think upon eternity," Brown calmly replied, "Governor, I have, from all appearances, not more than fifteen or twenty years the start of you in the journey to that eternity of which you kindly warn me; and whether my tenure here shall be fifteen months, or fifteen days, or fifteen hours, I am equally prepared to go."[42]

Tried for treason in proslavery Virginia, Brown's execution was a foregone conclusion, and he seemed to relish the idea of his impending martyrdom.[43] During the trial, he answered questions and gave statements with an almost eerie serenity. "If it is deemed necessary that I should forfeit my life for the furtherance of the ends of justice," he told the court in his final speech after the verdict of guilty was pronounced, "and mingle my blood further with the blood of millions in this slave country whose rights are disregarded by wicked, cruel, and unjust enactments, I say, let it be done." The jury took only forty-five minutes to find him guilty, and the judge pronounced a sentence of death forthwith. He was hanged a month later.[44]

Abolitionists knew good propaganda value when they saw it, and images of Brown's righteous martyrdom suffused abolitionist literature. Ralph Waldo Emerson, who had met Brown before the raid, likened him to Christianity's most revered figures: "That new saint, than whom none purer or more brave was ever led by love of men into conflict and death—the new saint awaiting his martyrdom, and who, if he shall suffer, will make the gallows glorious like the cross."[45] Even those who had little use for Brown or his tactics prior to his execution now discovered a nobility in the man heretofore unnoticed. As antislavery minister Henry Ward Beecher rather indelicately put it, "Let no man pray that Brown be spared. Let Virginia make him a martyr. . . . His soul was noble, his work miserable. But a cord and a gibbet would redeem all that." Others agreed. "By the gallows you have triumphed," read a resolution adopted by citizens meeting in Natick,

Massachusetts, to express their support for Brown two weeks before his execution, "Virginia will hang your body, but she will not hang John Brown. . . . Had you not done as you have, you would have died a living death for treason against God, as he spoke to you in the depths of your own soul."[46]

But for more moderate antislavery Americans like Lincoln, Brown's martyrdom posed a dilemma. If they agreed with Brown's purpose of ending slavery, most disagreed with his violent tactics. Members of the Republican Party felt compelled to tread carefully, given that their Democratic opponents and many proslavery Southern whites were convinced the Harpers Ferry raid was a clandestinely sanctioned Republican operation.

Many Republicans subsequently tried to draw a careful distinction between Brown's tactics (wrong) and his principles (right). His death provided a degree of cover for this distinction. He had died nobly and well, making praise of his principles easier and suggesting at the same time that however misguided his tactics, he had paid an appropriately high price for his failings.[47]

As Brown's trial proceeded during the latter part of October and into early November 1859, Lincoln coincidentally found himself in Kansas, where Brown had first made a name for himself with the Pottawatomie murders. Lincoln was touring the territory just after its citizens had adopted a Free-Soil constitution, so the various controversies that had roiled "Bleeding Kansas" regarding slavery over the last few years were uppermost on everyone's minds, and with Brown's trial receiving great national publicity, Lincoln felt compelled to say a few words on the matter. During a speech in Elwood, Kansas, he stated that he "believed the attack of Brown [on Harpers Ferry was] wrong for two reasons. It was a violation of law and it was, as all such attacks must be, futile as far as any effect it might have on the extinction of a great evil." He then occupied ground familiar among other members of the Republican Party, praising Brown for having "shown great courage, [and] rare unselfishness" but reiterating that "no man, North or South, can approve of violence or crime."[48]

He returned to the subject a few days later in Leavenworth, by which point Brown was dead. "Old John Brown has just been executed for treason against a state. We cannot object, even though he agreed with us in thinking slavery wrong," Lincoln declared. This time he did not speak at all to the man's character, noting only that Brown's antislavery convictions "cannot excuse violence, bloodshed, and treason. It could avail him nothing that he might think himself right." In a second speech, Lincoln reiterated his disapproval, noting that while he did "sympathize" with Brown's "hatred of slavery," he had no use at all for the Harpers Ferry raid and stated his belief that "the old man [was] insane."[49]

By 1860, even the faintest allusion to Brown's martyrdom as a courageous act, or to any private sympathies with his antislavery principles, had vanished from Lincoln's public statements. In February, he delivered an important speech at Cooper's Union in New York City. By this point, a congressional investigation led by prominent Democrats (including future Confederate president Jefferson Davis) had tried hard to establish a direct link between the Republican Party and Brown's raid. Lincoln expressed indignation at the very idea. "Harper's Ferry! John Brown!!" he exclaimed. "John Brown was no Republican; and [Democrats] have failed to implicate a single Republican in his Harper's Ferry enterprise. . . . Persisting in a charge which one does not know to be true, is simply malicious slander." He proceeded to heap scorn on the raid, again voicing no admiration or approval of its leader's motives. "John Brown's effort was peculiar," Lincoln pointed out. "It was not a slave insurrection. It was an attempt by white men to get up a revolt among slaves, in which the slaves refused to participate. In fact, it was so absurd that the slaves, with all their ignorance, saw plainly enough it could not succeed. That affair, in its philosophy, corresponds with the many attempts, related in history, at the assassination of kings and emperors. An enthusiast broods over the oppression of a people till he fancies himself commissioned by Heaven to liberate them. He ventures the attempt, which ends in little else than his own execution."[50]

Lincoln made a sound political decision in distancing himself from Brown's martyrdom. Any talk of Brown's "triumph at the gallows" or the like would have placed him in the company of the more radical antislavery elements he earnestly wished to avoid as he began laying plans to capture the Republican nomination for the presidency in 1860. Radicals found Brown's death redemptive, while more moderate antislavery Americans found his death politically useful, providing a way to express sympathy for the man without being tarred by his violent tactics.

Lincoln avoided talk of the former and did precious little of the latter; Brown the martyr was far too controversial. For Lincoln, death in the political realm, as with so much else involving this politically astute man, was a careful calculation. By 1860, he was a seasoned politician, unlikely to get carried away with his own emotions as he delivered a speech or expressed an opinion. He knew how to use a death when it suited his purposes, as in the Clay eulogy, and how to carefully avoid the highly emotional content of a political martyrdom, as with John Brown.

More generally, Lincoln's ideas about death were dualistic and somewhat contradictory. His taste in poetry, literature, and Shakespeare, along with his biblical fatalism, gave him an appreciation of death's mystery and un-knowability, an appreciation that was emotive and deeply attached to the gut-wrenching suffering he had witnessed in the deaths of his loved ones since an early age. But his legal training and political instincts taught him that death was also a thing that could be rationally analyzed, defined, and manipulated in a more detached manner. He would carry both sets of ideas with him into the White House.

4. ELMER

Elmer Ellsworth's death began and ended almost in the same instant: a loud blast reverberating down a stairwell, punctuated by the smell of gunpowder and wreathed in smoke. He lived only a few more brief moments, the hole in his chest quickly gurgling away his life's blood. He had just celebrated his twenty-fourth birthday.

When Lincoln first met Ellsworth sometime in 1860, the young man presented a somewhat curious mix of fiery bravado, ambition, and neediness. He was of average height, around five foot six, with a slight, compact frame. But he exuded an outsize charm that belied his ordinary size. Everyone who met him remarked on his effortless charisma, his good looks, and especially his athleticism. He was well coordinated and lithe, and he excelled in anything requiring physical activity or manual dexterity, "noted for his supremacy in all games requiring quickness of eye or limb." A friend recalled that while "he was less than the medium size, yet his strength was extraordinary; he seemed made of tempered steel."[1]

But athleticism and handsomeness were his only real assets; Ellsworth struggled much of his short life merely to gain respectability. His father's finances were wrecked in the Panic of 1837, and the young man was forced to cast about for work as he grew up, first in Mechanicville, New York, then New York City and Boston, and eventually Chicago. He peddled newspapers on a train, sold linen as a merchant's clerk, ran errands as an assistant to an engineer, and then for a time set type in a printing office. He did not last very long at any of these jobs, and none provided a stepping-stone to anything more lucrative or satisfying. His story was, according to an early biographer, "a weary history of uncongenial labor and foiled ambition."[2]

He made the acquaintance of Abraham Lincoln, and sometime in the spring or early summer of 1860, he began reading and studying for the Illinois bar in the office of Lincoln and Herndon in Springfield. Like nearly everyone else, Lincoln took a shine to the young man. Maybe he saw a little of himself in Ellsworth's penniless but intensely determined character, his constant casting about for a way to make something out of his life regardless of his humble background. By this point, Lincoln was an established, senior member of the Illinois bar, and although he was only fifty years old, he often cast himself as an older father figure for younger lawyers and men on the make. Ellsworth fit the mold, toiling away at Lincoln and Herndon's behest in their downtown Springfield law office, struggling to master Blackstone's *Commentaries* and the other seminal texts required of an attorney, all the while hoping for something more.[3]

Their relationship extended beyond Ellsworth's pursuit of a legal career. Lincoln "loved him like a younger brother," recalled Lincoln's private secretary, John Hay, and the president later wrote that their friendship was "as intimate as the disparity of our ages, and my engrossing engagements, would permit." Ellsworth became good friends with Hay and John Nicolay (Lincoln's other secretary), two fellow up-and-coming young Springfield men. At some point, Ellsworth also met Lincoln's family, and he developed a strong older-brother bond with the three Lincoln boys. Mary grew quite fond of him, and he became a regular visitor at the house on Eighth and Jackson Streets.[4]

Ellsworth was also a staunch Republican—he arrived in Springfield just as Lincoln began making his push to acquire the Republican Party's 1860 presidential nomination—and during the fall delivered several speeches on behalf of Republican causes and candidates; he was a "persuasive stump speaker," according to Hay. On the day Lincoln cast his own vote in the presidential election, Ellsworth (along with Herndon and several other friends) accompanied him to the polls. When he passed the bar exam early in 1861,

Ellsworth had to a certain extent arrived. He was now a bona fide lawyer and part of the president-elect's inner circle.[5]

But the military was always his real passion. He was especially fascinated by the exploits and reputation of French troops called Zouaves. Serving primarily in Algeria since the early 1830s, the Zouaves enjoyed an international reputation as crack troops, highly trained in marksmanship, drill, and skirmishing tactics. They were distinguished by their uniforms: brightly colored baggy pants, short braided jackets, and an idiosyncratic form of headgear called a *tarboosh*. Ellsworth sent away to Europe for books on Zouave tactics and their drill system, combining it with the U.S. Army's system (which he also absorbed through late-night reading sessions) to create complex and athletic drill routines that he performed for admiring onlookers at a Chicago gymnasium.[6]

His reputation gained him command of a company of like-minded young drill enthusiasts, the Rockford Grays, who staged displays of their drilling prowess at fairs and other gatherings around Illinois. They quickly gained a following, as did their handsome commander. Ellsworth had found his niche. The law was always something of a struggle—"it takes on an average half an hour to [read] each page" of Blackstone, he dejectedly wrote in his diary—but military organization, drill, and command came naturally. "Attended meeting of cadets' committee on ways and means," he wrote, happily adding, "all my propositions accepted."[7]

Lincoln knew of his student's martial enthusiasm. "That young man has a real genius for war!" Herndon remembered him exclaiming. In fact, Ellsworth knew very little about war. He had never seen combat or a battlefield. He did not know what a war zone looked like, and he had no clear idea regarding the damage and dislocations a real war created for those unfortunate enough to be caught in its wake. Most of all, Ellsworth had little conception of war's central, dark truth: violent and unremitting death. He had never seen someone die in battle, and he did not really know what a bullet, sword, or cannonball could do to a human body.[8]

But then again, few antebellum Americans knew wartime death, because few knew what *any* war looked like. There was the war with Mexico and the handful of desultory and infrequent combat encounters that sometimes arose with Native Americans. But this all took place far away and inflicted relatively few casualties, and it was an age when the national media, such as it was, was either unable or unwilling to shine a light into the darker corners of warmaking.

There was a battlefield version of the Good Death in antebellum America's popular imagination, and it looked much like the peacetime version. The dying soldier in the American mind was a man with God, country, and duty uppermost in his thoughts and the presence of mind to prepare himself for a noble death. "'Is not that the parley beating on the enemy's side?'" ran a popular account of the last words of an American officer during the Revolution. "'Have I not been fighting even to death to hear that sound? It is gladsome music to my, now, faint hearing—it ends this glorious war, and the colonies are now forever free. . . . Oh!—it's glorious!—my country is—is—free!'" At that, according to the story, "He fell back, dead!"[9]

None of this bore much resemblance to the grim realities of battle, yet such stories and images dominated the mental landscape of most antebellum Americans. For Lincoln to have been convinced that Ellsworth possessed a "real genius for war" reveals naïveté on the president-elect's part regarding the nature and hard truths of warfare. But his innocence merely reflected the larger American culture in which both he and his young friend dwelt.

It also reflected Lincoln's own circumstances; he had never seen much of war. His sole military service came when he was twenty-three, during the 1832 Black Hawk War. Lincoln served as a volunteer in the Illinois state militia, raised to thwart an invasion of the state by Sauk, Meskwaki, and Kickapoo Native Americans seeking to reclaim tribal lands. Lincoln was elected captain of his company, but not because he possessed any military skill or expertise. He knew little about drills or maneuvers, and he was not much of a disciplinarian; he was once forced to wear a wooden sword as punishment for allowing some of his men to discharge their weapons while in camp. He saw no combat, later joking, "I had a good many bloody struggles with the musquetoes; and, although I never fainted from loss of blood, I can truly say I was often very hungry."[10]

Throughout the 1850s, when talk in both the North and the South of a sectional conflict frequently devolved into hints of a fratricidal war between Americans, Lincoln consistently denied the possibility. War seemed at best a product of fevered imagination on both sides. "There will be no war, no violence" over slavery, he confidently declared during his last debate with Stephen Douglas in 1858. "It will be placed again where the wisest and best men of the world, placed it," on the path to "ultimate extinction." As Lincoln could not fully comprehend that there were large numbers of proslavery white Southerners who might be willing to destroy the Union to save slavery, so too did he fail to appreciate that they might kill or be killed in the pursuit of that same goal. War in Lincoln's mind was political and often metaphorical; it had not much to do with actual, violent death.[11]

As he prepared to travel to Washington, D.C., for his inauguration, the talk of war in the national press and from various public figures around the country steadily increased. Some believed bloodshed was inevitable; others did not. But Lincoln was reluctant to even mention the possibility, perhaps thinking that merely speaking of a civil war out loud might give it more concrete form or encourage that entire line of thinking. At no point between the time when he was elected and his departure for the nation's capital did he publicly use the word *war*.

Nor did he prepare himself or the nation for the possibility. Perhaps the most eloquent indicator of his attitude in this regard was his choice for secretary of war, Simon Cameron, a man with no military experience who would prove to be a poor administrator of the nation's military affairs. But when Lincoln chose him in early 1861, he never seems to have considered the possibility that his new secretary of war might not be up to the task. The choice was purely political; Cameron was a powerful Pennsylvania Republican, and he had provided crucial support for Lincoln's nomination and election. "War" in president-elect Lincoln's head was at best only a dim theoretical possibility.[12]

Again, in this Lincoln was not alone. Even those Americans who actually had witnessed a war and knew its human costs possessed no conception of what lay on the horizon in 1860. There simply was no available paradigm for the coming carnage. Few Americans, North or South, saw the bloodbath coming, and those who did were widely ridiculed. A fundamentally decent, cerebral man, Lincoln believed reason would prevail in the South—that and a sense of community binding Americans together, North and South. "Let us at all times remember that all American citizens are brothers of a common country, and should dwell together in the bonds of fraternal feeling," he told a gathering in Springfield soon after his election. He genuinely believed in that feeling.[13]

He should have paid more attention to the tone of many of the letters that were pouring into his office in Springfield—bags full of hate mail, many written with a deep-seated savagery that presaged the war's paroxysm of bloodletting. "May the hand of the devil strike you down before long—You are destroying the country. . . . Damn you—every breath you take," read a letter signed "Hand of God against you." Another letter from one R. A. Hunt pleaded with Lincoln to take the threats to his life seriously. "I have heard several persons in this place say that if you ever did take the President Chair that they would go to Washington City expressly to kill you," he wrote. "For you wife and children sake dont take the Chair if you do you will be murdered by some cowardly scoundrel." Hay kept a bulging folder marked "assassination," and in early 1861, Henry Whitney recalled, Lincoln "showed me several vulgar letters, all having Southern postmarks, containing threats against his life." And yet, Whitney noted, Lincoln "not only took no precautions against assassination himself, but allowed none to be taken on his behalf."[14]

Thus began a persistent theme in Lincoln's life, almost from the moment he became president and dogging him thereafter: his own mortality. Up to now, he had not spoken or written much about his own death. There was no compelling reason why he would have done so. He was in 1861 a healthy man with a robust physical constitution. He would turn fifty-two the day after he left Springfield for the capital, one of the younger presidents to that point in American history.[15]

All those death threats do not seem to have effected much of a change in his thinking. His chief worry was that the hate mail might fall into Mary's hands, and he instructed his secretaries to see to it that it did not. As Whitney noted, he took no precautions for his own security. He did not make out a will (nor would he ever do so), and he did not seem to take the threat of his own violent death seriously. "Neither he nor the country generally then understood the true facts concerning the dangers to his life," his friend and fellow lawyer Ward Hill Lamon later remembered.[16]

But if he did not comprehend just what exactly had been loosed with his election, he does seem to have felt, in a distant way, the rumblings of what was to come. As he boarded a train in Springfield for the journey east to Washington, D.C., he hinted at a sense of foreboding in his farewell speech at Springfield's train depot. "I now leave, not knowing when, or whether ever, I may return, with a task before me greater than that which rested upon Washington," he told the crowd gathered in a rainstorm before him at Springfield's rail depot. He even made a rare reference to Eddy, gone almost nine years, speaking of the town as the place where his "children have been born, and one is buried."[17]

The threats of assassination continued. Lamon was worried enough that he armed himself with multiple pistols, daggers, a blackjack, and brass knuckles and posted himself at the entrance to Lincoln's railway car. And there was also Elmer Ellsworth.[18]

By 1861, Ellsworth had developed a national reputation as a precision drillmaster. He was engaged to teach his drilling methods to the Governor's Guard in Madison Wisconsin, and in April 1859, he was elected captain of the U.S. Zouave Cadets of Chicago, a unit whose intricate drilling and marching skills earned it headlines nationwide and eventually an invitation to perform for President James Buchanan on the White House lawn in August 1860. Ellsworth rather cockily published a broadside pronouncing his unit of forty-two men (accompanied by an eighteen-piece band) "the best organized and drilled military company in the country" and issuing a challenge to all comers to prove otherwise. They embarked on a tour of the United States during the summer to prove their point, with a crowd estimated at ten thousand people seeing them off in Chicago. "There is not one member who is not a gentleman as well as a soldier," enthused a New York newspaper account. "The drill is most arduous, but; notwithstanding, every movement, no matter how complex, is executed to perfection."[19]

Returning home to Springfield after the tour, Ellsworth dutifully resumed his law studies throughout the summer and fall of 1860 and into early 1861. After Lincoln's election, he joined Lamon, Hay, Nicolay, and the president-elect's family for the trip east. Though he did not walk about with pistol butts and daggers protruding from his pockets, as the rather flamboyant Lamon was wont to do, Ellsworth did his part to help with security, checking arrangements for crowd control and the like. Like everyone else on the train, he worried about Lincoln's safety, and he stayed busy. "It will be absolutely impossible for me to leave the party for an hour," he wrote to his fiancée.[20]

Following the inauguration and the Fort Sumter crisis, and responding to Lincoln's call for seventy-five thousand volunteers to suppress the rebellion, Ellsworth traveled to his native state and recruited a new regiment, the 11th New York, specifically targeting the young men who manned New York City's firefighting brigades. "I want the New York firemen for there are no more effective men in the country," he proclaimed. "Our friends at Washington are sleeping on a volcano and I want men who are ready at any moment to plunge into the thickest of the fight." His recruiting circular sounded a highly patriotic note: "We are entering upon a struggle for the maintenance of our government, our institutions, and our national honor. . . . The firemen of New York must give an account of themselves in this contest."[21]

Two thousand men tried to enlist in his regiment, twice as many as he could accept. His "Fire Zouaves" quickly became one of the North's most celebrated military units, and Ellsworth found himself in demand. "I find myself surrounded by hosts of friends, of whose existence I *never dreamed* before," he wrote, and "who think they have discovered that *my stock*, is rising, and it *will pay to invest*."[22]

He had emerged as the North's beau ideal of a soldier. Other units copied his Zouave uniforms and drill routines, and he was keenly aware that his and his men's behavior was now prominent in the public eye. While in New York, he tailor designed the Fire Zouaves' uniforms, at one point taking the trouble to sketch out a special cap design for a New York haberdasher. The 11th New York was indeed a natty outfit, dressed in red shirts, short gray jackets, and gray pants. Ellsworth sported a sword, a "very heavy revolver," and "an enormously large and bloodthirsty-looking bowie knife, more than a foot long in the blade," according to John Hay.[23]

Leading his men on the journey from New York to Washington, Ellsworth enforced strict standards of behavior, mirroring his own. "Not one member of the company is allowed to indulge in the use of intoxicating drinks, or to visit places where drinks are sold," according to one newspaper reporter. Hay knew better; the Fire Zouaves had been recruited from some of the city's tougher neighborhoods, and Lincoln's private secretary called them "a jolly, gay set of blackguards . . . in a pretty complete state of don't care a damn, modified by an affectionate and respectful deference to the Colonel." When some Fire Zouaves engaged in shenanigans in Washington, Ellsworth sent several of them home and paid for the damages out of his own pocket.[24]

This was Elmer Ellsworth's war: impeccably dressed and drilled gentlemen with high moral standards embarked on a crusade for right and glory. There was no room in his war for boorish behavior, and their superlative marching and drilling made their warrior expertise seem all the more apparent, especially in those early days. "Much is hoped from the gallant Colonel's Bloodtubs," Hay observed. "They step together well and look as if they meant business." Matters as serious as death and dying hardly entered into the calculation. War for Ellsworth was a parade, and for his men, something of a lark. "They don't see what they were brought here to the 'war' for, as they can have more fighting any time in New York!" noted an amused reporter.[25]

Ellsworth's war was Lincoln's war as well, at least to a point. Lincoln lacked Ellsworth's youthful expectations of stainless character among men;

he had seen too much of the harder side of life, especially in his years litigating courtroom cases involving all sorts of bad behavior, to harbor unrealistic expectations. Nor did Lincoln possess Ellsworth's enthusiasm for all things military—at no point in his life was Abraham Lincoln enamored of war or military matters generally. He never did learn how to properly return a salute, and some soldiers were already remarking on their new commander in chief's frumpy and decidedly unmilitary bearing. A "source of worriment is your own personal manners," wrote a man named Robert Colby to the president in early May. Colby had been hearing complaints from soldiers. "For God's sake consult somebody, some military man, as to what you ought to do on [military] occasions. . . . You ought to assume some dignity for the occasion even though your breeding his not been military."[26]

But if he was not much given to romanticizing war, the president did not have any better understanding than Ellsworth of how painful and deadly a real war could be—at least not yet. His days after the bombardment of Fort Sumter were spent with administrative details, politics, patronage requests—what one would expect of a president dealing with the first harried days of a rapidly sprawling military conflict. Much of what he saw had an unreal quality. The famous abolitionist Cassius Clay burst into his office on April 22, for example, sporting three pistols and a huge knife, shades of Ward Hill Lamon, and looking (according to Hay) "like an admirable vignette to 25-cents-worth of yellow-covered romance." Three days later, a "jolly-hearted old Shaker from N[ew] H[ampshire] came in and filled the room with the freshness of his presence," Hay wrote, noting that the man apologized profusely for his late arrival in coming to defend the capital.[27]

Ellsworth was a frequent visitor at the White House, as he had been at the Lincoln home in Springfield. He again struck up his friendship with Willie and Tad, and he saw them frequently enough that he contracted measles from the two boys; all three were briefly bedridden early in 1861. In the meantime, the president tried to find a job for Ellsworth that was commensurate with the "genius for war" Lincoln thought he possessed. "I have been, and still am anxious for you to have the best position in the military which can be given you," he wrote to Ellsworth the day after the Sumter bombardment. He tried to have Ellsworth appointed inspector general for the militia but ran into a wall of opposition from more experienced military men. He then hoped to have Ellsworth appointed "chief clerk" in Cameron's War Department, but nothing came of that either. If Ellsworth was admired by many in the general populace, he rubbed others the wrong way, especially professional military men and those with political ambitions who resented Ellsworth's easy access to the president. "The jealousy of the staff officers of the regular army . . . was productive of very serious annoyance and impediment to Ellsworth," Hay recalled.[28]

Lincoln was never quite so naïve as to equate Ellsworth's talent for drill and organizational charts with expertise in real combat. The jobs Lincoln sought for his young friend were administrative and clerical, and Lincoln admitted that he was not yet, only two months into his presidency, a good judge of who might be good at war and who might not. "Ever since the beginning of our acquaintance, I have valued you highly as a person [and] friend," Lincoln wrote on April 15 to what was apparently becoming a frustrated Ellsworth, "and at the same time (without much capacity of judging) have had a very high estimate of your military talent." That qualification, "without much capacity of judging," is a telling little phrase; unlike so many other Americans in those early days of the Civil War, Lincoln knew what he did not know.[29]

Virginia seceded from the Union and joined the new Confederacy two days after Lincoln wrote that letter to Ellsworth, and the state's defection placed Confederate territory nearly on Lincoln's doorstep. Visible from the White House was a Confederate flag flying from a rooftop in Alexandria, Virginia, across the Potomac River. The flag seemed to mock Lincoln, mock what many in the North saw as a flailing administration that was too supine to mount an effective response to secession and the new Southern nation.

More to the point, Alexandria was a strategically important little town, located as it was so near the nation's capital, with both a railroad depot and telegraph office that could serve the new Confederate army, should its leaders decide to menace the national capital. Union planners wanted the town occupied and began massing units to mount a determined assault. Colonel Ellsworth saw an opportunity and presented himself and his command for the honor of leading the vanguard in the capture of Alexandria.

When the Fire Zouaves geared up for their mission on the evening of May 23, 1861, the war was only a little over a month old and had so far cost few lives. No one died at all during the war's first bona fide battle, from April 12 to 14, when the Confederates bombed a U.S. Army garrison stationed in Charleston Harbor's Fort Sumter (though two soldiers did die afterward from injuries they received when a cannon exploded during a one-hundred-gun salute fired during the lowering of the Fort's American flag).

Four soldiers died during a riot when their unit passed through heavily prosecessionist Baltimore on April 19. Six days prior to the Alexandria operation, Union gunboats exchanged cannon fire with a Confederate battery situated at Sewell's Point in Virginia; to this day, no one is sure whether anyone died during this "battle." Such was the Civil War by May 23.

Ellsworth and the men of the 11th New York, around a thousand strong, boarded three civilian steamers that had been pressed into service as military transports. They docked at Alexandria's wharves in the predawn hours on May 24. A few desultory musket shots rang out from Confederate sentinels scattered around the riverbank, who then quickly fled. Ellsworth and his men met no resistance as they walked down the gangways and formed up in the street running along the wharves. It was five o'clock, with sunrise not far away.

They saw drowsy civilians here and there as they spread out through the town but no Confederate soldiers, the darkness gradually giving way to early morning gray. Ellsworth was busy giving orders, deploying guards and sending companies to seize key points in the town. Severing Alexandria's communications was especially important; more Union units were scheduled to arrive, and keeping the town isolated from Confederate reinforcements and a possible counterattack was paramount. Ellsworth peeled off Company E and sent them toward Alexandria's rail depot. Company A he pointed toward the town's telegraph office.

He took a few steps down the street toward the telegraph office himself, thinking to accompany his men in accomplishing that vital mission. But the secession flag that everyone had seen from Washington, D.C., now fluttered overhead nearby, its folds clearly visible in the dawning light. It was affixed to a pole atop the roof of the Marshall House, a three-story hotel. "Boys, we must have that down before we return," he said. Detailing several men to accompany him, he marched up the steps and entered the hotel's front door.

A clerk and a few others—hotel boarders, perhaps—stared at the young colonel and his men as they entered the lobby. Ellsworth demanded to be shown the way to the roof. No one moved. Spying a staircase, Ellsworth ordered four of his men to remain on guard, while he and the remaining Zouaves clambered up the stairs.

In a hallway leading down the second floor from the stair landing, they saw an elderly man, standing half-dressed in only a shirt and trousers, with a sleepy, disheveled look. The sound of the soldiers' feet on the steps had apparently roused him from bed. "Who put that flag up?" Ellsworth demanded, his men crowding behind him. The man retorted with a sullen air, "I don't know. I am a boarder here." They left him standing in the hallway and continued to the roof.

The men climbed out onto the steeply sloped roof, using a ladder they had found in the hotel's attic, and cut the enormous flag down. The colonel picked up the folds and, with his men, began descending the staircase. In front was Corporal Francis Brownell, followed by Ellsworth and the rest. Ellsworth was unarmed, having handed his revolver to a comrade while he tried to stuff the flag into a manageable bundle.

They had nearly reached the second-floor landing again, when there appeared from the hallway that same half-dressed old man, now wielding a double-barreled shotgun. He was no mere boarder; his name was James Jackson, and he was the proprietor of the hotel. The sleepy look had given way to rage. Ellsworth was carrying his flag.

What happened next was a cacophony of split-second noise and confusion. Jackson leveled the shotgun at Ellsworth, who did not immediately see him, occupied as he still was with the unwieldy flag. Standing in front of his commander, Corporal Brownell swung his musket around to knock the shotgun barrel away. He swung so hard that he tripped and momentarily lost his balance, giving Jackson time to recover. The hotel proprietor pointed the gun again at Ellsworth and fired one barrel, hitting the young colonel at point-blank range. The concussion in that narrow space would have been deafening, the echo clanging down the stairwell, eyes stinging and ears ringing from the smoke and noise.

Brownell managed to regain his footing as his momentum carried him stumbling onto the second-floor landing where Jackson stood. Jackson swung the shotgun around at him and fired the other barrel, but adrenaline, the noise, and general confusion caused him to miss entirely. The buckshot buried itself into a door near the corporal's head, pieces of wainscoting and splinters showering down. Brownell stuck his musket right in Jackson's face and fired, adding a third report reverberating down the stairwell and hallway. He could not tell whether his shot had hit the mark—the smoke was blinding—and still seeing Jackson's shadowy figure before him, he thrust the long bayonet at the end of his rifle into Jackson's body, running him through. "My God!" Brownell heard someone scream from within the cloud of smoke. Only later did he realize it was Ellsworth.

The entire encounter was over in only a few seconds. "Who is hit?" yelled one of the men back up in the stairwell. They could hear the hotel's occupants stirring in their various rooms. Brownell quickly reloaded his weapon and pointed it right at the door damaged by Jackson's errant shotgun blast. The door began to open; pulling the musket's stock up to his shoulder and sighting down the barrel, Brownell drew a bead and yelled that he would kill anyone who emerged. The remaining Zouaves had by this point crowded onto the landing, weapons at the ready and pointed down the hallway. "There were quite a number [of boarders] converging to the point where we stood," recalled one. The nervous little band of Zouaves realized they were outnumbered, in a tightly confined space, and facing a possibly unruly crowd. Only their loaded weapons and the general shock kept them at bay.[30]

Jackson's shotgun blast had blown Ellsworth back onto the staircase. "It was at first difficult to discover the precise locality of his wound, for all parts of his coat were equally saturated with blood," a Zouave remembered. The men gingerly loosened his belt and began to unbutton his coat when they saw a hole, slightly smaller than a man's fist, gaping just above and to the left of a brass button, over his heart. All those searing hot buckshot pebbles had shredded the aorta, broken Ellsworth's third rib, and passed through his lung, burrowing into the spine and breaking two vertebrae. Bright streams of blood poured from his chest, soaking his clothes, his face, and much of the flag. A gold medallion Ellsworth carried in his lapel pocket had been slammed deep into his chest; a doctor would later dig it out during the autopsy.[31]

His pallor was rapidly turning a sickening pale bluish-white as blood drained away from the body. "None of us had any medical knowledge," admitted a soldier, "but we saw that all hope must be resigned." They nevertheless sent for the regimental surgeon, who arrived in a few minutes. By that point, Ellsworth was dead.[32]

So was his assailant. Brownell had fired his weapon at nearly point-blank range, the bullet and powder blast from the muzzle tearing into Jackson's face and leaving a wound "so appalling that I shall not attempt to describe it," recalled an onlooker. A reporter later wrote that Brownell's bullet "blew [Jackson's] brains out," suggesting a ghastly mess. The blast and bayonet thrust had thrown Jackson down the stairs to the lobby floor. He lay there facedown, the empty shotgun underneath him, an angry crowd gathering around. It included Brownell's wife, "wild almost to insanity" as she stared at her dead husband's body and wondered aloud whether her children would now be killed. Jackson's sister soon appeared as well, mumbling, "Of course they wouldn't shoot a man dead in his house about a bit of old bunting."[33]

Someone found a red blanket, in which they hastily sewed Ellsworth's corpse. Wrenching a door loose from its hinges, the Zouaves turned it into a makeshift stretcher. By now the regiment had secured the town, and a crowd of onlookers watched as the body was removed from the stairwell, carried out of the hotel, and taken down the street to one of the steamers for the journey back to Navy Yard at Washington, D.C. There he was laid on a bench in the engine room, the red blanket was removed, and he was surrounded with the customary civilian accoutrements of mourning: black crepe on the building and a wreath of flowers on his breast ("shockingly lacerated by the slug shot," noted an onlooker).[34]

This was a military affair, and there were customs regarding how a dead soldier was to be honored. He was still dressed in his Zouave uniform, and the bench on which he lay was covered in the national flag. Flags similarly adorned the engine house's exterior, and he was afforded an honor guard—a military variant of the civilian practice that bodies should be guarded by vigilant family members until the actual funeral. Flags were flown at half-mast, both at the Navy Yard and soon at other military installations around Washington.[35]

Lincoln learned of Ellsworth's death later that day, when a messenger from the War Department's telegraph office arrived at the White House to deliver the news. A newspaper correspondent and Senator Henry Wilson of Massachusetts happened to call on the president soon afterward, and they found him in the library, staring out the window at the Potomac River below. "He did not move until we approached very closely," wrote the correspondent, "when he turned round abruptly, and advanced toward us, extending his hand: 'Excuse me,' he said, 'but I cannot talk.' . . . To our surprise the President burst into tears, and concealed his face in his handkerchief."[36]

The president and the First Lady arrived at the Navy Yard the next morning. After spending some time gazing at Ellsworth's body, Lincoln personally supervised his removal to the White House's East Room; deceased presidents William Henry Harrison and Zachary Taylor had both lain in state in that room. Ellsworth was now ensconced in a flag-draped coffin, set on a bier draped with an American flag, white lilies on his breast. The coffin had a glass covering to reveal Ellsworth's head and upper body; some thought his complexion had an unnatural hue, a "livid paleness," one report wrote, that "contrasted strongly with the ruddy glow of health that always characterized the Colonel in his lifetime." The secessionist flag, still bloodstained, lay on the bier nearby.[37]

Like the viewing at the Navy Yard, Ellsworth's East Room service had a military air, with honor guards flanking the coffin and prominent army officers in attendance. General Winfield Scott was resplendent in full dress uniform (though badly hampered by his great girth and the gout), along with various other high-ranking commanders from the army and navy.[38] There were also at least two women present, exceptions to the prewar custom that women should not attend funeral services: the First Lady and Julia Taft, the teenage daughter of a Patent Office lawyer who had come to know both Ellsworth and the Lincoln family when she brought her two younger brothers to the White House as playmates for Willie and Tad. Mary placed a photo of Ellsworth on the coffin, and Julia a wreath of white flowers. In Ms. Taft's case, the moment proved nearly overwhelming. "It made me quite faint," she recalled. "I had never looked on one dead."[39]

Lincoln's deep involvement in the mourning and funeral for his young friend was evident in the unusual circumstance of how Ellsworth's body was preserved: he was embalmed, a procedure that was rare before the war and was undertaken at the president's personal behest. The man considered to be the "father of embalming," Dr. Thomas Holmes, performed the service. Secretary of State Seward brought Holmes to the president's attention while Lincoln directed preparations for Ellsworth's funeral. How Seward knew of Holmes is unknown; the doctor had advertised his skills as a professional embalmer in Washington newspapers and only four days before Ellsworth's death was appointed as a surgeon in the U.S. Army, with his stated duty being to "embalm all those killed in battle," according to a *New York Times* reporter. The fact that Holmes would be expected to preserve the remains of every Civil War battle casualty is eloquent testimony to how unprepared the nation was for the coming carnage. Whatever procedure Dr. Holmes performed on Ellsworth's corpse was apparently to the president's satisfaction; while some thought the body was too pale, Lincoln remarked on the corpse's lifelike quality.[40]

The Reverend J. Smith Pyne of St. John's Episcopal Church in Washington, D.C., performed the service. St. John's was a traditional place of worship for

American presidents, dating back to the days of James Madison. Lincoln was still not a regular churchgoer, but he did attend Reverend Pyne's services soon after his arrival in Washington, accompanied by Seward. Following the service, large numbers of people filed through the East Room to gaze on the coffin, so many that army authorities had difficulty keeping the crowd orderly; some people even cut swatches of cloth from the secessionist flag as souvenirs. The coffin was then carried by Zouave pallbearers to a waiting hearse, followed by a procession down Pennsylvania Avenue, Lincoln riding in a carriage just behind the coffin. Crowds lined the street as they passed, and thousands more would come to view Ellsworth's body when it was transported to New York City several days later. Church bells rang and flags flew at half-mast throughout the North.[41]

The day of the funeral, Lincoln wrote a letter of condolence to Ellsworth's parents. "In the untimely loss of your noble son, our affliction here, is scarcely less than your own," he wrote. "So much of promised usefulness to one's country, and of bright hopes for one's self and friends, have rarely been so suddenly dashed, as in his fall." Lincoln reiterated his faith in Ellsworth's talents and military capacity. "His power to command men, was surpassingly great," the president noted, and "this power, combined with a fine intellect, an indomitable energy, and a taste altogether military, constituted in him, as seemed to me, the best natural talent, in that department, I ever knew."[42]

Lincoln carried his grief for some time afterward. "He was a great pet in the [Lincoln] family," noted Mary's cousin Elizabeth Grimsley, who was visiting the White House at the time, "and Mr. Lincoln feels it very much."[43] He was moved to tears both while looking at Ellsworth's body at the Navy Yard and while attending the East Room service. "I felt an impulse to tell the President about our pleasant visit to Colonel Ellsworth the day before he was ordered to Alexandria," Julia Taft recalled, "but I was told that the President wept at the mention of Ellsworth and I was afraid it would make him grieve." This man who was described by nearly everyone who knew him as being in tight control of his feelings seemed barely able to do so where the subject of Elmer Ellsworth was concerned.[44]

He was genuinely shocked by Ellsworth's death. He of course knew that young men would die, probably in large numbers, in the war that was now the defining fact of his presidency. For that matter, he was mature enough to know—as so many nineteenth-century Americans knew—that he would probably lose at least one child to illness, as had occurred with Eddy, and death was an omnipresent feature of his early frontier life. Americans of his time spoke constantly of death, created elaborate rituals to wrap around the great central fact of death, made of death a familiar specter.

But Ellsworth's demise, sudden and messy as it had been, put a name and a face on wartime death that previously had not existed, and it occurred in a war Lincoln had not really expected. As an athletic, energetic young man with a "genius for war," Ellsworth did not seem like the sort who would die, who *should* die, before having a real chance to prove his mettle in combat, at the hands of a disgruntled, half-dressed old man wielding a shotgun, no less. "I have ventured to address you this tribute to the memory of my young friend, and your brave and early fallen child," Lincoln wrote to the Ellsworths. "Early fallen child" was not just a reference to Elmer's youth; it also seemed as if he had died far too early in his soldier's career.[45]

Lincoln's shock was the nation's shock. "All classes seem to regard [Ellsworth's] death as a personal affliction," Hay wrote. "Our citizens are filled with grief and wrath at Colonel Ellsworth's death," Chicagoan Joseph Medill wrote Lincoln, "A Virgin[ia] traitor would fare no better at our hands than at those of his 'Pet Lambs' if we could get at the thieving assassins."[46]

The idea of Ellsworth having been "assassinated," rather than being a more legitimate combat victim, was common in the North, whose citizens characterized it as the wanton murder of an American soldier doing his duty by a crazed secessionist hothead. "He has been assassinated!" read Ellsworth's obituary in the *New York Times*, "He has lived a brief but an eventful, a public and an honorable life. His memory will be revered, his name respected, and long after the rebellion shall have become a matter of history, his death will be regarded as a martyrdom, and his name will be enrolled upon the list of our country's patriots."[47] Other newspapers around the country offered similar encomiums. "The entrance into Alexandria was attended by an event which has cast a deep gloom over this community," said one Ohio newspaper. "Colonel Ellsworth, who had hauled down the secession flag from the Marshall house, was soon afterwards shot by a concealed foe."[48]

Prints of Ellsworth's death soon appeared. "Murder of Colonel Ellsworth of the Fire Zouaves" depicted a heroically fallen hero, still clutching the flag he had removed from the Marshall House's steeple. "The Murder of Colonel Ellsworth" was the title of a similar illustration on the front page of the June 15 issue of *Harper's Weekly*. Various reproductions of Ellsworth's photographic portrait became popular, as did a photograph of Corporal

Brownell, posed with his musket and one foot standing on the flag Ellsworth had removed. He was awarded the Medal of Honor.[49]

In the South, Ellsworth's assailant was commemorated as a fallen hero, "the first martyr in the war for Southern independence." Jackson had actually been an inconsequential man, but Southern culture cast him as a martyred hero of Confederate independence. In 1862, a pamphlet biography of Jackson appeared throughout the Confederacy, portraying Jackson as an aggrieved homeowner defending his hearth from a rapacious Yankee. "He is lauded as a hero," read the pamphlet's introduction, "loved for his devotion to the flag of his country, and the terrible determination with which he defended it."[50]

The outpouring of stories, artwork, songs, and the like underline the fact that while Ellsworth's death was profoundly personal to Lincoln and Elmer's other friends, it carried political implications as well. When Northerners described Ellsworth's death as a "murder" or an "assassination," they were essentially delegitimizing the entire Southern enterprise of creating a viable, separate nation, for as a mere murderer, James Jackson represented nobody and was a martyr to nothing. Ellsworth, on the other hand, was in his martyrdom the embodiment of Northern resolve and legitimacy, his death proving to be a very effective recruiting tool. New regiments would name themselves "The People's Ellsworth Regiment" and the like, and a desire to avenge his death was a motivating factor for some Northern men to enlist. Songs were written on the theme of Ellsworth's inspiring patriotism, and a poem exhorted:

> Brave Fire Zouaves! your leader's name
> Is left you for a battle-cry;
> Let Ellsworth's pure and spotless fame
> Lead you to conquer or to die.[51]

But Lincoln never used Ellsworth's death for political purposes or to fire up Northern resolve. The letter he wrote to Ellsworth's parents, unlike later letters he wrote with an eye toward their public consumption, seems not to have had any larger audience or purpose other than comforting Elmer's grieving parents. In July, when he sent his first major address to Congress following his inauguration, Lincoln did not directly reference Ellsworth's death or the notion of dying for one's country at all, instead concluding with the simple exhortation for loyal Americans to "go forward without fear, and with manly hearts."[52]

New at his job, and never much inclined toward using death for political purposes, Lincoln seems not to have thought of using the death of his friend as a propaganda device. But he would soon learn. He would discover how to put more emotional distance between himself and battlefield death, and he would learn how to speak, with more eloquence than any other American president before or since, of the martyrdom of the battlefield dead and its higher political meaning. But first he would experience a death even more personal, more shocking, and more profound than even the demise of the young colonel.

5. WILLIE

Following Ellsworth's funeral, Jackson's secessionist flag, which had been displayed at the funeral services in both Washington and New York, was presented to the First Lady. Mary could hardly stand to look at the blood-stained thing. She hid it away in a bureau drawer.

But eight-year-old Tad Lincoln was inordinately fascinated with the flag and got into the habit of digging it out of the drawer and displaying it at the most inopportune and embarrassing moments. One such occasion was a troop review, during which Tad stood behind his father, waving it while Lincoln stood holding the Stars and Stripes. "The sight of a rebel flag caused some commotion," Julia Taft remembered, "and when the President saw what was happening he pinioned his bad boy and the flag in his strong arms and handed them together to an orderly, who carried the offenders [into the White House]."[1]

Older brother Willie, who was ten when the Lincolns arrived in Washington, was sometimes Tad's partner in crime, other times not. He shared Tad's roguish streak, at least to an extent, but lacked his younger brother's more troubling tendency toward peevishness, as well as Tad's physical difficulties—a cleft palate made Tad's speech difficult to understand, and the boy could sometimes grow frustrated. Tad may also have suffered from a learning disability, as he found reading difficult and experienced problems with basic daily functions like dressing himself.

But Willie was a bright young lad. "He had a decided literary taste, and was a studious boy," remembered Mary Lincoln's seamstress, Elizabeth Keckly.[2] He was not nearly as given to moodiness as the eldest Lincoln son, Robert, and he had a strong analytical bent that pleased his father. Willie liked to memorize railroad timetables and would calculate times and distances for imaginary trips from Chicago to New York. He was, Hay later wrote, "a child of great promise, capable of close application and study."[3]

Lincoln loved all his sons, but Willie's cheerful disposition and intellectual bent suited him best. "He was his father's favorite," Keckly thought, observing that "they were intimates—often seen hand in hand." Lincoln saw Willie (and usually Tad, despite his various challenges) as a kind of quiet spot, an oasis of innocence in a sea of bloodshed and brutality; they were his only retreat into something resembling normalcy. "When the president came into the family sitting room and sat down to read, the boys would rush at him and demand a story," Julia Taft recalled. "Tad perched precariously on the back of the big chair, [and] Willie on one knee."[4]

But Willie and Tad saw their father less and less, as he was now fully engrossed in the war. The entire White House was inundated with war, full of soldiers and the ubiquitous presence of all things military. Willie and Tad both were given miniature Zouave uniforms—probably patterned after those of Ellsworth's Fire Zouaves—and in the summer they camped out in a military-style tent on the White House lawn. They also recruited playmates as enlisted men in a unit they called "Mrs. Lincoln's Zouaves," with the Lincoln boys as officers, and they drilled in and around the White House. They annoyed the groundskeepers by digging "rifle pits" in the gardens, and they sometimes accompanied Lincoln and other adults on visits to army camps in the city.

When the Sanitary Commission of New York sent the boys a doll dressed in a Zouave uniform, Willie and Tad played with the doll by staging mock trials for "desertion," followed by an "execution" by firing squad using Tad's toy cannon. They then proceeded to bury the doll, named Jack, with all the trappings of a full military funeral, both boys apparently having seen enough of such things (or recalling the Ellsworth funeral in the East Room) to approximate the real deal. Mary's only reaction was to worry that Jack's "grave" might wreck the rose garden where the boys performed their "funeral."[5]

There is no evidence that either Abraham or Mary was particularly concerned about their young children immersing themselves in so much that was related to war—a war that was to quickly evolve into an ugly bloodbath. Nor were the Lincoln boys unique. In playing soldier, Willie and Tad were doing what many other young boys were doing during the Civil War. Children's magazines, juvenile novels and fictional short stories, artwork, and toys engrossed America's children North and South with the business of war. Most parents tried not to unduly expose their children to war's endemic encounters with death. But children surely often sensed that beneath the surface of wartime adventure stories, toy soldiers, and toy guns lurked grimmer realities.[6]

For all the whimsy that surrounded the Lincoln boys' mock trials of Jack and other war-related play—the president once wrote out a pardon for Jack, only to be told in total seriousness by Willie and Tad that sentence had already been pronounced—those deadly realities were never far away. The boys would have daily seen soldiers in and around their home, witnessed their father conferring with generals and military planners, and possibly overheard talk of battlefield body counts, burial details, and the like. Willie got into the habit of wandering down to the White House stables and reading battle reports to the employees, reports that surely contained statistics on the dead. And when the Lincolns began in midsummer 1861 to relocate to a large cottage called the Soldiers' Home on the outskirts of the capital city to escape Washington's oppressive heat, the boys would have seen maimed and disabled soldiers from the nearby convalescent facility from which the cottage got its name.[7]

None of this is to suggest that Abraham and Mary were bad parents in allowing their boys to be constantly exposed to reminders, large and small, of war's violence. Given the war's ubiquity in their lives—indeed, in every American's life—such exposure was unavoidable. Willie and Tad would have come to understand, if only in a dim fashion, that the war involved an ever-increasing number of men suffering and dying. As the summer advanced and the first sizable battles occurred at Bull Run, Wilson's Creek, and elsewhere, they surely overheard bits and pieces of conversations among uniform-clad men, the household staff, and their own parents regarding the nation's growing casualty lists.

One death hit especially close to home. In October, the president learned that an old friend from Illinois, Edward Baker, had perished in battle. Lincoln knew Baker from their days serving together in the Illinois militia during the Black Hawk War and later as fellow circuit lawyers and representatives in the state house. Charming, eloquent, but also somewhat combative and intensely ambitious, Baker was often Lincoln's political rival, though this inflicted no lasting damage on their friendship. Lincoln thought well enough of Baker that he had named his son Eddy after him.[8]

Baker's demise came during a dreadful little debacle at a place called Ball's Bluff in Virginia, where Union units tried unsuccessfully to dislodge a Confederate force from high ground on the banks of the Potomac River near Leesburg. Baker commanded a regiment in the assault, and he followed the custom holding that officers should lead by example and risk their lives with their men. He stood ten paces out in front of his men, directing their fire and urging them to "keep cool now, and fire low"—common advice, as excited soldiers had a tendency to aim their muskets high. Baker saw a man on a white horse emerge from the smoke and in the confusion thought he was a fellow Union officer. He was actually a Confederate cavalryman, who rode up and emptied his revolver—either five or six shots—into Baker. Baker may also have caught the attention of other Confederates, for afterward an examination of his body counted nine musket balls, including two embedded in his hat. He died instantly.[9]

When Lincoln heard the news, he was borne down with sorrow, more so than at any time since Ellsworth's death. "He seemed, indeed, to feel the loss as if of a brother," reported the *New York Tribune*, "and [he] paced the floor of his room through the night in the greatest grief." Both the president and First Lady announced the following day that they would receive no visitors at the White House. Later in the war, Lincoln told journalist Noah Brooks that "the keenest blow of all the war was at an early stage, when the disaster of Ball's Bluff and the death of his beloved Baker smote upon him like a whirlwind from the desert."[10]

The president requested that Baker's body be brought to the East Room, as with Ellsworth. But as a reporter observed, this was "not practicable" because Mary's various White House renovation projects had begun, and the East Room was a mass of exposed plumbing and disassembled wood-work.[11] The viewing was instead held at the private Washington residence of a fellow army officer and friend of Baker's, Major James W. Webb. Baker's body was embalmed, a difficult procedure, given the number of bullets that struck him, at least one of which had carried away part of his head. In their haste, the embalmers were unable to complete the job, and one newspaper correspondent observed that a wound "above the left ear is open to sight." The Senate chaplain delivered the eulogy, after which Baker was given a large procession through the city, the cortege moving "with solemn and measured tread . . . while the muffled tones of the bells sounded out their solemn cadence."[12] That evening, after what Hay described as a "heavy day," Lincoln sat talking about the matter in quiet tones with General McClellan. "There is many a good fellow that wears the shoulder-straps going under the sod before this thing is over," McClellan remarked. Lincoln responded, "I want you to take care of yourself."[13]

Mary's heartache nearly equaled Abraham's. When the First Lady learned of Baker's death, she canceled her public receptions and refused to see anyone. She had known Baker a long time, dating back to the days before her marriage, when Baker was a regular guest in her brother and sister-in-law's Springfield home. He had attended the Lincolns' wedding and been a frequent guest in their circle of friends. The day before his death, Baker had breakfasted with the Lincolns in the White House.[14]

There is a story that Mary created a public scandal by attending Baker's funeral dressed inappropriately for such an occasion, in a lilac dress and accessories, rather than the usual black. When a member of Washington's social set remonstrated with her, so the story goes, she supposedly replied in a huff, "I wonder if the women of Washington expect me to muffle myself up in mourning for every soldier killed in this great war? . . . I want the women to mind their own business; I intend to wear what I please." This tale has been widely disseminated by historians and cited as evidence of Mary's flouting of social convention and etiquette in what was fast becoming a hostile Washington social set.[15]

The hostility was real enough, as were Mary's occasional social missteps. But the wearing of lilac was not of itself scandalous, since lilac and other muted lavender colors were considered "half-mourning," the donning of full black being generally reserved for the funerals of spouses, children, and other close relatives. There is no reliable evidence that Mary attended Baker's funeral at all; newspaper accounts from the time do not mention her presence, referring only to the president's attendance. Nor does she seem to have accompanied her husband in the procession afterward.[16] Whatever mistakes Mary made as First Lady, they did not include public violation of mourning conventions and funeral etiquette.

Willie knew Baker as a visitor to his parents' house in Springfield and sometimes also a caller at the White House. After he breakfasted with the Lincolns the morning before he left for battle, Baker and the president relaxed under a tree on the White House lawn while Willie and Tad rustled among the autumn leaves nearby. Willie was also surely aware that his parents had named his deceased brother, Eddy, after Baker. Willie was moved enough by Baker's death that he wrote a poem to commemorate it, which he submitted to the *Washington, DC, National Republican* for publication:

> There was no patriot like Baker,
> So noble and so true;
> He fell as a soldier on the field,
> His face to the sky of blue.
>
> His voice is silent in the hall
> Which oft his presence graced;
> No more he'll hear the loud acclaim
> Which rang from place to place.
>
> No squeamish notions filled his breast,
> *The Union* was his theme;
> *"No surrender and no compromise,"*
> His day-thought and night's dream.
>
> His Country has *her* part to pay
> To'rds those he has left behind;
> His widow and his children all,
> She must always keep in mind.[17]

The repercussions from Baker's death lingered well into the winter. In early December, the new congressional Joint Committee on the Conduct of the War began to hold hearings. Later that month, Lincoln entered the Senate chamber—a rare event; presidents did not often enter congressional chambers—to hear eulogies delivered by Baker's former Senate colleagues, like Massachusetts's Charles Sumner, who praised Baker as the "Prince

Rupert of battle and debate." That same day, Baker was buried with full military honors in faraway San Francisco. Lincoln received a telegraph describing the "immense cortege" that escorted Baker's body to the city's Lone Hill Cemetery.[18]

Sometime not long afterward, both Tad and Willie fell ill. No one knows for certain what ailed them, but it was reported in one newspaper that they had contracted "typhoid fever"—the same illness that had carried away Ann Rutledge.[19] While there are other possibilities—scholars over the years have argued for malaria, bronchopneumonia, and even a variant of a genetic disorder called Marfan syndrome—typhoid is the most likely explanation. The source of their illness was probably the White House's dank basement, where the boys frequently played. The White House sewage system was shaky at best, and runoff water from a number of contaminated sources could have found its way into the basement. There were several army camps nearby, and Civil War camps were notorious for their unsanitary conditions.[20]

Typhoid is caused by the mixture of excrement, animal or human, with water that is then ingested. The bacteria *Salmonella typhi* grow in the victim's intestines, a slow process—usually around two weeks—after which the symptoms become apparent. Willie and Tad would have left the White House dining table without eating much, probably complaining of stomach pains and seeming more tired and lethargic than should have been the case with these two typically boisterous youngsters. At about the same time, they would have begun manifesting the first signs of the fever that was the disease's defining feature.[21]

As when Eddy became ill, the Lincolns possessed at best only an imperfect understanding of what was happening with their children. Typhoid was often confused with "typhus" and other similar maladies, which were often lumped under the catchall term "bilious fever." Not until after the Civil War would physicians and researchers identify the specific bacteria causing typhoid and begin to understand its symptoms and characteristics. During the war, typhoid was common, especially in military facilities, but beyond a vague understanding that it was somehow caused by "contaminated" food and water, no one really understood its causes, prevention, or treatment.[22]

Whatever their exact symptoms might have been—likely fever and stomach cramps, as well as recurring and painful bouts of diarrhea—Tad and Willie were bedridden sometime in late January or possibly early February 1862. Their parents' feelings about the boys' illness are difficult to ascertain.

Perhaps the memory of Eddy's fatal illness ten years previously led the Lincolns to react with immediate alarm. But the boys had been sick before; Willie in particular had suffered what his father described in July 1860 as a "hard and tedious spell of scarlet-fever."[23]

Unlike with Eddy, the Lincolns now had plenty of help in caring for their sick children. Mary Jane Welles, the wife of Secretary of the Navy Gideon Welles and Mary Lincoln's close friend, stayed for a time at the White House to help nurse the boys. So did Eliza Browning, the wife of Senator Orville Browning, Lincoln's old friend and colleague from Illinois. Mary's seamstress and close confidant, Elizabeth Keckly, an astute and compassionate African American woman, also helped, sometimes to the point that she was "worn out with watching" at the boys' bedsides late into the evening.[24]

The Lincolns also consulted at least three doctors. Robert Stone was a prominent Washington physician whom the Lincolns employed as their family doctor when they moved to the capital city; he was Tad and Willie's primary physician. He was assisted by James Hall (another well-known Washington doctor) and an ex-governor of New Jersey, William Newell, who knew Lincoln from their days as fellow Whigs and who had a medical background.[25] Typhoid exhibited an array of different symptoms, and Doctor Stone and his colleagues had at their disposal a wide variety of possible treatments. The fever would have received much of their attention, and they probably prescribed the treatments common at the time: cold compresses and frequent bathing in cool or lukewarm water. Diarrhea and the stomach ailments associated with typhoid called for the administration of any of a number of possible drugs, especially mineral acids, which were thought to ease the victims' painful intestinal cramping that sometimes also caused vomiting and distended stomachs. The boys' loss of appetite continued, though doctors of the day agreed that patients required some sort of nourishment and suggested milder food and drink—warm milk, oatmeal, veal, and chicken broth. Hygiene was an ongoing difficulty, given the boys' extended period in bed; Mary, Keckly, and their friends would have been kept busy changing bedding to prevent blisters and bedsores and to deal with the ongoing effects of chronic diarrhea. Tad and Willie were assisted by a small army of caretakers—and they were needed.[26]

It soon became clear that Willie's case was more severe than his brother's.[27] The fever caused him to slip in and out of consciousness, "painfully productive of mental wandering and delirium," according to one observer.

He often called for his playmate Bud Taft, Julia's little brother, who was brought to his bedside and "stayed with him most of the time," according to Julia. One evening, the president came into the room and found Bud standing by Willie's bed as the boy was sleeping. "You ought to go to bed, Bud," Lincoln gently told him as he stood stroking Willie's hair. Bud replied that he wished to stay. "If I go he will call for me," he explained. Later in the evening, the president found Bud asleep in the room and carried him off to bed.[28]

As cruel as Eddy's situation had been ten years previously, this was in some ways worse, because typhoid tends to follow an erratic and unpredictable course. Ann Rutledge's experience was a sudden, relatively quick ending over the course of a few days, and Eddy's tuberculosis caused a long, steady decline. But Willie's health ebbed and flowed; as a New York correspondent put it, the illness was "an intermittent fever, which gradually merged into the ordinary typhoid." The intermittent aspect was evident during the early days of February, when he oscillated between periods of stress and then relative recovery. Lincoln spent most of Friday, February 7, at Willie's side and then canceled a scheduled reception the next day as the boy's condition worsened. But a week later, a Washington, D.C., newspaper reported that both boys were "on the mend." Four days after that, John Nicolay wrote that Willie was again much worse, saying, "The President despairs of his recovery."[29]

The ups and downs of Willie's condition caused agonizing dilemmas for Mary and especially for Abraham. Their answer was to take matters one day at a time, having no set policy for keeping or breaking engagements but using their best judgment given the circumstances of the moment. They canceled numerous activities throughout February, but they also sometimes kept other scheduled events and meetings, as need and circumstances required. On Saturday, February 8, they canceled a scheduled White House reception, but Lincoln found the time to write a note to General McClellan asking for more information about various military matters. The following Monday, he took nearly the entire day off to spend time with both Willie and Tad, and he continued to do so until Friday, when he felt it necessary to hold his regular weekly cabinet meeting and transact other pressing business.

The Lincolns' dilemma was painfully apparent during a large gathering at the White House on the evening of February 5. Several hundred invitations had been issued to leading citizens and dignitaries in the capital, and the Marine Band was scheduled to perform. Seeing Willie's illness worsen that afternoon, Mary wanted to cancel the whole affair. But Lincoln knew there would be a stiff social price to pay for his wife—already the subject of endless rounds of vicious gossip in Washington society circles—and perhaps a political price for him as well, so he urged that Dr. Stone be consulted before they took such a drastic step. The doctor told the First Lady and president that Willie "was in no immediate danger," and the party went on as scheduled—"the most superb affair of the kind ever seen here," noted a Washington paper. But throughout the evening, Mary broke away when she could to look in on Willie, "the rich notes of the Marine Band in the apartments below [coming] to the sick room in soft, subdued murmurs," according to Keckly. Noting the anxious and depressed mood of his wife, the president forbade any dancing during the evening.[30]

By February 19, the *Washington, DC, Evening Star* felt confident enough to report that Willie's condition, though he was "critically ill," was "somewhat easier." That day Lincoln received a note from Dorothea Dix, superintendent of nurses in the Union army. She offered the president the services of a nurse to help care for the two sick boys. He replied with a brief note thanking Dix for her offer but politely declining, writing that "they do not, just now, need the nurse."[31]

The next day, Willie died. Julia Taft's mother and brother Bud happened to be at the White House that day, and around noon, Julia received word from her mother that Willie had held Bud's hand and seemed to be improving. But at five o'clock, he passed away.[32]

"A shadow has fallen upon the White House," read the widely reprinted obituary reporting Willie's death. Keckly helped prepare Willie's body. "I assisted in washed him and dressing him, and then laid him on the bed," she wrote. As she finished the task, the president came into Willie's room. "I never saw a man so bowed down with grief," she recalled. "He came to the bed, lifted the cover from the face of his child, gazed at it long and earnestly, murmuring, 'My poor boy, he was too good for this earth. God has called him home. I know that he is much better off in heaven, but then we loved him so. It is hard, hard to have him die!'" He then burst into "great sobs." Later that day, the president walked into Nicolay's office. "Well, Nicolay, my boy is gone," Lincoln said. "He is actually gone." He burst into tears again and left.[33]

A coffin was brought into the Green Room, and Willie was laid to rest therein, dressed in a military uniform his parents had provided for him, yet another manifestation of the White House's martial atmosphere. Through their experiences with Ellsworth and Baker, the Lincolns had become admirers of the embalming process, and they allowed Willie to be preserved in that fashion. The procedure was administered by five physicians, under the supervision of Orville Browning, who handled the funeral and burial arrangements. They used the methods pioneered by a French professor named J. P. Sucquet, using zinc chloride rather than the standard arsenic as the primary preserving agent. Sucquet's process did not involve removing the heart and brain (as did other methods) or draining of the body's fluids. The zinc chloride was injected into either Willie's carotid artery in the neck or the femoral artery in the upper thigh.[34] The results were "a perfect success," said a newspaper correspondent. Willie's "countenance wore a natural and placid look," remarked one observer, "the only signs of death being a slight discoloration of the features."[35]

The funeral took place at two o'clock on February 27 in the White House's Green Room. The entire building was bedecked in black crepe, and visitors "spoke in subdued tones when they thought of the sweet boy at rest," according to Keckly. Willie's body, dressed in "his accustomed pants and jacket," was adorned heavily with flowers on his breast, in his hand, and in bouquets and wreaths around the bier. The Lincolns chose a "plain, metallic case" for the coffin, inscribed simply with his name and the dates of his birth and death, draped in white crepe.[36]

The service was conducted by Phineas Gurley, reverend of the New York Street Presbyterian Church in Washington, D.C. Gurley was a low-key sort, an excellent orator and blessed with a fine singing voice. He was antislavery but not inclined to shout his politics from the pulpit, something Lincoln found appealing. Gurley was well trained in the Calvinist theology, which emphasized surrender to God's unknowable divine will and with which Lincoln had been familiar since he was a boy. At Willie's funeral, the reverend spoke in these same terms. "All those events which in any wise affect our condition and happiness are in his hands, and at his disposal," Gurley declared. Why an innocent little boy like Willie might die in this fashion seems an unfathomable mystery to his grieving loved ones, and yet, Gurley declared, "It is still *His* dealing; and while they mourn He is saying to them . . . 'What I do ye know not now, but ye shall know hereafter.'"[37]

The ceremony was attended by an array of political leaders, diplomats, cabinet members, and other dignitaries; Congress suspended business for the day so members could attend the funeral. General McClellan was also present, and one observer saw him moved nearly to tears during the proceedings. Robert Lincoln accompanied his father, who sat in a circle with cabinet members around the bier, the rest of the crowd arranged behind. There was little precedent for exactly how the deceased child of a sitting president was to be memorialized, but people agreed that the affair was handled well. "The occasion was a most impressive one," noted a Washington newspaper correspondent, "and the large crowd present seemed to be deeply affected by its solemnity."[38]

Afterward, Willie's body was removed from the Green Room and borne through a blustery gray winter day to the Oak Hill Cemetery in nearby Georgetown, his hearse drawn by the white horses traditionally associated with the death of a child. He was interred in a mausoleum owned by a Supreme Court clerk named William Carroll—a temporary location until his parents could arrange for their son's remains to be sent home to Illinois. Government offices were closed that day, and church bells rang throughout the city. Both houses of Congress adopted resolutions of sympathy.[39]

Mary was not present, and her later detractors made much of this fact. But as we have seen, Ellsworth's funeral notwithstanding, Mary generally followed the custom of the times, which held that women should not attend funerals. She did write to Julia Taft's mother, asking her to keep the Taft boys—Willie and Tad's constant playmates—away during the day of the funeral. "It makes me feel worse to see them," she wrote. Just as the service was beginning in the Green Room, she sent word from upstairs that she wished to have the bouquet of flowers that was clasped in Willie's hands, and it was carefully removed before the lid was closed. She spent the day in seclusion in the White House.

The hour before the service was reserved for a private viewing by the president, Mary, and their sons and close friends of the family. The president felt a special sympathy for Bud Taft, the boy who had been at Willie's bedside constantly throughout the ordeal. During the private viewing, he sent for the boy to see Willie in his casket one last time. He meant it as a kind gesture, but it backfired. "Bud had to be carried from the room," Julia Taft remembered, "and was ill for some days after."[40]

Lincoln was outwardly composed during the service, or at least none of those present commented otherwise, though one observer thought he was "bent now with the load . . . staggering under a blow like the taking of a child." The funeral was attended by a great many dignitaries, cabinet members, and other high-ranking officials, so he may well have felt it best to maintain a stoic facade. "He gave no outward sign of his trouble," Hay later wrote about Lincoln in the days following Willie's death, "but kept about his work the same as ever."[41]

But out of the public's view, Lincoln teetered close to the emotional shattering his friends claimed he had risked following Ann Rutledge's death. One newspaper noted that he "was in a stupor of grief, and seemed to care little even for great national events" throughout Friday evening and well into the weekend following Willie's death. He was so depressed and physically exhausted that some feared Lincoln had contracted a disease and fallen ill.[42] But by Sunday evening, he had pulled himself together. He "began to recover from the shock," remarked a reporter on Friday, February 28, "and is now though deeply bowed down by his great affliction, in nowise incapacitated for the duties of his position."[43]

No one criticized the president for his bereavement. In fact, he may even have been helped in public opinion by those who saw a father stricken with grief, rather than a president and a politician. Those who noted Lincoln's distraction during Willie's illness were more inclined to praise rather than scold him. "His anxiety does him honor," argued one newspaper correspondent. "Mr. Lincoln is one of the most warm-hearted men in the country, and the dangerous illness of any member of his family at once fits him for the ordinary duties of life . . . for no one would like to see the president so much of an executive that he would suppress the feelings of the father."[44]

Some noted the poignancy of a man who was presiding over a war of unprecedented bloodletting while at the same time wrestling with the grief of a close personal loss. Others took note of the irony that the Union cause had just scored important (and relatively rare) battlefield victories at Forts Henry and Donelson in Tennessee, but the president was unable to celebrate. "The affliction is brought the more forcibly to the heart of Mr. Lincoln by the contrast forced upon him," noted a correspondent for the *New York Evening Post*, as "all Washington and the country rejoices over the good news of victory."[45]

The effects of Willie's death rippled outward for a long time. The Lincolns did not host a public reception again in the White House until New Year's Day 1863, and even then, Mary was compelled to leave early, feeling too much of an emotional connection between the White House and her son's death. "From this time until spring each day will be a most gloomy anniversary," she wrote a few days before the reception. She oscillated between anger and despair over the higher meaning of Willie's death. "How often, I feel rebellious, and almost believe that our Heavenly Father, has forsaken us, in removing, so lovely a child from us!" she wrote. "Yet I know, a great sin, is committed when we feel thus." At other times, she was wracked with guilt over what she saw as divine retribution, "God's chastising hand." "I had become, so wrapped up in the world, so devoted to our own political advancement that I thought of little else besides," she believed. "Our Heavenly Father sees fit, oftentimes to visit us, at such times for our worldliness . . . when we are thus so severely tried."[46]

It also left its mark on Abraham and Mary as parents. Whatever inclination they may have felt toward disciplining Tad disappeared. The boy became "the most absolute little monarch ever known at the White House," according to one observer. "After the death of his brother Willie . . . [Tad] installed himself as the absolute tyrant of the Executive Mansion," Hay irritably wrote. "He was idolized by both his father and mother, petted and indulged by his teachers . . . [and had] no opinion of discipline."[47]

But Tad also lingered under Willie's shadow. Seeing the toys he had enjoyed with Willie became so difficult that the Lincolns arranged to have them shipped back to Springfield. When Julia Taft paid a visit in 1864 to the White House, where she had not been since Willie's death, Tad on seeing her "threw himself down . . . and kicked and screamed and had to be taken out by the servants." Mary attributed Tad's behavior to the association between Julia's presence and his deceased brother bringing up memories related to happier days. "You must excuse him, Julia," she said. "You know what he remembers."[48]

Mary also grew more protective of Robert. The Lincolns' eldest son saw other Northern men his age enlisting in the army, and he wanted to do so as well, but Mary was bitterly opposed. "We have lost one son, and his loss is as much as I can bear," she complained to the president, who replied that "many a poor mother has given up all her sons." Mary would have none of it. "That may be," she retorted; "but I cannot bear to have Robert exposed to danger." Abraham and Robert's will eventually prevailed, and Robert served as a staff officer for General Ulysses S. Grant, far enough away from the battlefield to at least somewhat soothe his mother's anxiety.[49]

Her husband, of course, had much to distract him. "The burdensome and responsible duties of the nation rests heavily on the mind of the honored Chief Magistrate," read a sympathetic news report, but after having been "prostrated in both mind and body" by Willie's loss for a time, "he is now recovering." By early March, his daily diet of cabinet meetings, consultations with generals and congressmen, diplomatic ceremonies, and the like looked much the same as it had before Willie died. "So things began to look vigorous," Hay wrote in his diary in early March.[50]

Mary also knew better than to make a public spectacle of her suffering. To the outside world, she presented a steady appearance. Mrs. Lincoln is "calm and even in her disposition," wrote one person who saw her a few days after the funeral, and she is "less demonstrative and more guarded. Hence, she is able to control her feelings in such a manner that few, even those in the White House, will know how deeply she has felt this affliction." She courted scandal in a variety of ways, but she was always careful—dating back to the days of Eddy's death—to avoid public missteps in the socially and culturally important matters of funerals and mourning.[51]

Throughout the rest of the winter of 1862, Mary entered into a period of seclusion, seeing few people outside her immediate circle and avoiding the public limelight. Part of the reason was Tad's illness. The little boy remained sick for some time after his brother died, and Mary was preoccupied with his care, even though the nurse Abraham had previously rejected was now on hand, along with others, to help. Mary's social calendar remained light well into the spring, but in March, she did host a gathering at the White House that was intended primarily to honor soldiers and their families, an event that had been scheduled several months in advance—before Willie and Tad had fallen ill—and that Mary believed she could not properly cancel. She was "somewhat better" at this point, according to one newspaper report, but another characterized her as "a most unhappy, broken-hearted woman." Rumors circulated that she was in poor health and had been secluded away because of some undisclosed illness.[52]

Some Confederate papers—and a few hostile Northern ones, as well—castigated Mary for staging a "ball" in the midst of a ruinous war, arguing that such an event threw into sharp relief the Lincoln White House's frivolity and extravagance.[53] But there was no newspaper commentary to the effect that she was mourning her dead son too much or with undue emotional excess. At least one person was impressed by the fact that she had "sufficiently recovered from her recent severe bereavement" in June to resume her visits to military hospitals, with "kind gifts and kinder words to our sick and wounded soldiers."[54]

She wore the usual full mourning black, adorned with white trimming, as was the custom with a child's death, though she temporarily put the black aside for a brighter blue and white velvet dress for the spring White House gathering. Otherwise, she was careful to wear attire that was not only appropriate to the occasion but also of high quality, knowing full well that her actions were scrutinized. Appearances always mattered to her, and never more so than now. "I want the crape to be the *finest jet black* English crape," she wrote to a dressmaker in May, with "white and black face trimmings— Could you obtain any black and white crape flowers?" She had developed something of a reputation for sumptuous fashion, ornate even to excess, but in mourning Willie, she wanted to cut against this grain, actively seeking mourning dress that was "very fine" but "plain."[55]

She wore mourning for a long time. The poet Walt Whitman, who lived along the route the president took between the White House and the Soldiers' Home, observed Mary riding with Lincoln one day in mid-August 1863, "dressed in complete black, with a long crape veil." This was eighteen months after Willie's death, but by the standards of the day, which held that mourning attire for a close family member called for a lengthier period in full mourning, Mary's black attire was not remarkable. Whitman did not seem to find it inappropriate, and apparently neither did anyone else at the time.[56]

The president also donned the mourning attire suitable for a grieving father: a strip of "dusty, puffy crepe," according to an Englishman who met him in June, wrapped around his signature stovepipe hat. The black cloth was stitched over the hat's original band and remained in place until he wore the hat on the evening of his assassination three years later. This was itself a stretch; normally fathers in mourning for their sons removed black crepe from their clothing after a brief period of a few months at most. But no one seems to have thought it odd; most people probably did not even notice a bit of black cloth on a black stovepipe hat, perched on the head of a man who habitually wore black clothing.[57]

By early April, the Washington press was reporting that the First Family was collectively recovered from illness, and life in the White House had outwardly returned to something resembling normalcy. The president visited the Navy Yard, the First Lady began to receive an occasional visitor, Tad received a gift of some white rabbits from a well-wisher to occupy his time, and Elizabeth Edwards returned home to Springfield in June. They presented a stalwart and dutiful public face, did the Lincolns, and the newspapers, those omnipresent guardians of American public behavior, made no mention of any problems.[58]

But if Mary managed to maintain a careful public image of appropriate mourning, in private she was an emotional wreck, more so than was thought proper by her family and friends, even for a mother who had suffered such a tragic loss. "Mrs. Lincoln's grief was inconsolable," Keckly remembered, adding that when Mary saw Willie's body right after he died, "the pale face of her dead boy threw her into convulsions." She may well have been unable to assist Keckly in washing and dressing Willie's body, as was thought the fitting duty for a dead child's mother.[59]

Her "convulsions" continued, along with long periods of uncontrollable sobbing. She secluded herself in her room for days on end, and when she did reappear, she was drawn and depressed. "Mrs. Lincoln was an altered woman," Keckly believed. As Mary's close confidant and friend, she saw the private pain Mary tried to hide from the public, her feelings percolating just below the surface. "The mere mention of Willie's name would excite her emotion," Keckly remembered, "and any trifling memento that recalled him would move her to tears." Mary never again could bring herself to enter the rooms in the White House where Willie died and was embalmed.[60]

Lincoln was worried. He "tried in many ways to distract Mary's mind from the grief which was consuming her," Elizabeth Edwards later wrote. He attempted to keep her busy by scheduling concerts and social affairs at the White House.[61] When this did not have much of an effect, he tried sterner measures. At one point, Keckly recalled, he led his sobbing wife to a window and pointed to what Keckly called the "lunatic asylum" in the distance (probably St. Elizabeth's Hospital, a facility that in 1855 was designated to house the city's mental ill residents), saying, "Mother, do you see that large white building on the hill yonder? Try and control your grief, or it will drive you mad, and we may have to send you there."[62]

As much attention as this little vignette has received from historians regarding Mary's state of mind, we should also consider what it tells us about her husband. Throughout his life, Lincoln was flummoxed by the sorts of emotional displays to which Mary was prone. As a young man, he had associated girls with frivolity and a lack of seriousness—one reason he avoided their company—and as a husband, he frequently responded to Mary's outbursts by simply scooping up the boys and leaving the house for a while.[63] Women who came to the White House during the war believing their tears would move the president to sympathy were often rudely disappointed. On the occasions when distraught mothers of soldier sons appeared at the White House begging for presidential discharges or the female relatives of imprisoned Rebel soldiers and accused Rebel spies collapsed in tears before him, Lincoln often grew annoyed and uncharacteristically short-tempered.[64]

His threat regarding the mental hospital was entirely in character, as was his general response to Mary's emotional crisis: he backed away and called on the aid of other women. The day of Willie's funeral, he found time to scrawl a quick note to Alice Sumner, wife of Senator Charles Sumner and one of Mary's close friends, asking her to visit the White House. "Mrs. L. needs your help," he wrote on a small card he had delivered to the Sumner home. "Can you come?" Since Tad was still sick, he likely had in mind help with the nursing chores, but he probably also wanted Mrs. Sumner (along with Elizabeth Edwards) to find a way to help Mary get past the worst stages of her grief.[65]

Mary understood that she needed to escape her anguish, if only temporarily. This appears to have been one of her motives in moving the family to the Soldiers' Home, beginning in the spring of 1862 and every summer thereafter. It was a good way to put some distance between herself and the White House's constant reminders of Willie, though even at the Soldiers' Home her pain was never very far from the surface. One newspaper correspondent who visited her at the home that summer was unnerved by Mary's fragile emotional state. The correspondent found that the First Lady was clad in full black mourning when she entered the room. "As I took the hand which she extended to me," the writer remembered, "she burst into a passion of tears and gave up all effort at self control. . . . She could neither think nor talk about anything but Willie."[66]

6. GHOSTS

In December 1863, Mary's half-sister Emilie Helm visited the White House under a safe-conduct pass from the president; "just arrived from Secessia," as Hay tartly put it. Her visit was controversial. She was a Southerner and a member of a family that supplied soldiers to the Confederate army. Emilie's late husband was a Confederate general, no less: Benjamin Hardin Helm, killed at the Battle of Chickamauga. Nevertheless, the president went to some trouble—and risked scandal—to bring her to the White House.[1]

Emilie did not like what she was seeing in her older sister. Mary's smiles "seemed forced," and Emilie caught what she took to be an odd, bright glint in Mary's eyes. She talked to the president about the matter. "Her nerves have gone to pieces," Lincoln wearily said. "She cannot hide from me that the strain she has been under is too much." He urged Emilie to stay the summer with them in the Soldiers' Home. "You and Mary love each other," he said. "It is good for her to have you with her."

Later that evening, Mary knocked on Emilie's bedroom door. When she opened it, Emilie noticed that even though her sister's face glistened with tears, she was smiling. "I want to tell you, Emilie, that one may not be wholly without comfort when our loved ones leave us. . . . If Willie did not come to comfort me I would still be drowned in tears. . . . He lives, Emilie!" Emilie stared in shock at Mary, whose voice assumed a tone that, Emilie said, "I can never forget." Mary then described how her dead son came to visit her every night. He "stands at the foot of my bed with the same sweet, adorable smile he has always had," she said, and "he does not always come alone; little Eddie is sometimes with him." Emilie was alarmed. Mary was acting "unnatural and abnormal," she observed; "it frightens me."[2]

Mary was not the only one who seemed haunted by Willie's memory. "Do you ever find yourself talking with the dead?" Lincoln's secretary of the treasury, Salmon Chase, recalled the president asking him. "I do. Ever since Willie's death I catch myself involuntarily talking to him as if he were with me—and I feel that he is!" Artist Francis Carpenter, who became acquainted with Lincoln while commissioned to do a painting of the president and his cabinet, recalled that one day in 1864, Lincoln called a staff officer into the room where he had been reading alone and quoted aloud a passage from *Hamlet* referring to the loss of a child. "Did you ever dream of a lost friend, and feel that you were holding sweet communion with that friend, and yet have a sad consciousness that it was not a reality?" he asked the man. "Just so I dream of my boy Willie."[3]

Two years after Willie died, the White House stables caught fire. The president saw the flames from the White House and sprinted out the door in a frenzied dash that shocked everyone present. "When he reached the boxwood hedge that served as an enclosure to the stables he sprang over it like a deer," recalled an army officer who witnessed the scene, ". . . and with his own hands burst open the stable door. A glance within showed that the whole interior of the stable was in flames, and that the rescue of the horses was impossible. Notwithstanding this, he would apparently have rushed in had not those standing around caught and restrained him." Led back to the White House, Lincoln wandered into the East Room and watched the fire from a window. "He was weeping," remembered the officer. Tad was also present; he saw the officer's perplexed look and explained that "the stable contained a pony that belonged to [Willie]. The thought of his dead child had come to his mind as soon as he learned the stables were on fire, and he had rushed out to try to save the pony from the flames."[4]

As deeply wounded as Abraham and Mary were by Willie's passing, none of this was particularly unusual. Even Lincoln's intimation that he continued to commune with Willie's spirit was not so odd. Christians in the Civil War era fervently believed in an afterlife; they felt their deceased loved ones had gone on to a better place, where they would not only reunite with each other after death but also provide a spiritual bridge between the living and God. People sometimes spoke of death as a "veil," a thin border through which the shapes of the dead's spirits could be discerned by the living.

The war also provided an incessant, thrumming background noise the Lincolns could not escape. When Willie died, many thousands of Americans—not just soldiers but also refugee civilians and others swept up in the war's wake, including other children—were languishing and dying as well. The war had become an impossibly big, grinding, growling thing that filled the Lincolns' lives from horizon to horizon—and death was its defining feature. Their loss of Willie was a personal piece of what had become the new American normal. "We presume that Mrs. Lincoln will now be able to sympathize as she could not do so before, with the thousands of mothers throughout the land who were mourning the sudden bereavement of a son," thought one grim observer.[5]

In April, the nurse detailed by Dorothea Dix to attend to Tad during his illness, a young woman named Rebecca Pomeroy, received a letter, bound neatly in a white ribbon, from Reverend John Pierpont of Boston, who called on her in Washington and, knowing her acquaintance with the Lincolns, asked that the letter be delivered to the First Lady. The letter was purported to be from a spiritual medium, who had supposedly received it from the dead Willie Lincoln's ghost. Writing to his mother, Willie's ghost sought to assure Mary that "he is happy, and wants her to feel him as always around her; but she heeds him not, and when she is so tired in heart, closing the eyes of those dear ones committed to her care, he wishes to try to commune with her, and try to ease her mind and make her happy." Pomeroy was not convinced of the letter's authenticity, even as Reverend Pierpont—who apparently was—pressed her to get Willie's communique to his bereaved mother. When she firmly refused to do so, Pierpont stormed angrily away.[6]

Spiritualists like the anonymous author of this letter were a fact of life for the Lincolns from the war's outset, offering the president unsolicited advice, predictions, and opinions. A man named J. S. Hastings, "an undoubting believer in Spiritual communion," wrote Lincoln in August 1861 that a medium of his acquaintance had accurately foreseen the Union army's calamity at First Bull Run. On other occasions, Spiritualists wrote long, curious missives with no apparent point. "I wish you to weigh these things and see if there is not an equal balance the Devil has taught man that their neighbors was doing forever wrong and he was himself doing right and this comparatively speaking is the great cause of disharmony over the earth sphere the Devil has controlled affairs long enough," read a rambling and punctuation-free communique from "God," dictated through a medium named Lydia Smith, who insisted the president meet with her at "the Fitzgeralds" in Washington, D.C., where she would reveal "just what to do that will terminate this Devilish war."[7]

Most of the Spiritualists operating in mid-nineteenth America were pre-occupied not so much with fortune-telling or channeling God's will as with contacting the dead. In December 1861, Lincoln received a letter from the dead ghost of Edward Baker via a New York Spiritualist named I. B. Conklin. "You will no doubt be surprised to receive this from me," said Baker's ghost, "but, I like millions of other disembodied spirits feel a desire to convey ex-pressions of gratitude and hope to earthly friends. I am not dead. I still live, a conscious individual, with hope, aspirations and interest; for the Union [is] still alive." Baker's ghost actually did not have much in the way of other-worldly wisdom to impart to his friend, except the bland observation that "Man lives on Earth, to live elsewhere, and that elsewhere is ever present."[8]

Lincoln probably did not find Mr. Conklin's letter helpful or amusing, the wound of his friend's death still being fresh. Three years later, he received another letter from Baker's ghost, this time via another New Yorker named R. A. Beck. Baker's ghost was here more exact in his advice, informing the president that God was on his side, that the Union "armies are loyal [and] you have no traitor at their head," and that "this national conflict [will] end in a tryumphant victory." The ghost then insisted that out of gratitude for having communicated with him from the afterlife, the president must answer two earlier letters sent to him by Beck.[9]

Lincoln could not have been surprised by any of this, for Spiritualism had been an increasingly popular pastime among Americans since the 1840s. An-tebellum Spiritualists such as Andrew Jackson Davis, Cora L. V. Scott, and Kate and Margaret Fox believed they could achieve contact with the souls of the dead, either words and conversations with the deceased or "rappings," loud, sometimes coded knocks on tables, walls, and floors—presumably by ghosts who could find no more direct way to converse. Exactly how people could go about contacting the dead varied from one Spiritualist to the next. Sometimes it involved mesmerism, named after its inventor, an eighteenth-century German doctor and scientist named Franz Mesmer, a trancelike state of hypnosis during which the dead spirit temporarily inhabited the body of the person who was thus entranced. Others used a séance, French for "a sitting," in which practitioners were seated in a circle, often holding hands, and recited an incantation to summon ghostly spirits. Still other Spiritualists used artwork, claiming that their renderings were created by some unseen ghostly will guiding their pen or paint brush.

There were endless variations, tailored to a given Spiritualist's particular set of beliefs and idiosyncrasies. Spiritualism was a widespread phenomenon during the antebellum era, especially among middle-class white Americans, but the war sent Spiritualism to greater heights of popularity. Spiritualist tracts, pamphlets, and newsletters and works of fiction dealing with Spiritualist themes were in high demand as the war progressed and the casualty lists lengthened. It was an impulse exacerbated by the fact that for a great many American families, the fate of their loved ones was never known. Most Civil War soldiers did not carry dog tags or any other identification of the sort that could survive a battle. Often their parents, wives, and other relatives and friends discovered their fate only when the letters stopped arriving; small wonder, then, that their grief drove them into the arms of Spiritualists who claimed they could establish some form of contact with their deceased soldiers.[10]

But for all its popularity, Spiritualism was controversial. While its roots lay in the evangelical fervor of the "Burnt-Over District" in upstate New York, it was frowned upon by many clergy: Henry Ward Beecher, for example, was so disturbed by rumors of his Spiritualist tendencies that he circulated in 1856 a strongly worded letter stating that he was a "stout unbeliever" in mediums, séances, and other Spiritualist practices. Other critics wrote books or toured the country denouncing Spiritualism's tenets. "Spiritualism has become a gigantic evil," declared Reverend Hugh A. Brown during a typical anti-Spiritualist lecture in Rockford, Illinois, in 1854. "It is most pernicious and soul ruining in its teachings."[11]

Some people equated Spiritualism with a species of witchcraft; others saw it as mere hucksterism dressed up as theology. It was also associated with the more radical reaches of nineteenth-century American politics. Spiritualist practices were egalitarian where gender was concerned; women and men were equally capable of contacting the ghosts of the dead, many Spiritualists taught, and this led to charges that their gatherings were immoral, "free love bagnios" on a par with Unitarianism and other suspect factions. Others lumped Spiritualism indiscriminately (and without much logic) with commitments to labor and racial equality: "Millerism, Spiritualism, Freeloveism, and lastly the horrid disease of Niggerism," according to one pungent indictment. Another story held that groups of Spiritualists in Boston "sit in circles perfectly undisguised with clothing, that is to say in *puris naturalibus*—men and women indiscriminately."[12]

Lincoln was not the sort who indulged in serious thinking about those very matters that so preoccupied the Spiritualists. "By reason of his practical turn of mind Mr. Lincoln never speculated any more in the scientific and philosophical than he did in the financial world," noted law partner William Herndon. Billy could not seem to get his friend engaged in conversations about metaphysics and the like, which "he brushed aside as trash—mere scientific absurdities."[13]

Events related to Spiritualism occurred in Lincoln's Springfield, but they were about equally pro and con. Merchants in town advertised the sale of Spiritualist tracts, but they also sold books debunking Spiritualist ideas and beliefs. In 1858, a woman named Emma Hardinge delivered a series of lectures on Spiritualism's past and future in downtown Springfield, not far from Lincoln's law office. But Springfield also hosted Spiritualism's critics: a man named Leo Miller, for example, who in March that same year launched a hard-hitting attack on Spiritualism in the town's concert hall "without gloves," according to one account, in which he "clearly show[ed] Spiritualism to be an arrant delusion."[14]

After the war, a Springfield man named J. Ridgely Martin, who claimed to have been Lincoln's neighbor and to have studied law in the same building where Lincoln's law office was located, wrote that Lincoln habitually attended séances conducted by a medium named Thorp, whom Lincoln used to try to contact the dead spirits of his mother and Ann Rutledge. It is impossible to ascertain whether Martin's account is true.[15] In any event, there were serious political risks involved for Lincoln, the always ambitious antebellum politician, to be seen in the company of mediums or other Spiritualists. He avoided association with the radical politics commonly associated, fairly or not, with Spiritualism. He also labored under the rumor that he was a religious infidel, and while many Christians saw no contradiction between mainstream Christian orthodoxy and Spiritualism, plenty of others did. The same Abraham Lincoln who had to go out of his way during the election of 1846 to announce he was no "scoffer at" organized Christian religious principles was not the sort who wanted to revisit that particular scandal by being seen in attendance at a local séance or Spiritualist lecture.

Once in Washington, he was surrounded by Spiritualists of various stripes. Secretary of the Navy Gideon Welles and his wife, Mary, consulted a medium in an attempt to contact their own dead children, and various military men and government officials close to the president dabbled in Spiritualism. The city as a whole hosted a vigorous Spiritualist scene that predated the war; an 1852 visitor to the capital noted that "frequent meetings or circles were held at different places [in Washington], for the purpose of investigating the different phenomena classed under the head of spiritual manifestations."[16]

There were rumors afoot among the Spiritualists that the president was quietly one of their own. A tale made the rounds in the early days of his presidency that while en route to Washington for the inauguration, Lincoln secretly called on a well-known New York medium looking for "spiritual association with the patriots of the past." Newspapers around the country printed rumors to the effect that Lincoln dabbled in Spiritualist beliefs, and in 1864, the National Spiritualist Convention, meeting in Chicago, endorsed his reelection bid, albeit for the decidedly temporal reason that they saw him as a champion of "liberty over tyranny." "Current report has it that President Lincoln is a firm and enthusiastic believer in modern spiritualism, and that regular meetings are held at the White House," read a typical newspaper declaration, but no one could offer any real evidence to substantiate these rumors.[17]

In October 1863, Lincoln received a letter from Joshua Speed, an old friend from his Springfield days, who provided an introduction for a Mrs. Cosby and her companion, a Spiritualist named Nettie Colburn. "They are both mediums and believers in the spirits," Speed wrote, "and are I am quite sure very choice spirits themselves." Speed's letter had a snickering undertone—"it will I am sure be some relief from the tedious round of office seekers to see two such agreeable ladies"—and just how seriously Lincoln took his friend, from whom he had drifted apart over the years, or indeed how serious Speed was himself, is difficult to ascertain.[18]

But even if Lincoln had been disposed to meet with such people, he had to have realized he would be playing with political fire. "Is President Lincoln a Victim of Spiritualism?" inquired a headline in the virulently anti-Lincoln

New York World in May 1863. The article claimed (with no evidence) that famous Radical Republicans Thaddeus Stevens and Charles Sumner were Spiritualists who prevailed on the will of a weak president to do their bidding because Lincoln "is a very firm believer in ghosts." The *World* did give Lincoln some benefit of the doubt by suggesting that when told by Spiritualists of the political will of the dead, "he frequently remarks that the communications from the other world are often delusive."[19]

Many Americans ascribed Spiritualism and séances to darker impulses than radical politics. It would not have taken much to connect the president with literal devilry, had it become known that he met with mediums or took their beliefs seriously. One anti-administration critic did just that, producing a nasty little booklet in 1863 called *Interior Causes of the War: The Nation Demonized, and Its President a Spirit-Rapper,* in which the author, under the pseudonym "A Citizen of Ohio," claimed that the president was "not only a spiritualist of the Abolition school, but has his media around him, and is and has been, from the beginning of his term, directing the war under the direction of spirit rappings." Several anti-administration newspapers hawked the book, one observing that "it contains, in a small space, many plain political truths, adapted to the times, and is forcibly written."[20]

That endorsement by the Spiritualist Convention may have made Lincoln wince in a save-me-from-my-friends way. "It is well known that the infidels, atheists, free-thinkers, free-lovers, Spiritualists and 'progressive Christians' have always been ardent admirers of Mr. Lincoln and his policy," noted a hostile Philadelphia newspaper, "and no one will be surprised to hear that [the Spiritualists] have now publicly ratified [Lincoln's nomination]."[21]

One of the women Speed mentioned in his letter, Nettie Colburn, later claimed to have staged a séance in the White House that Lincoln attended. Ms. Colburn was an earnest sort; she possessed absolute faith in her special powers as a channel for the ghosts of the dead, who would periodically inhabit her body and cause her to speak with their voices while in a trance. She was the source of many of the claims regarding Lincoln's supposed predisposition toward Spiritualism.

According to Colburn, she met the president in the White House sometime in late 1862. She had been making inquiries among various Washington officials in an attempt to obtain a furlough for her soldier brother, who was ill, and wanted badly to meet the president, both to help her brother and apparently also to provide Lincoln with advice from the spirit world. She knew she would be successful in the endeavor because a "little messenger of [her] spirit circle" whom Colburn referred to as "Pinkie," assured her this would be so.

Having gained entrance to the White House, she claimed to have met the president in the Red Room, accompanied by several other friends and sympathizers, one of whom was suddenly seized by the "master hand" of a dead spirit and began to bang away at a nearby piano with such authority and force that "the heavy end of the piano began rising and falling in perfect time to the music." Lincoln, she recalled, came down the staircase to the room with his steps keeping perfect time to the music's tempo. "So this is our 'little Nettie,' is it, that we've heard so much about?" the president remarked when he met her.

From there, Colburn's account becomes even more bizarre. While speaking to the president, she fell into a trance for over an hour, channeling "some strong masculine spirit force," in which she told Lincoln in stentorian tones that he must not renege on his promise to issue an Emancipation Proclamation a few days hence. When she finally awoke, the president was *sitting back in his chair, with his arms folded upon his breast, looking intently at [her]*. One of the onlookers pointed to a nearby portrait of Daniel Webster and suggested to the president that it was Webster's ghost, his "masculine spirit," who had spoken through Colburn. Lincoln seemed to agree. "Yes, and it is very singular, very!" he replied. He then told Nettie, "My child, you possess a very singular gift" and opined that hers was surely a "gift from God."[22]

If Colburn made such a deep impression on the president at this encounter, which she claims occurred in December 1862, it is curious that she appeared ten months later in a letter of introduction from Joshua Speed as if she were a complete stranger.[23] In any event, no reliable corroborating evidence exists for Colburn's account; we have only her word and the contents of her 1891 book, *Was Abraham Lincoln a Spiritualist?*, which she could manipulate to suit her purposes. As a Spiritualist and a medium, she had an obvious vested interest in making her claims. Enlisting Lincoln as a fellow traveler could only bolster her personal career and the cause of Spiritualism generally. While Speed's letter indicates that Lincoln at least vaguely knew her name, there is no hard evidence that he ever actually met her, that she impressed him with her "gift from God," or that she tried on his behalf to contact the spirits of the dead.[24]

Another widely circulated story appeared in various newspapers during the spring of 1863, describing a "spiritual soiree" in the White House, attended by a Spiritualist lawyer, judge, and author named John W. Edmonds; Abraham and Mary; Secretary of War Edwin Stanton; Secretary of the Navy Gideon Welles; and several others. According to the story, written by a correspondent for the *Boston Gazette*, the medium in question, one Charles Shockle, induced invisible "manifestations" to pinch Stanton's ears and twitch Welles's beard. He then conjured the ghost of Henry Knox, who, after consulting with the ghosts of Napoleon, Lafayette, Washington, Benjamin Franklin, and the British abolitionist William Wilberforce, proceeded to give the president a great deal of unsolicited advice regarding the war. This was accompanied by various rappings on the walls, dimmed lights, and a rattling of the portrait of Henry Clay, hanging on a nearby wall. Lincoln supposedly asked the ghost of Knox, via Mr. Shockle, to ascertain the ghost of Stephen Douglas's opinion on the war. The Douglas-Knox-Shockle apparition duly replied that Lincoln needed to attain at least two more battlefield victories, to which the president replied, "I believe that, whether it comes from spirit or human."[25]

Leaving aside the manifest silliness of the story—one wonders whether the *Gazette* article is actually political satire—there is no reliable evidence that it occurred. In his voluminous diary, Welles made no mention of this event, and Edmonds wrote a public letter denying that he had ever met the president, save on one official occasion during which no dead spirits were consulted. When the account made its way into the papers, one anti-administration paper declared that the story "will have the effect to degrade the President, his office and his people in the eyes of the whole civilized world." True enough, which is why it probably never happened.[26]

On the whole, there is no reliable evidence that Lincoln tried to contact ghosts via a séance or other Spiritualist ceremony. To believe the stories regarding Lincoln's wartime dalliances with Spiritualism, one would need to accept that this man, who was rightly recognized as a master politician in his time, was so overcome with desire to contact the dead—suddenly finding a passion for subjects related to the afterlife he never expressed before the war—that he disregarded his own better political judgment regarding the risks associated with Spiritualism and its connection in the minds of many Americans with radical politics, and this at a time when moderate and conservative support was critical to the success of his policies. We must also accept that he would attend séances in the White House (or elsewhere) while never once mentioning the fact, or anything related to Spiritualism at all, in any extant public or private document.[27]

One would also need to accept at face value the claims of Spiritualists like Nettie Colburn. Possibly she was telling the truth or some version of it. But it is more likely that she and her fellow Spiritualists—a segment of Civil War–era society that was peppered with more than its fair share of people who were charlatans or delusional, or both—either greatly embellished their claims or manufactured them entirely out of whole cloth.

Lincoln's private secretary John Nicolay had it about right when he wrote after the war that the president's dalliances with ghosts were much exaggerated. Like many people during that time, Lincoln "might have had some curiosity as to Spiritualism," Nicolay conceded, but "he was not superstitious, nor did he have any spiritualistic tendencies. . . . I do not remember that even curiosity ever impelled him to attend a séance. He had more important business on hand during those days."[28]

For Mary, however, matters were more complicated. Willie's death was a profoundly traumatizing event, and given Spiritualism's popularity during the war among some of her friends, such as Mary Welles, it is not surprising that she sought help from mediums in trying to contact his dead spirit. Nettie Colburn claimed to have had close and repeated contact with the First Lady. She may or may not be reliable in this regard; again, her book is our only source for much of this information. But other sources do indicate that Mary was making the rounds of Washington's Spiritualist community, trying to find someone who could help her contact her lost child. Orville Hickman Browning, a congressman and old friend of the Lincolns from their Springfield days, wrote in his diary on New Year's Day 1863 that Mary told him she had visited a local medium who "had made wonderful revelations to her about her little son Willy," though Browning did not note what those revelations entailed.[29]

Elizabeth Keckly also possessed some degree of interest in Spiritualism. Sometime soon after Willie's death, Keckly discussed Spiritualism with Mary. In particular, Keckly introduced Mary to a man named Charles J. Colchester—"Lord" Colchester, as he styled himself. He claimed to be the long-lost son of an English duke and a medium capable of contacting the dead by means of inducing rappings and other noises from the nether regions.

In fact, "Lord" Colchester was a fraud, albeit of a charming and imaginative variety, who managed to ingratiate himself with quite a few important personages in Washington, including several congressmen. He was later prosecuted for illegal juggling (performing jugglery and sleight of hand required a twenty-dollar license), and during his trial he argued that he was not actually "juggling," but rather acting while under the influence of ghosts who were moving his body without his awareness, "under the guise of spiritual control." He lost the case.[30]

Mary was soon taken in by Colchester's charm. She invited him to the Soldiers' Home, where he contacted Willie for his mother's benefit. In a darkened room, he performed a ceremony inducing Willie's ghost to produce loud knocking on a table and scratches along a wall. "Mrs. Lincoln told me of these so-called manifestations," remembered wartime correspondent Noah Brooks, who had become acquainted with the Lincolns, "and asked me to be present at the White House when Colchester would give an exhibition of his powers."

Brooks was not impressed. Soon after Mary approached him, the reporter availed himself of the opportunity to attend one of Colchester's sessions at another Washington home (the event cost him a dollar), where he discovered that the erstwhile Spiritualist, who claimed to have conjured knocks, bells, and drumbeats from dead spirits in another darkened room, was producing these sounds himself. Brooks got into a scuffle with Colchester—caught red-handed with the drum—during which the "Lord" made his escape. With more than his share of cheek, Colchester appeared at the White House a few days later, begging Mary for a War Department pass to New York and strongly hinting that he was willing to blackmail the First Lady by making public their connection. Frightened by the blackmail threat, Mary sent for Brooks, who confronted Colchester, called him a "scoundrel" and a "humbug," and told him to leave Washington forthwith, which he then did.[31]

Lincoln was aware of his wife's Spiritualist explorations, particularly the Colchester episode, and when he found out about the séance in the Soldiers' Home, he reacted not as an enthusiastic Spiritualist believer, or even as a curious onlooker, but rather as a rational skeptic and a husband who feared his wife might have been the victim of a con man. He asked Joseph Henry, head of the Smithsonian Institution, to investigate Colchester. Henry did briefly speak with the man but learned nothing of note—and soon thereafter, Noah Brooks exposed the Englishman as a fake.

Colchester never did perform a séance in the White House, and there is no hard evidence that any séances were held there, once we discard the uncorroborated word of Colburn and others with a vested interest in exaggerating and fabricating their connections with the Lincolns. And there were contrary voices from people who knew Lincoln well: his friend and fellow lawyer from Springfield, Ward Hill Lamon, who sniffed that Lincoln "was no dabbler in divination—astrology, horoscopy, prophecy, ghost lore, or witcheries of any sort"; Reverend Gurley, who observed that "Mr. Lincoln was greatly annoyed by the report that that he was interested in spiritualism"; and Nicolay, who saw him on a regular basis during the war and wrote, "I never knew of his attending a séance of Spiritualists at the White House or elsewhere. . . . That he was in any sense a so-called 'Spiritualist' seems to me almost too absurd to need contradiction."[32]

A fundamentally rational man, Lincoln was not at all given to extended explorations of the ghostly, more esoteric dimension of death. But he was steadily transitioning toward a deeper spiritual understanding, a process that did not much involve a belief in ghosts, "rappings," or the like. And while Willie's death no doubt played a central role in that process, the true catalyst was the battlefield.

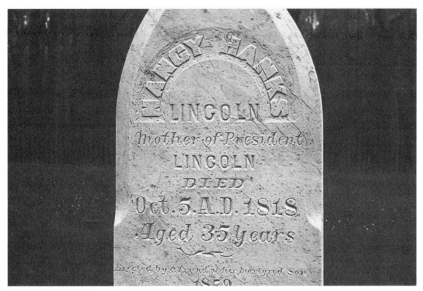

Gravesite of Nancy Hanks Lincoln in Spencer County, Indiana. Nancy died from "milk sickness" in 1818 and is buried on a knoll not far from the family's Indiana homestead. AUTHOR'S PHOTO.

Thomas Lincoln, Abraham's father. A devoutly religious man, Thomas endured a distant and strained relationship with his son, who did not attend his father's deathbed or funeral. COURTESY ABRAHAM LINCOLN LIBRARY AND ARCHIVES, HARROGATE, TENNESSEE.

Eddy's tombstone. The stone was discovered lying face-down and forgotten in the Oak Ridge Cemetery during the 1950s; it is currently on display at the Abraham Lincoln Presidential Library. ABRAHAM LINCOLN PRESIDEN-TIAL LIBRARY AND MUSEUM, SPRINGFIELD, ILLINOIS.

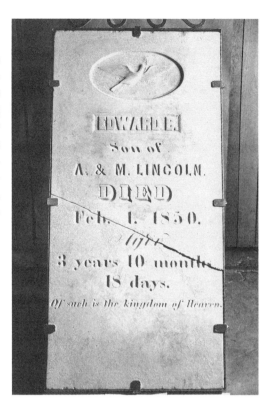

Henry Clay. This image of Lincoln's "beau ideal of a statesman" was taken not long before his death in 1852. Lincoln used his eulogy of Clay to reenter politics, hitching his own views of the Union and slavery to those expressed by Clay. LIBRARY OF CONGRESS.

Elmer Ellsworth. He was considered to be the ideal Union soldier and was a close friend of Lincoln and his family. Ellsworth's death during the early days of the war traumatized the First Family. LIBRARY OF CONGRESS.

Colonel Edward Baker. This congressman and close friend of Lincoln's was killed at the Battle of Ball's Bluff. Accepting his death was very difficult for the president. LIBRARY OF CONGRESS.

Willie Lincoln. Abraham's favorite son died from typhoid fever in 1862. Willie's death was probably the most difficult personal experience endured by Lincoln during the war. LIBRARY OF CONGRESS.

Mary Lincoln. She wore full mourning for a lengthy time following her son Willie's death, as she verged on emotional collapse. LIBRARY OF CONGRESS.

Dead soldiers on the Antietam battlefield. By the fall of 1862, these sickening sights were an all too familiar part of American life. Earlier in the war, Lincoln did not know how to guide his countrymen through this trauma. LIBRARY OF CONGRESS.

Anti-Lincoln cartoon. This image depicts the president requesting a ribald song while standing in front of the dead and wounded at the Battle of Antietam. The scandal surrounding Lincoln's visit to this battlefield, with wildly inaccurate stories of his alleged inappropriate behavior, proved to be effective political propaganda for his enemies. LIBRARY OF CONGRESS.

Lincoln's Gettysburg Address, November 19, 1863. At the Pennsylvania cemetery's dedication, shown here in this only known extant photo, the president confronted the higher meaning of the war's dead and his own lack of control over the war's staggering human costs. LIBRARY OF CONGRESS.

Gravediggers at work following the Battle of Cold Harbor in Virginia. This battle was part of General Ulysses S. Grant's deadly campaign around Richmond and Petersburg during the spring and summer of 1864. By this point in the war, Lincoln had found ways to persevere with a dogged determination, even as lists of the dead grew longer. LIBRARY OF CONGRESS.

Lincoln delivering his Second Inaugural Address in Washington, D.C. He had finally, by this point, arrived at a certain understanding of the war's dead. LIBRARY OF CONGRESS.

7. BATTLEFIELDS

Any major Civil War battle created a horrifying patch of earth: "a little spot of hell," as one eyewitness described the area around Bull Run, where not one but two battles ravaged the landscape. Wrecked cannons, wagons, and caissons; flattened buildings and fences; broken and abandoned equipment; rotting carcasses of dead horses and mules (and sometimes cattle caught in the crossfire); blackened and charred trees and underbrush: battlefields were assaults on the senses and on the very land itself. Bizarre idiosyncrasies stood out. Bits and pieces of half-consumed breakfast meals were scattered helter-skelter in the remains of a camp suddenly shelled by artillery fire at Wilson's Creek in Missouri. A snow and sleet storm, a rarity given that most battles were fought in the sunny South, fell on the Fort Donelson battle-ground, powdering the wrack of war with an incongruously peaceful-looking white blanket. After the Battle of Franklin in Tennessee, one could hear the screams of horses given mercy deaths as they lay in pools of their own blood and intestines; one was a general's horse that "had his fore feet on one side of the [enemy's] works and his hind feet on the other, dead."[1]

The dead soldiers were the most shocking: all those bodies, bloated and blackened, their limbs twisted in grotesque shapes caused by rigor mortis or blown away entirely by shell fire, arms and legs scattered about. Sometimes the dead fell in rows, incongruously uniform from the way a volley of musket fire had laid them out with an odd neatness. Others lay in piles, one atop the other. Hogs, vultures, and other animals sometimes descended on the remains. On some occasions, soldiers from the opposing side deliberately mutilated the corpses of their foes. "I saw one of our dead soldiers with his mouth crammed full of cartridges until the cheeks were bulged out," noted a disgusted Union soldier walking the field after the Battle of Shiloh. "Several protruded from his mouth." The man's comrades gave as good as they got, digging only shallow pits in which they unceremoniously dumped the Rebel dead. "Some of our boys were disposed to kick the secesh into these pits," he wrote. "One fell in with a heavy dump on his face. The more humane proposed to turn him over. 'O, that'll do,' said a Union Missourian, 'for when he scratches, he'll scratch nearer hell.'"[2]

The war had quickly evolved (or devolved) from the earliest days, when the death of one soldier such as Elmer Ellsworth evoked extensive commentary. Americans treated Ellsworth's death almost like a peacetime homicide, but as the casualty lists grew ever longer, they were no longer inclined to refer to a dead soldier as having been "murdered" on the battlefield. The soldiers themselves grew callous to the sight of a corpse, and whatever outrage they felt regarding the war dead had become more generalized, their sensitivity to combat casualties more numbed to the war's cruelties. "Death is so common that little sentiment is wasted," observed a young Union officer during the Peninsula Campaign. "It is not like death at home."[3]

The war was now vast fields of Ellsworths, each with his own story but all blended together in what was a roiling sea of suffering. "Many of our dead and wounded were still on the field. . . . Many are hid away in the bushes who will never have burial, and years hence their bones will be discovered bleaching in the sun. Such is the case on every battle-field," wrote a witness to the aftermath of the Battle of Pea Ridge in Arkansas. "The scenes over this field of carnage beggars all description. Sights calculated to chill the blood and strike the mind with horror meet you on every side. Here is a human body with the mangled remnants of a head which a cannon-ball has torn to fragments. There lies another with both legs shot away. Here is one the top of whose skull is gone, leaving the brain all exposed to the weather, and see! he is still alive."[4]

As Lincoln stepped onto the Antietam battlefield the morning of October 4, 1862, he stepped into the war's darkest place, bounded and defined by violent forms of death he had never seen and probably never even imagined. But it was not his first battlefield. While serving in the Illinois state militia during the Black Hawk War of 1832, he was among the soldiers who occupied a battle site in an area around Sycamore Creek in northern Illinois. On a hill near the creek, twelve militiamen in an advance scouting party were surrounded and killed by Native Americans. Lincoln took no part in that fight, but he was among the main body of men who came upon the little battlefield afterward and found the bodies. The sight made a lasting impression. "I remember just how those men looked," he recalled years later. "The red light of the morning sun was streaming upon them as they lay, heads toward us, on the ground, and every man had a round red spot on the top of his head, about as big as a dollar, where the redskins had taken his scalp." It unnerved him. "It was frightful, but it was grotesque," he confessed, "and the red sunlight seemed to paint everything all over." The next day, Lincoln helped bury the men—the first and last time in his life he was directly involved in burying a dead body.[5]

Antietam was exponentially worse. More than twenty-two thousand men were killed and wounded in a twelve-square-mile area around the town of Sharpsburg, Maryland, and Antietam Creek during an approximately fourteen-hour span on September 17, making it the deadliest single day in American history. When the sun finally set and the fighting died away, the sheer number of bodies left from the battle was indescribable. One short stretch of road—later nicknamed "Bloody Lane"—contained over five thousand dead and wounded Rebel soldiers: a "ghastly flooring" four and sometimes five layers deep. "The Confederates had gone down as grass before the scythe," wrote one observer. "They were lying in rows, like the ties of a railroad. . . . I recall a soldier with a cartridge between his thumb and finger, the end of the cartridge bitten off, and the paper between his teeth when the bullet pierced his heart, and the machinery of life—all the muscles and nerves—came to a standstill."[6]

The aftermath was an imposing exercise in mass body disposal. "In every direction around men were digging graves and burying the dead," noted a Union officer riding across the battlefield the next morning. He stopped near a patch of woods bordering what would become known simply as the

Cornfield, a scene of particularly ferocious slaughter, "where lay two or three hundred festering bodies, nearly all of [them] Rebels, the most hideous exhibition I had yet seen. Many were black as Negroes, heads and faces hideously swelled, covered with dust until they looked like clods. . . . Here was a long grave of ours, made in a rain-washed gulley, certain to be washed out the first time it rained hard." He said as much to a gravedigger, who simply replied, "To be sure they will," and resumed digging.[7]

People tried to staple the norms of the antebellum Good Death over these scenes. Comrades of dead soldiers wrote home to grieving parents that their loved ones had given inspiring speeches as they lay dying, bidding family and comrades farewell and urging them on to victory and observance of their duty. "One young fellow from Massachusetts lay dying his comrades trying to sooth," a Wisconsin private wrote his family. "He said to them, 'Go on and save Massachusetts; don't stop for me I shall soon be out of trouble.'"[8]

Many letters home contained miniature eulogies of the deceased. "As a soldier, there could be none better," Captain James Pierpont of Massachusetts reassured the parents of Corporal T. S. Yates, shot through the eye at Antietam. "Ever ready for his duty, and one of the bravest of the brave, he had won the love and respect of all that knew him." Pierpont also reassured Yates's parents that he had in his possession the corporal's watch, "the only thing of value with him," which he would return if they wished—a talisman of death reminiscent of the prewar locks of hair and other cherished mementoes of the dead.[9]

Many such letters were written to relatives by the friends and commanding officers of the deceased, and they probably helped some. But they were of little comfort, especially when battlefield death was so shocking and new. In the wake of the massive bloodletting that was Antietam and the other big early battles of the war, people struggled in their attempt to make sense of this strange new way of dying.

Politics played a role in the public perception of battlefields from the war's earliest days. Soldiers who saw their comrades die on the field voiced a renewed determination to kill enemy soldiers by way of retaliation. "Three of my most intimate friends were shot down by my side," wrote a Rhode Island soldier to his parents, "one of them having his head shot from his body, and another had his leg taken entirely off, the blood flying in my face. I felt so badly I almost fainted, but I rallied immediately, and clenching my teeth, went in, and every shot I fired I made it tell, as I can assure you that I saw five of the rebels fall dead, and I thought the death of my friends avenged."[10]

Rumors of battlefield atrocities—many of dubious accuracy—motivated men to enlist, the idea of Northern men not just dying at Bull Run but dying wrongfully giving an extra spur. "O! Sir," exclaimed a new recruit to a man in Iowa, who asked why there were so many men lined up to enlist, "since they read the account of how our wounded soldiers in the hospital and on the battle field at Bull Run were murdered, nothing could restrain them." A newspaper editor in Lincoln's hometown of Springfield, Illinois, opined, "When we look away to that scene of carnage [at Bull Run] all strewed with the bodies of patriotic men who courted death for themselves, that their country might live, and then look upon the homes which their fall has rendered desolate forever, we realize—what I think the popular heart in its forbearance has never completely comprehended—the unspeakable and hellish atrocity of this rebellion."[11]

Some tried to use the casualties as a shaming device, pressing reluctant men to enlist. There was an edge now to the criticisms leveled at those who would not volunteer or tried to find other ways to stay off the battlefield. One individual with a poetic bent penned a few lines aimed at those who joined Home Guard rather than frontline combat units:

> Let dogs delight to bark and bite,
>   I have no taste for war;
> My joy is not in fire and fight,
> In cannon's roar and bullet's flight,
> And nasty pools of gore.
> . . . .
> Let others fight, let others fall,
>   Let others wear the bays,
> But of the military ball
> Let me alone adorn the festive hall
>   Where brass and buttons blaze.[12]

The dead could give an extra edge to the blame assigned by the president's critics to his (real and perceived) mistakes. For the Bull Run defeat, "Abraham Lincoln alone is responsible," argued one Democratic newspaper, which also stated, with no apparent sense of contradiction, that the "awful responsibility" for what had occurred rested with numerous Republican Party leaders, all of whom had pressured the Union army into premature action and had gotten men killed. "When we publish the cold record of names of those that have futilely perished in battle recently," explained a Democratic newspaper, "it seems to us that each one, though mute in death, speaks to those dear to him, imploring that they ask themselves whether these calamities were not the result of a delusion and a political deception practiced by [Republican] fanatical leaders."[13]

In the early months of his presidency, Lincoln struggled to find an effective response. He did not do much to harness the energy of those whose assessment of the war, sobered by the battlefield dead, involved a stiffening of the spine and renewed resolve to do their duty. He made no public calls to revenge the dead, and he did not try to shame anyone to enlist in the face of those first casualty lists. His direct encounters with wartime death—primarily Elmer Ellsworth and Edward Baker—were more personal than anything else, of a piece with the private mourning he experienced when Willie and Eddy died or, going even further back, the deaths of his mother, sister, and Ann Rutledge. He understood the need to mourn these deaths with public propriety, keeping his grief hidden away and only occasionally allowing it to surface, and he also understood the need to keep Mary's grief behind closed doors as much as possible.

But none of this translated, at least early in the war, into an understanding that death during such a massive civil war was essentially a public matter. Battlefields were a public square, a grim sort of polis, and as president and commander in chief, Lincoln occupied a prime role in shaping how the war dead would be understood and the meaning of their sacrifice articulated in this public realm. The battlefield had flipped the ordinary order of death. Eddy and Willie, Edward Baker and Elmer Ellsworth—these were private losses with a public dimension. But battlefields were at their core public deaths, which then filtered down into the homes and hearts of ordinary Americans. They required a new understanding, a new paradigm.

Lincoln did not fully grasp this, at least not right away. His first major address to the nation following his inauguration, sent to Congress's special session on July 4, 1861, contained nothing regarding wartime death and what it might mean, because the war to that point had caused very few casualties. But even at the end of the year, after First Bull Run, Wilson's Creek in

Missouri (a smaller but quite nasty little fight) and numerous other violent encounters had killed or wounded thousands of men, Lincoln said little about the war's fallen soldiers in his first annual address to Congress.[14]

The first truly massive battles of the war—Shiloh in April 1862, Second Bull Run that August, and the various battles constituting General George McClellan's peninsula campaign earlier that summer—also elicited little in the way of a direct public response from the president. These battles put lists of dead soldiers in the columns of newspapers around the country, and they called forth a shocked, painful new national reckoning with the war's mortal seriousness. But there was no campaign emanating from the White House designed to explain these deaths. Lincoln's first proclamation of prayer and fasting, issued in August, made no mention of the fallen or any acknowledgment of the battlefield dead beyond a general reference to the affliction of "faction and civil war."[15]

This is not altogether surprising, given the limitations of his office. Lincoln inherited in the presidency an institution that was not yet structured for such work. Presidents before him did little to shape public opinion. The idea of what we might call today "media management" barely existed.

It also may not have yet fully dawned on Lincoln that he needed to do something from the White House to shape the public's perception of wartime death, because before the war he was not inclined to see death as a political matter. He never spoke much about dying for a cause or about death serving a higher moral cause, and he had always avoided rhetoric that smacked of political martyrdom. Equating dying with politics before the war was a radical thing, the stuff of extremists who spoke and wrote of sacrificing themselves (and others) to end human bondage, shades of John Brown. Lincoln wanted no part of this.

But now the politics of death was omnipresent, a powerful subtext in the debates swirling around wartime policymaking. When the finger-pointing inevitably began regarding the Union army and navy's setbacks, those fingers jabbed that much sharper because everyone knew that somewhere in the background lurked graves. "Since the late disastrous affair at Bull's Run, our people are beginning to inquire who is responsible for the misadventures of our armies?" noted a New York journalist in late July 1861.[16]

Antietam created a fresh round of such queries, particularly after the president announced soon after the battle that he planned to issue an emancipation proclamation. Now all the thorny, ugly questions about slavery and race in American life would be wedded to the battlefield dead. Would white men be willing to die for African American freedom? Would black men be willing to die for their own freedom? Were they all dying for the same reasons?

Up until the fall of 1862, Lincoln had done little to shape this dialogue. If anything, he seems to have understood battle, at least to this point in the war, as a matter of abstract calculations—the sanitized, unemotional approach to death he had learned long before from Blackstone and in the courtrooms. "I state my general idea of this war to be that we have the *greater* numbers, and the enemy has the *greater* facility of concentrating forces upon points of collision," he wrote to General Don Carlos Buell in early 1862; "that we must fail, unless we can find some way of making *our* advantage an over-match for *his*; and that this can only be done by menacing him with superior forces at *different* points, at the *same* time; so that we can safely attack, one, or both, if he makes no change; and if he *weakens* one to *strengthen* the other, forbear to attack the strengthened one, but seize, and hold the weakened one, gaining so much."[17]

His visit to Antietam was ostensibly a matter of these considerations, for he had come to believe, with good reason, that his commanding general, George McClellan, lacked insufficient drive to aggressively pursue the enemy. McClellan's army held the field after the battle, yet he did nothing to impede the Confederate army's retreat into Virginia. "Little Mac" was also becoming the focal point for much of the political opposition to Lincoln, to the degree that some wondered whether the general was purposely hindering an aggressive approach to the war by way of appeasing the peace wing of the Democratic Party, whose nomination for the presidency he wished to pursue in 1864. McClellan denied this, insisting he had no designs on the White House or any other political career. But the rumors persisted.[18]

More generally, and a bit surprisingly for a West Point graduate and experienced soldier, McClellan was shocked by the human cost of battle. He had seen combat before the war, having served as an engineer and artillery officer under General Winfield Scott during the war with Mexico and as an official U.S. Army observer of the Siege of Sevastopol during the Crimean War. He was not an especially squeamish sort, and he well knew that war was a violent and deadly enterprise. McClellan was also quite capable of militant bravado. "Soldiers! I have heard there was danger here," read an early war proclamation he had issued to his men. "I have come to place myself at your head and share it with you. I fear now but one thing—that you will not find foemen worthy of your steel."[19]

The war produced its share of officers who reveled in this sort of bombast and were callous about the war's human cost. But in McClellan's case, the bombast masked an inner unease with battlefield death. Whatever his faults as a battlefield tactician—and they were many—and whatever his personality defects (a healthy ego and overweening arrogance), George McClellan was a fundamentally humane man. He had grown to love his men, perhaps too much, and the sight of their dead corpses horrified him. "I feel sure of success," he wrote to his wife after touring the Fair Oaks battlefield in June 1862. "But I am tired of the sickening sight of the battlefield, with its mangled corpses & poor suffering wounded! Victory has no charms for me when purchased at such cost." As the casualty lists from his Peninsula Campaign lengthened, he confessed to her, "Every poor fellow that is killed or wounded almost haunts me! My only consolation is that I have honestly done my best to save as many lives as possible."[20] While this was an expression of his private moral compass, it contained a political component as well. McClellan wanted to win the war—he was no traitor, as some would later claim—and yet he also wanted that victory to be as bloodless as possible, not only for his own men but for the Rebels as well.

Lincoln was not a bloodthirsty or callous man—quite the contrary. From his childhood days in Indiana, when he avoided hunting, he was never comfortable with violence. He had begun what would become a steady habit of commuting capital offenses by soldiers if at all possible, putting his thumb on the scales of war death. In September 1861, he penned a letter to General McClellan, asking that a Vermont private be spared the firing squad for falling asleep while on guard duty, after receiving a personal visit in the White House by a delegation of the man's comrades. The story of the president saving the lowly private made the newspapers and quickly became part of the Lincoln legend. "Captain, your boy shall not be shot," Lincoln is supposed to have remarked to the officer in charge of the Vermont delegation. The man's life was spared, and variations of that tale and other similar incidents persisted throughout the war and after, reinforcing a growing popular image among many Americans of Lincoln as a fundamentally compassionate man who tried to spare common soldiers' lives whenever possible.[21]

He took a less popular course regarding executions following a massive Native American uprising in August 1862, when Dakota Sioux warriors attacked white settlements in western and southern Minnesota, killing several hundred civilians and nearly eighty soldiers. In suppressing the uprising, army and civilian authorities took over five hundred Sioux prisoners, three hundred of whom were sentenced to death by highly dubious drumhead trials, some lasting only a few minutes.

Public opinion tended to side with the white Minnesotans, particularly when grisly stories—some true, many others not—made the rounds in the Northern press of atrocities visited by Dakota warriors on the settlers. Lincoln was under considerable pressure to allow the executions. "A great necessity is upon us to execute the *great majority* of those who have been condemned," read one letter Lincoln received from Minnesota. "This is required as a satisfaction to the demands of public justice."[22]

To his credit, Lincoln resisted such considerations. He ordered an immediate halt to the executions and personally reviewed the trial records of the condemned, and this at a time when he could easily claim to have had bigger fish to fry—emancipation was imminent, as was yet another ill-fated assault on Richmond by the Army of the Potomac. But he read every document and threw out most of the convictions, allowing only those to stand where proof was available that the defendant in question had acted with wanton cruelty. In the end, thirty-eight Sioux were hanged the day after Christmas 1862. If the president would not allow executions of individual Union soldiers in the name of enforcing military discipline, so too did he choose not to allow the deaths of Dakota Sioux in the name of political expediency. When told that his stance had cost Republicans support in the state, he retorted that he "could not afford to hang men for votes."[23]

He was actually not so very different from his commanding general in his wish to mitigate the war's deadlier aspects. But unlike McClellan, Lincoln came to believe that the war would require risking a revolution, of the sort that might create many more corpses, and the centerpiece of that revolution would be African American freedom. Sometime in the early summer of 1862, he made emancipation official Union wartime policy. In doing so, he understood that he was now linking the body count directly to the dark inner demons of race hatred and resentment his fellow white Americans harbored. He knew what sort of toxic combination race, slavery, and battle death might create. "See our present condition—the country engaged in war!—our white men cutting one another's throats, none knowing how far it will extend," he bluntly told a meeting of African American ministers at the White House in August 1862, "and then consider what we know to be the truth. But for your race among us there could not be war, although many men engaged on either side do not care for you one way or the other." The president's abolitionist critics were appalled that Lincoln seemed here to be blaming the war on African Americans and slaves, and while historians and Lincoln biographers have debated the meaning behind his words where slavery and American race relations were concerned, it seems clear that, emancipation policies aside, the war's volatile mix of death, violence, and race worried Lincoln a great deal.[24]

When McClellan launched his long-awaited assault on Richmond via the peninsula area in eastern Virginia in the spring of 1862, Lincoln followed his progress—or lack thereof—with keen attention. By midsummer he resolved to visit the army, amid stories of impending disasters and alarming dispatches from McClellan that he was being overwhelmed and driven back from Richmond by Confederate forces. The president boarded the USS *Ariel* on July 7 with a retinue of army officials and landed at McClellan's headquarters the following morning. After conferring briefly with McClellan aboard the *Ariel* soon after his arrival, he disembarked and made his way to the army's lines, where he inspected the entrenchments guarding their frontlines. It was almost, if not quite, an actual battlefield. He did not come under enemy fire, nor did he see dead bodies, but he had inched closer to the war's dark heart.

Two and half months later, he was returning to Antietam on a similar mission, a second visit to the Army of the Potomac, which reflected Lincoln's ever-increasing frustration toward his commanding general. McClellan had won the battle, more or less, having blunted a Confederate invasion of the North and compelled Confederate general Robert E. Lee's badly mauled force to fall back into Virginia. But despite Lincoln's repeated urgings, McClellan made no attempt to follow. The president was again restless and worried, and his decision to pay a second visit to the army was impulsive. Gideon Welles called on the president at the White House and was surprised to learn of his absence, though he guessed the reason. "I have no doubt he is on a visit to McClellan," Welles wrote in his diary. "None of his cabinet or not more than one, I think, can have been aware of this journey."[25]

Lincoln boarded a train this time, leaving Washington, D.C., on October 1. He was accompanied by Ward Hill Lamon, an Illinois friend and fellow lawyer, who now acted as the president's impromptu bodyguard and was the marshal for Washington. Also along for the trip was Oziah Hatch, another

Illinois friend; the railroad's president, John W. Garrett; and General John A. McClernand.[26] They paused briefly at Harpers Ferry while Lincoln reviewed the troops stationed in the area, arriving at McClellan's headquarters near the battlefield the following evening. The army put the president up for the night in a tent and serenaded him with a cavalry unit's band.

He was spared the goriest aspects of Antietam. The battle had occurred several weeks before his arrival, and by the time of Lincoln's visit, nearly all the corpses were underground or otherwise removed. Lincoln saw no fresh signs of the carnage. His time was instead occupied with reviewing live soldiers, members of General Ambrose Burnside's corps, and conferring with McClellan at his headquarters three miles south of the battlefield.

Lincoln's mood was dark. He wondered if the army's terrible sacrifice on this ground had been for naught, because the commanding general lacked the vigor to pursue the enemy and prosecute the war to a successful conclusion. Standing on a hill overlooking the Army of the Potomac that morning after breakfast, the president turned to Hatch and asked him what he saw. Peering down at the sea of white tents beneath them, a perplexed Hatch said, "It is the Army of the Potomac." "So it is called," the president sarcastically replied, "but that is a mistake. It is only McClellan's bodyguard."[27]

McClellan suggested they review General Fitz-John Porter's corps, several miles away. The party boarded ambulances, Lincoln sitting "with his long legs doubled up so that his knees almost struck his chin," and set out for Porter's campsite. His reception among the men was positive enough, for the most part—enlisted men cheered the president as he rode by—though some were unimpressed. "Republican simplicity is well enough, but I should have preferred to see the President of the United States traveling with a little more regard to appearances," grumbled one soldier, who thought Lincoln "not only is the ugliest man I ever saw, but the most uncouth and gawky in his manners and appearance."[28]

The atmosphere between Lincoln and McClellan was tense, and the president's mood grew increasingly somber. As the men rumbled along in their ambulances between one campsite and the next, he asked Lamon to sing a song he remembered from their days riding the circuit together as lawyers in Illinois. Sensing the president's sadness, Lamon sang "two or three little comic things" by way of lightening the mood.[29]

His efforts did not help; Lincoln was distracted and uncharacteristically jumpy. While the party stood on a knoll near a portion of the battlefield,

McClellan began to describe for the president the order of battle, when the president suddenly interrupted him by saying, "Let us go and see where Hooker went in," referring to Union general Joseph Hooker's corps, which had been badly mauled during an assault on the morning of the battle. En route to the site of Hooker's assault, Lincoln's ambulance took a different path than the rest, at which point the president abruptly called off the tour entirely and returned to McClellan's headquarters without notifying the general, who for several hours had no idea where the president was. Reviewing Porter's corps the next day, the president rode by the men in silence, without "a word of approval, not even a smile of approbation."[30]

It was not an auspicious visit, and on his return to Washington, Lincoln discovered himself in the middle of a controversy, what Lamon called a "tempest of defamation." Rumors began making the rounds of various newspapers—especially the Democratic Party organs—that Lincoln had made light of the battlefield dead by asking his companions to sing songs as they strode among the soldiers' graves. "It is a fact that President Lincoln, when he visited the battle field of Antietam, before the corpses had been buried, called upon an officer, who had been reported to him as a good songster, to 'step out and sing me a song,'" reported a correspondent using the pseudonym "Manhattan." The correspondent identified the president's preference as a tune called "Jim along Josey," an old folk tune, "and then, in an open plain, in hearing of the dying, and in sight of the sightless dead, the officer sung for the President of the United States." The correspondent acidly concluded his account by observing "what a splendid but much abused ruler old Nero was. He fiddled while Rome was burning, but he never called out one of his officers to sing 'Jim along Josey.'"[31]

Press commentary was scathing. "It is mortifying beyond measure that the chief magistrate of the American people should thus be represented before the eyes of the world," declared one New Hampshire paper. A San Francisco commentator noted that the story "lends him into apparently trivial conduct, and to make jests on apparently very malapropos occasions." The *New York Sunday Times* related a highly embellished account of the incident, in which Lincoln asked for the song while McClellan stood by with "trembling lip," and Union officers who stood nearby quickly took their leave so they would not be present when the song desecrated the "sod that covered the bones on that battlefield, of their once gallant comrades." Another version had McClellan pointing out a portion of the battlefield containing the graves of four thousand dead Union and Confederate soldiers, whereby Lincoln turned and requested the singing of a song called "Picayune Butler."[32]

Memories of the affair lingered. In August 1864, nearly two years after Lincoln had visited Antietam, a supporter sent him a news clipping from "a vile Copper head sheet" published in New Jersey that had resurrected the controversy with an eye toward the impending presidential election by reprinting rumors that Lincoln wanted a "comic negro song" sung to him as he trod over the graves of the dead. In this version, Lincoln had asked Lamon to sing some funny tunes they both knew, dating back to their days together as lawyers on the Illinois Eighth Judicial Circuit.[33]

This new story made fresh rounds among the nation's newspapers. "Abraham Lincoln called for a comic negro song when he was surrounded by corpses upon the battlefield of Antietam," claimed the *Cleveland Plain Dealer*. A more detailed and imaginative version, printed in a Connecticut paper, had Lincoln's party arriving in the ambulance at "Burnside's Bridge," a stone bridge that was the scene of heavy fighting. Here, "where the dead were piled highest," went the tale, "Mr. Lincoln suddenly slapp[ed] Marshal Lamon on the knee, [and] exclaimed: 'Come, Lamon, give us that song.'" A stunned McClellan is supposed to have replied "with a shudder," "'Not now, if you please, Marshal.'"[34]

The scandal picked up steam just as the nation headed into the presidential election's final stretch, Lincoln's opponents growing increasingly shrill—and creative. One account had Lincoln requesting the song to "drown the sighs of the living and the groans of the dying" as he walked among the battle's casualties. Another had the "manly officers" of Lincoln's entourage purposely lagging behind while Lamon sang his song, "leaving the heartless and ribald President to his own chosen companion and degradation." Still another described one of the officers present upbraiding his commander in chief, saying, "This is not the place or the time, Mr. President, for such a song as that." Accusing Lincoln of "a callous, cold blooded, ribald indifference to the sufferings of others," an Ohio newspaper recalled the story and described the president as "call[ing] upon a parasite," presumably Lamon, "for a ribald negro song . . . amid the dead and dying, the maimed and suffering soldiers who fell in that great fight."[35]

The accusations stung. Worse, there was a striking lack of response by way of defending Lincoln in the various pro-administration newspapers, as if the editors, taking into account the president's well-known penchant for jokes and songs, thought the Antietam tale was at least plausible. Some of the president's supporters were worried. "Is there any good authority for the World's story of Mr. Lincoln asking for a comic song on the battlefield of Antietam?" asked an anonymous writer in the *New York Tribune*?[36]

For Lincoln's enemies, the contrast with the prim and proper military man George McClellan, who was now Lincoln's opponent in the 1864 presidential election, was telling, and the repeated characterization of the tune as "Negro" injected yet another racial overtone in a campaign that was already deeply infused with racist accusations leveled against the author of the Emancipation Proclamation. "Abraham Lincoln called for a vulgar negro song at Antietam," declared one especially virulent anti-Lincoln Philadelphia newspaper on Election Day, and "Geo. B. McClellan rebuked him for his levity on the field of battle. Freemen! To-day give your votes to the man who, in the hour of sadness, deeply sympathizes with the soldier, instead of filling his ears with a comic melody!"[37]

One critic made of the incident a nasty poem, titled "Lincoln at Antietam." The poem pulled together in one place all the imagery associated with the suffering and dying on a Civil War battlefield and contrasted it with Lincoln's supposed indifference and inappropriate behavior:

> Dead upon dead were huddled thick,
> The very air with death was sick;
> The wounded waited, with ebbing life,
> Their turn for the surgeon's tired knife.
>> But carelessly rode Old Abe along,
>> And called in that scene for a negro song.
>
> Youth and manhood lay weltering there,
> With the sweat of agony matting the hair;
> And the bravest of the brave heard with awe
> The crunching sound of the busy saw.
>> But carelessly rode Old Abe along,
>> And called in such a scene for a negro song.
>
> Mothers, daughters, sisters, wives,
> Knit by love to those precious lives,

How must your hearts for news athirst,
Have throbbed and sunk, and bled, or burst,
    While carelessly Old Abe rode along,
    And called 'mid those graves for a negro song.[38]

Aspersions on his character, wild rumors based on half-truths and out-right lies, were nothing new for the president, who had suffered the slings and arrows of his political enemies since the earliest days of his election. He endured them largely in silence, rarely contemplating a direct response, and at first he believed silence was the best response to the "Antietam song-singing." "There has already been too much said about this falsehood," he told Lamon, who urged him to make a public refutation. "Let the thing alone." But the characterizations of him as "The Joker of Antietam" (as one paper put it) were impinging on something quite sensitive: the battlefield dead and his relationship with all those fallen soldiers.[39]

This eventually led him to contemplate the extraordinary measure of having Lamon publicly issue a denial. Lincoln himself wrote out the document—another unusual act. In it, Lamon admitted that Lincoln had asked him to sing a "little sad song" and that he had done so, but they were nowhere near any gravesite or burial ground, and the song was not considered inappropriate to the occasion. "Neither Gen. McClellan or any one else made any objection to the singing," went the statement; "the place was not on the battle field, the time was sixteen days after the battle, no dead body was seen during the whole time the president was absent from Washington, nor even a grave that had not been rained on since it was made."[40]

In the end, Lincoln believed that silence was his best response. "I dislike to appear as an apologist for an act of my own which I know is right," he told Lamon. He chose not to have Lamon issue the denial. On the other hand, he did tell his friend to "keep the paper, and we will see about it."[41]

But while he did not publicly refute the Antietam rumors, he did begin to pay closer attention to the need for articulating a public—and necessarily political—defense of battlefield death. It was not enough that he (and for that matter, Mary) knew and observed the proper rituals of mourning when death struck their private lives, as Willie's father and Edward Baker and Elmer Ellsworth's friend. Lincoln knew how to properly conduct a funeral, what to wear and what to say, and how to put on a brave public face in the wake of private loss.

But this all was still essentially prewar death, of a kind with Eddy's death so long ago: the same basic rituals, the same gestures, albeit on a grander scale. Not so with battlefield death. The dead of Antietam and other Civil War battles were radically and strangely new to Lincoln, as with every other American. They were all in effect renegotiating a new relationship with death in the war's awful wake. Lincoln would find the need to do so as well.

8. CONTROL

Lincoln grew harder after Antietam. He could be pressed past the limits of his considerable patience, and those who importuned him with unreasonable or frivolous requests, or added to the endless barrage of grousing, sometimes found themselves subject to the president's ire. "I sincerely wish war was an easier and pleasanter business than it is," he snapped after receiving a complaint from one man, "but it does not admit of holy-days."[1]

From the first days of the war, he had pressed for vigorous offensive action from his generals, but by the end of 1862, that aggressiveness acquired an edge. He grew increasingly angry with what he saw as his generals' maddening unwillingness to pursue the enemy and incessant excuses for delay. On receiving a typical detailed explanation from one general as to why it was impossible for him to move his army from Missouri into Kentucky, Lincoln's despair was palpable. "It is exceedingly discouraging," he scribbled at the bottom of the general's letter. "As everywhere else, nothing can be done."[2]

McClellan was a particularly vexing problem. After Antietam his army sat idle in Maryland, licking its wounds, while the Confederate army he had beaten returned to Virginia unmolested, to regroup and fight another day. Days turned into weeks, and still the Army of the Potomac did not move.

Lincoln grew ever more exasperated, and McClellan felt the sharp end of the president's tongue. When in one message McClellan pleaded tired horses as a reason not to deploy his cavalry more aggressively, Lincoln snapped. "I have just read your despatch about sore tongued and fatigued horses," he wrote. "Will you pardon me for asking what the horses of your army have done since the battle of Antietam that fatigue anything?"[3]

He fired McClellan in November, but it proved of no immediate benefit. McClellan's replacement was Ambrose Burnside, an affable Ohioan with good intentions and limited ability. "I have my fears that [Burnside] has not sufficient grasp and power for the position given him or for so large a force," Gideon Welles confided in his diary, "but he is patriotic, and his aims are right."[4]

Taking Lincoln's injunctions to aggressively assault the enemy a bit too simplistically, Burnside marched the Army of the Potomac more or less straight at Lee's Confederate army, which was well emplaced behind strong fortifications at the Virginia town of Fredericksburg on the Rappahannock River. Burnside's assault against Lee's army produced the most lopsided battlefield defeat for the Union in the entire war. Over twelve thousand men were killed or wounded between December 11 and 14, creating yet another corpse-littered, battered piece of earth.

The slapdash disposal of unidentified bodies, now a new American normal, was made more urgent by the bitterly cold December weather. Even Southerners were moved by the scene. "I witnessed with pain the burial of many thousands of Federal dead," wrote a Confederate officer. "The night before, the thermometer must have fallen to zero, and the bodies of the slain had frozen to the ground. The ground was frozen nearly a foot deep, and it was necessary to use pick-axes. . . . It was a sad sight to see these brave soldiers thrown into trenches, without even a blanket or a word of prayer, and the heavy clods thrown upon them." In their haste, one burial party stuffed a local farmer's icehouse with bodies, where they were not discovered until after the war, a "hecatomb of skeletons."[5]

No other military setback produced quite so much utter disbelief in the North. "The repulse of our gallant army at Fredericksburg has caused a feeling of despondency throughout the North unequalled by any other event of the war," claimed a Vermont newspaper. The shock quickly (and predictably) turned to furor. The Joint Committee on the Conduct of the War opened a fresh investigation and grilled Burnside's subordinate commanders such as General Joseph Hooker, who told the committee that "all the troops in the world could not have taken the rebel position." The lopsided ratio of casualties—approximately three Union soldiers died for every Confederate—gave the criticisms added bite. Union officers called to testify before the committee tried to sound a dispassionate, technical note, citing equipment issues, particularly the failure of pontoon bridges to arrive in a timely enough fashion to allow the army to cross the Rappahannock before Lee could firm up his defenses; miscommunication between parts of the army and the Washington high command; and various difficulties caused by the frigid weather.[6]

The Northern press was not nearly so detached. "A stunning and fatal blow to public confidence," declared the *New York World*, asking, "Of what advantage are our unparalleled resources if they are to be thus squandered by administrative and military incapables, who, as often as they send our brave soldiers to battle, send them to a fruitless butchery?" Another newspaper referred to the tremendous waste of soldiers' lives as "criminal" and casting a "dark pall [that] seems to have enshrouded all ranks, and conditions of the people—the high, the low, the rich, the poor, the dwellers in the palace as well as those of the humbled roof, whether numbered with the long list of widowed wives, orphaned children and bereaved relatives and friends or not." "Disheartened, humiliated, crushed by the terrible blow which has fallen on them, the loyal men of America can with difficulty possess their souls in calmness sufficient to review the horrible history which has been enacted within the past week," read one editorial. The Army of the Potomac was now "almost an army of martyrs," bravely marching to their deaths without protest, for "of what avail has it been found to protest against the madness which rules at Washington? . . . Such was the soldierly spirit that animated that magnificent army every man of whom felt that the crossing [of the Rappahannock] was marching into the jaws of death. All honor to them, and some day a monument to the thousands who lie on the bloody fields around Fredericksburg, fallen in hopeless obedience to the Government of the United States."[7]

Many Northerners placed the responsibility for the dead directly on the president's shoulders. "Again have you, Abraham Lincoln . . . sent death to thousands of our brothers and friends, again desolation into the homes and hearts of the people; death that gives no life to the perishing nation, and sorrow which no patriotism can console," declared a New York newspaper.

An article headlined "The Fredericksburg Butchery" blamed "the fearful and fruitless slaughter of our gallant soldiers" directly on the president. McClellan was still popular in many quarters, particularly among anti-Lincoln people and Democratic Party stalwarts, and they wasted little time in castigating Lincoln for his decision to remove Little Mac from command. "All this has resulted directly from Abraham Lincoln's wicked interference with Gen[eral] McClellan's plans," thought one observer, "and his treacherous determination to prevent that noble patriot and accomplished commander from achieving a success that would have rendered his name and fame immortal and saved the country from impending anarchy." Whatever his faults, Little Mac had not gotten so many men killed so quickly, and in such higher numbers than the Confederates on the same battlefield.[8]

Lincoln signed the Emancipation Proclamation a little over two weeks after Fredericksburg. More conservative elements in white Northern society conflated black freedom, the aggressiveness of Radical Republicans who called for a more vigorous pursuit of the war, and piles of dead bodies. "'Spades to the rear,' was the cry of the abolitionists when McClellan was removed," observed a Maine newspaper. "But spades, it seems, went to the front after the battle of Fredericksburg and dug the graves of some thousands of our soldiers."[9]

Dead white Union soldiers and freed black Americans—here was a potent brew for any critic of Lincoln to stir fresh rounds of racially tinged anger and resentment. Rumors abounded among Democrats that Lincoln was interested in prolonging the war—and the dying—because he wanted a complete and revolutionary subversion of American race relations. There were those who thought Lincoln had deliberately withheld reinforcements from McClellan during the Peninsula Campaign for just this reason. "Had not the president, by his own personal orders deprived McClellan of the supporting columns promised him, Richmond would have been ours last spring, and the rebellion crushed," thought a hostile editor from the president's own hometown in Springfield, Illinois. "But no. The solution of the slavery conflict was involved, and it would not do to permit McClellan to close the war until the negro was free."[10]

Worst of all, Fredericksburg's death toll seemed an exercise in futility. The public tolerated high casualty rates, at least to a point. But Fredericksburg seemed meaningless, death in the service of nothing. "Soldiers who fall in a noble cause under worthy and skillful leaders count it a joy to die on the field of battle," opined the *New York World*, "but [not] when a whole nation is put in mourning because blundering incompetence and charlatanism direct the movements of armies and deluge the land with blood shed to no purpose beyond which further forbearance would be a crime."[11]

Reeling from the casualty lists and the hostile press, Lincoln tried to put the Fredericksburg debacle in a positive light. He issued a public decree to the Army of the Potomac, congratulating the men for their bravery at Fredericksburg and arguing that while the assault was certainly "not successful, the attempt was not an error, nor the failure other than an accident." What the president meant by this was unclear. Perhaps he was referring to the "accident" of the tardy pontoon equipment. In any event, he praised the soldiers' courage and assured them and the country that he was "condoling with the mourners for the dead, and sympathizing with the severely wounded," and further observed that "the number of both is comparatively so small."[12]

His attempt to paper over the Fredericksburg disaster was unconvincing; if anything, he only added fuel to the fire. "The address of the President to the Army of the Potomac is a remarkable document," noted a newspaper in Philadelphia. "But, without quarrelling with Mr. Lincoln's adverb ['comparatively'] *was* the loss at Fredericksburg *small*? . . . We submit that the outrages and criminal blunders of this administration have been enough to put upon the American people, without such wretched attempts to deceive them. This is adding 'insult to injury.'"[13] It sounded a bit too much like a lawyer's attempt to make the best of a bad case, what modern Americans term political "spin." Even sympathetic Northerners were nonplussed by Lincoln's language. "It may have been no 'error' to make such an attack," laconically observed Union general Edwin Sumner, "but it certainly was a very costly method of learning that the enemy's position was impregnable."[14]

Aside from the damage Fredericksburg wrought on the Union's strategic plans and his administration's political prospects, the battle's death toll devastated Lincoln personally. Pennsylvania governor Andrew Curtin met with him soon after having visited the battlefield. The governor arrived at the White House late at night and was ushered into Lincoln's bedroom—such was the president's anxiety to hear the news—and when Lincoln sat on the edge of the bed and asked what Curtin had seen, the governor informed him that it was not so much a battlefield as a "slaughter pen." "I was sorry in a moment that I had said that," Curtin recalled, "for he groaned, wrung his hands, and uttered exclamations of grief." It was only with considerable difficulty, Curtin later remembered, that he was able to get Lincoln calmed enough to return to his bed. He told Curtin, "If there is a worse place than hell I am in it." In a similar vein, he soon thereafter remarked to a young officer in the War Department's telegraph office, "If there is a man out of perdition who suffers more than I do, I pity him."[15]

Such was the grim calculus of the war by the end of 1862. Everything depended on the army. As fortunes on the battlefield turned, so too did the national mood, and that mood waxed and waned in more or less direct proportion to the number of dead bodies on the field and whether that number had exceeded some arbitrary and vaguely unidentifiable threshold past which the casualty levels were unacceptable. "There is discontent in the public mind," Gideon Welles confessed in his diary. "Our army operations have been a succession of disappointments." "Things look badly around here politically," Hay wrote to his secretarial counterpart John Nicolay during a visit to Illinois in late October. "The inaction of the Army and the ill success of our arms have a bad effect." Hay was entirely correct; Republican candidates everywhere took a shellacking in the November elections.[16]

Lincoln faced a delicate task. He had to move the lines on the map in such a way as to demonstrate to the Northern populace that progress was being made toward victory, but the movement of those lines necessarily caused more battlefield deaths. If he hesitated—or allowed the generals to hesitate—this might slow the casualty rates, but the war's end would recede further into the distance. But if the casualties rose too high while the lines moved too slowly—or, as at Fredericksburg, not at all—then Lincoln faced a serious public backlash. The army and the public will that sustained it were after all assets that could be squandered away. The army could refuse en masse to fight; the Northern public could vote him and his party out of office, replacing them with political leaders who would sue for peace on the basis of separation.

Put bluntly, victory meant dying. This was an obvious fact of the war, and yet its stark reality was no less difficult for being so self-evident. Lincoln pressed, cajoled, sometimes begged his generals to hound the enemy without letup. Yet he knew—he had to have known—that his relentlessness, his unceasing urging of his generals forward to pursue the enemy without pause meant that more men would die.

His detractors understood this very well. "When the commander on the Peninsula [McClellan] protested, he was sacrificed," argued an anti-Lincoln writer, and "when the people of the United States protested with tremendous voice, they heard but derisive laughter from Washington, and they now hear repeated the insane orders—'Fight the enemy wherever you can find him!'; 'Move on the enemy's works!'"[17] Lincoln knew that the more he pressed his generals to fight, not only would more men die but also the criticism of his leadership, and often of him personally, would grow worse.

It could be argued that an energetic prosecution of the war would shorten its duration and save lives—the longer the war dragged on, the more men would die. This was a valid point, but it was not one that Lincoln made. Sending his second annual address to Congress on December 1, 1862, ten days before the Fredericksburg debacle and on the cusp of his issuing the Emancipation Proclamation, he made a strong case for emancipation as a means of shortening the war "and thus lessen[ing] its expenditure of money and of blood," but this was as close as he would get to suggesting that short-term high casualty rates might reduce the war's human toll in the longer run.[18]

He knew that his pivot toward emancipation as a central war aim would tear open the scab that covered the ugly American wound of white bigotry and racism and that he would now, as the Great Emancipator, be responsible for enraging white Southerners still further and motivate them to inflict still more deaths on the battlefield. "But for your race among us there could not be war," he bluntly told that deputation of African American leaders in August 1862.[19] This statement could be (and was) read by some indignant observers such as Frederick Douglass as Lincoln laying the blame for the war on African Americans. But perhaps Lincoln meant something more elemental here: that there was a direct connection between American racism and killing. Emancipation would surely only motivate Confederates to greater fury and violence. It might well speak to a higher cause and purpose, eventually proving to be, as he described the Thirteenth Amendment, which permanently abolished slavery, the "King's cure for all the evils" of the war. But until that time, it must add to the ever-lengthening butcher's bill.[20]

Emancipation, race, victory on the battlefield, party politics . . . everything swirled together into that tight apex of the war dead, and it was death of a sort that was different from the deaths Lincoln had previously encountered throughout his life. Now it was he who was responsible for the dying, not the caprice of disease that had carried away his mother, Ann Rutledge, and his two boys or the vagaries of childbirth that had killed his sister. Nor was Lincoln, as in his lawyer days, a dispassionate observer to deaths caused by circumstances in which he played no part. As president, *he* was now the circumstance.

He never intimated that there was a line beyond which he would not go, beyond which there would be too much dying for him to bear. He never even in private expressed a McClellanesque view holding that victory would not be worth it—would "have no charms"—if purchased at too high a cost in human treasure. But in making this choice to endure whatever the war threw at him, he was, as president and commander in chief, assuming a singular degree of personal responsibility for the war's dead.

His opponents rarely let him forget it. "The war is of Lincoln's making," went a typical editorial in a Democratic newspaper from Maine. "He and his party are responsible for its success. . . . The dominant [Republican] party at the North think of peace only as they think of political disgrace and ruin. Peace would be to that party death and annihilation. Lincoln himself has announced his resignation would precede any measure of pacification."[21]

To his more unkind critics, Lincoln reveled in this fact, reveled in the killing. Along with the spurious accusations that he dishonored the dead with ribald songs or that he consulted with ghosts before making important decisions, Democrats and other anti-war Northerners charged the president with being a callous, unfeeling butcher who deliberately sacrificed brave soldiers on the altar of his own incompetence and political ambitions. "Mr. LINCOLN, give me back my 500,000 sons!!!" begged a mournful Columbia, the female symbol of the United States, in one cartoon, only to be met with a rejoinder by a smirking Lincoln, "Well the fact is—by the way that reminds me of a STORY!" Others depicted the president dressed as a Roman soldier with a bloody sword or—following the lead of the Antietam song incident— making light of a field of dead and wounded men.[22] "He has exactly the demeanor of a man whose rest is broken by remorse, and to whose pillow tranquil sleep is a stranger," noted a hostile Washington correspondent. "God knows he has done enough to cause him a lifetime of remorse."[23]

Lincoln's legions of critics in the Confederate South were even more scathing. Anti-Lincoln propaganda in the Confederacy routinely portrayed the Union's president as a man with a great deal of blood on his hands. "Schemes of hellish cruelty and outrage, such as were never before conceived by the most bloody tyrants and or relentless savages, are freely and shamelessly discussed and advocated by the satanic press of the North," railed a typical editorial from a Memphis newspaper, "and an administration, whose folly is only surpassed by its intense and boundless wickedness, hastens to adopt and carry into action these diabolical counsels."[24]

It was small wonder that Lincoln turned increasingly to religion. By 1863, he was attending church on a more regular basis than at any other point in his life, primarily at the New York Avenue Presbyterian Church, where presided Phineas Gurley, the minister who had conducted Willie's funeral. Gurley had since become something of a spiritual advisor to the president, frequently visiting the White House, even as the president frequently attended his church. Noah Brooks saw the First Couple as they exited a Gurley service at the end of November 1862, both dressed in deep mourning for Willie, the president towering over the crowd of churchgoers, "his gait more stooping, his countenance sallow." On other occasions, Lincoln sneaked into a side room unobserved to listen to Gurley's sermon, trying to remain incognito and escape the favor seekers and others who hounded him even inside the church doors.[25]

When Lincoln spoke of God publicly, he adopted a reserved air. He never presumed to speak with any degree of certainty regarding God's will. "Unless I am more deceived in myself than I often am, it is my earnest desire to know the will of Providence," he told a delegation of Christian leaders. "These are not, however, the days of miracles, and I suppose it will be granted that I am not to expect a direct revelation." He also tried to put as brave a face as possible on the Union's military reverses and God's will. "While it has not pleased the Almighty to bless us with a return of peace, we can but press on," he declared in his December 1862 message to Congress.[26]

But in private, he had begun to seriously ponder the connections among the war's many deaths, God's will, and his own part in whatever grand plan the Almighty was following. "What has God put me in this place for?" he asked when learning of the news that so many men had died at Fredericksburg. He was too careful a politician to let the public hear him utter such thoughts aloud, but behind closed doors, he agonized over the war's cost and ultimate meaning—an unfamiliar place for a man who, before this point, had not been much given to theological or metaphysical musings.[27]

Sometime during that awful fall, he wrote down a few thoughts on the subject of God's will and the war—a scrap of paper that he meant no one to see. He had a lifelong habit of working out his private musings this way, and though we cannot know for sure the precise circumstances, it is easy to imagine him scribbling away in the wee hours of yet another sleepless night at the White House, perhaps having just read the casualty lists from Second Bull Run, or Antietam, or some other gruesome carnage.

"In great contests," he wrote, "each party claims to act in accordance with the will of God. Both *may* be, and one *must* be wrong. God can not be *for*, and *against* the same thing at the same time." Here was the familiar Lincoln of trigonometry-like logic. But then he ventured further:

> In the present civil war it is quite possible that God's purpose is something different from the purpose of either party—and yet the human instrumentalities, working just as they do, are of the best adaptation to effect His purpose. I am almost ready to say this is probably true—that God wills this contest, and wills that it shall not end yet. By his mere quiet power, on the minds of the now contestants, He could have either *saved* or *destroyed* the Union without a human contest. Yet the contest began. And having begun He could give the final victory to either side any day. Yet the contest proceeds.[28]

Emancipation was a strong subtext—it was surely among the things God could not be both for and against at the same time. The survival of the American nation was uppermost in Lincoln's mind when he wrote the words about saving or destroying the Union, and his thoughts also reflect his lifelong curiosity regarding the nature of God's will, given a sharp, almost desperate edge by the circumstances of the times.

But another theme is lurking beneath the surface, contained in that seemingly bloodless word *contest*, repeated several times on his little scrap of paper. *Contest* meant in this context fighting, bleeding, and dying on a large scale. Yet God willed the contest. God had a purpose—of that Lincoln was certain. God wanted something from the war. But apparently the only means at His disposal, given the frailties and sinfulness of humanity, involved the killing fields, the imperfect "instrumentalities" of an imperfect human race that could find no other, nonlethal alternatives in realizing God's plan. Lincoln here had begun to articulate a sense that the war's deaths transcended his personal preferences. "I shall do nothing in malice," he wrote. "What I deal with is too vast for malicious dealing."[29]

This was a revealing turn of phrase, perhaps even more revealing than his rejection of malicious intent in prosecuting the war. The war had become too big for Lincoln to claim any sort of direction or controlling influence. It had assumed a life of its own or, perhaps, to be more precise, a level of death all its own. Already by the end of 1862, the war had claimed a tremendous number of lives, with many more deaths yet to come. The war was fast becoming that very thing George McClellan so feared: a remorseless revolutionary struggle.

That Lincoln embraced the revolution—especially via emancipation—is not to imply that he did so with relish or with the hubris of a man imagining himself exercising any significant degree of control. Nor was he abrogating a sense of responsibility for the dead by placing the ultimate responsibility in the hands of the Almighty. He always knew he was the one giving the orders and directing the campaigns that killed people. But Lincoln was suggesting that the great, grinding engine of the war and the death that it produced was operating at a level far above his (and everyone else's) comprehension—that there must be a divine will at work here, something moving events that answered little (if at all) to his relatively minuscule sensibilities.

These sensibilities, developed at first in privacy on his little scrap of paper, began making their way into his public pronouncements. His first proclamation of a national "day of prayer and thanksgiving," issued in August 1861, was an anodyne statement that said little about the war's deadliness.[30] But nearly two years—and many thousands of dead soldiers—later, in March 1863, he responded to a Senate resolution asking him to set aside a day for national "prayer and humiliation" by dwelling at some length on the idea that the casualty lists were a counterbalance for America's collective sinfulness—slavery, perhaps, but more generally the sin of pride:

> Insomuch as we know that, by His divine law, nations like individuals are subjected to punishments and chastisements in this world, may we not justly fear that the awful calamity of civil war, which now desolates the land, may be but a punishment, inflicted upon us, for our presumptuous sins, to the needful end of our national reformation as a whole People?. . . . We have been preserved, these many years, in peace and prosperity. We have grown in numbers, wealth and power, as no other nation has ever grown. But we have forgotten God. . . . We have become too self-sufficient to feel the necessity of redeeming and preserving grace, too proud to pray to the God that made us![31]

Pride was, at bottom, the substitution of one's individual will for the will of God, and in so making the war's cost a form of atonement for national pride, Lincoln was here again—echoing his private musings—suggesting that the public function of death during the war transcended any individual motive or intent, even his own. "I claim not to have controlled events, but confess plainly that events have controlled me," he wrote.[32] It was a statement about emancipation and the fact that the very logic of the war dictated black freedom, but it also expressed his more general belief that the war had become a thing that, for all his power as president, was now functioning beyond him and his wishes.

Eight months later, he stood before a crowd gathered at the new cemetery in Gettysburg, Pennsylvania, the site of a battle that, for all its portents and promise of hope for the future, was all too familiar to Lincoln in terms of its human cost. The actual numbers were unprecedented—fifty-one thousand casualties total, with over seven thousand dead and many thousands more wounded or missing—but Lincoln and the rest of the country were by now numbingly acquainted with the scenes created in the battle's aftermath. Gettysburg was a charnel house of suffering, nearly every building and house having been transformed into a hospital or a makeshift morgue. Horror stories abounded about the dead bodies lying everywhere. "What spectacles awaited us on the slopes of the rolling hills around us!" wrote a Union nurse. "I never could have imagined anything to compare with it. Dead, dying, and wounded, in every condition you can conceive."[33]

But it was a decisive Union victory, whatever the cost. Lincoln's reaction, while celebratory, was even-keeled and rather subdued, more so than probably would have been the case earlier in the war. He understood that even as Northerners basked in their army's triumph, their mood was tempered by a sobering realization of its high cost. "While the nation's heart is cheered by the glorious success of our arms, routing if not destroying the rebel hosts who have invaded the North, our joy is chastened by the remembrance of those who have fallen in the contest, and the thousands of homes that are saddened by the loss of those most dear," observed a Connecticut newspaper.[34]

Lincoln responded from a White House balcony to a gathering of well-wishers on July 7, following news of the Vicksburg victory, with a paean to the recent Fourth of July celebrations and in the process echoed words he would later use in his Gettysburg Address: "How long ago is it?—eighty odd years—since on the Fourth of July for the first time in the history of the world a nation by its representatives, assembled and declared as a self-evident truth that 'all men are created equal.'" He thanked the Almighty for the Union's triumphs but also added the somewhat cryptic observation that "there are trying occasions, not only in success, but for the want of success"—possibly a gentle nod on Lincoln's part to the fact that many soldiers sacrificed their lives in such battles, regardless of the outcome.[35]

He was also given reasons not to be too enthused when the army's commanding general, George Meade, who like so many other Union commanders seemed painfully slow in following up his victory, allowed Lee's army to escape back to Virginia largely unmolested. On July 12, Lincoln received a message from Meade that he was only then at a point ready for his pursuit, and the president was dismayed. "They will be ready to fight a magnificent battle when there is no enemy there to fight," he remarked. He constantly goaded Meade to get on with it; "he paced the room, wringing his hands," recalled one observer who saw him in the War Department's telegraph office. "On only one or two occasions have I ever seen the President so troubled, so dejected and discouraged," Welles confided in his diary.[36]

Lincoln was absolutely convinced that the aftermath of Gettysburg was a golden opportunity not only to defeat Lee but also to end the war. When it became clear that Lee had indeed made his way back to Virginia, Lincoln's reaction was unusually harsh, perhaps because he was so painfully aware of how many men had died to afford Meade the opportunity he had now squandered. "Our army held the war in the hollow of their hand and they would not close it," he told John Hay. "We had gone through all the labor of tilling and planting an enormous crop and when it was ripe we did not harvest it." To Welles, he was more emotional: "It is terrible, terrible, this weakness, this indifference of our Potomac generals, with such armies of good and brave men."[37]

He drafted a message to Meade that dripped with anger and despair. "I do not believe you appreciate the magnitude of the misfortune involved in Lee's escape," the president wrote. "He was within your easy grasp, and to have closed upon him would, in connection with our other late successes, have ended the war. As it is, the war will be prolonged indefinitely.... Your golden opportunity is gone, and I am distressed immeasureably because of it." Lincoln knew his tone was hard, and upon reflection, he never sent the message.[38]

Piles of corpses, calculations of public reaction to the casualties, yet another commander slow to capitalize on a battlefield victory purchased in human blood—none of this was unusual for Lincoln. By 1863, he had seen it all before. Yet it was different; he was different.

Much has been written about that three-minute speech of only 272 words that he delivered four months after the battle, which historian Garry Wills (among many others) argues transformed America, with its invocation of the highest American ideals of democracy, freedom, and sacrifice. "The power of words has rarely been given a more compelling demonstration," Wills wrote. Lincoln "casts a spell" here with a "transcendental declaration," tying together the nation's past, present, and future as an experiment in self-government, rooted in equality, with "the chaste and graven quality of an Attic frieze."[39]

Wills is essentially correct. But if the address was a triumph, it was also more subtly a capitulation. It was a frank public admission of what the rising body count had been communicating to Lincoln since the war's opening days: that ultimately he exercised no real control over the dying.

He accepted relatively few speaking invitations during the war, and he never explained exactly why he went to Gettysburg or what he hoped to accomplish when he arrived. The affair was obviously important to him, given the care he took in both making the preparations for travel and writing the speech. Old myths that he hastily composed the address on the back of an envelope while en route to Gettysburg have long been debunked; Lincoln put extensive thought into what he would say, working his way through multiple drafts in the days prior to the speech.[40]

When he arrived on the evening of November 18, the new cemetery was far from completed, the project having encountered various delays and scheduling problems. Work crews were still busy disinterring bodies from the hastily dug sites in which they had been placed following the battle. "The dead were buried, friend and foe, on the field where they fell," noted one government report. "Many were not identified, but slight marks were put up to indicate how many each trench contained and to which side they belonged."[41]

Digging out these bodies and then reinterring them in an orderly fashion was a nasty and thankless task. Two Gettysburg men named John Hoke and Franklin Biesecker won the contract; they were paid $1.59 per corpse and were required to "open up the graves and trenches for personal inspection of the remains, for the purpose of ascertaining whether they are bodies of Union soldiers, and close them over again when ordered to do so." Hoke and Biesecker in turn contracted with two other Gettysburg men to supervise the exhumation of the bodies and surveying of new cemetery plots, and they hired a team of African American laborers to perform the actual task of digging up the bodies and parts of bodies, rifling through jacket pockets or searching shoes—where soldiers sometimes placed slips of paper with their names written on them for this very purpose—for some sign of identification. These bodies were months along in the decomposing process. Those buried on higher or drier ground tended to be skeletal, while bodies in wetter areas still had partially rotted strips of flesh, mingled with decayed uniforms and the other detritus of what amounted to a massive battlefield graveyard.[42]

When the crowds began to arrive for the dedication ceremony, there were still signs everywhere of only partial completion of this gruesome and time-consuming task. Marshals worked to steer people clear of the areas where graves were still freshly dug or marked for future burial, so it is unlikely that many people actually saw human remains waiting to be reburied. Still, the place had a raw funereal air. "The graves are fresh, for they are newly made," noted one correspondent. They are "marked as yet, at head and foot, only by bits of board stuck in the ground, numbered, or bearing the hastily written name of the dead soldier, the letter of his company, and his regiment. No flowers or tree are yet planted over them. No marble monument or lofty gateway guards the approach to these hundred[s] of sepulchers. That is the work of art and time, yet to be performed."[43]

Accompanied by Secretary of State Seward, the president toured the battlefield that morning. There is no record of what they saw, but it was Lincoln's closest proximity yet to the actual disposal and burial of dead soldiers. He must have been keenly aware of the presence of the dead, so close to where he stood as he rose to deliver his remarks later that day.[44]

An air of spiritual solemnity marked the occasion. Several newspapers referred to Lincoln's task at the ceremony as "perform[ing] the consecrational service," almost as if the president were pronouncing a benediction.[45] So it is not surprising that he sounded a spiritual note in tying the dead soldiers to an abiding idea of the sacred, alluding to the complex relationship among dying on the battlefield, the war's higher meaning, and God that he had been groping toward when he penned his private meditation a year earlier: "We cannot dedicate, we cannot consecrate, we cannot hallow this ground. The brave men, living and dead, who struggled here, have hallowed it, far above our poor power to add or detract."[46]

The divine had always been to Lincoln, broadly speaking, an incomprehensible thing, unknown and largely unknowable. By tying the Gettysburg dead to concepts like consecration and the hallowing of a space, he was elevating their deaths to a level that was too "far above" Lincoln's "power to add or detract" and even to fully comprehend. Men died at Gettysburg not in the service of Abraham Lincoln, their commander in chief, or their military leaders who designed campaigns and gave orders. They died in the service of an ideal, "a new birth of freedom" that was in turn ultimately tied to a greater, unknowable divine plan.

A close reading of his words at Gettysburg reveals a Lincoln who does not promise an end to the death toll. "It is for us, the living, rather to be dedicated here to the unfinished work which they have, thus far, so nobly carried on." "Unfinished" and "thus far" connote at the very least a war that is not yet won, and so might much of the crowd who listened to him have understood his meaning: the president wanted his audience to continue pressing forward to victory so that the Gettysburg deaths were not wasted in a lost cause. "It is rather for us to be here dedicated to the great task remaining before us."[47]

But there is more here than simply an exhortation to victory in the "great task" of winning the war, a gentle version of the prod he had so often applied to Meade, McClellan, and others to fight on. Lincoln did not here actually call on the American people to be dedicated to an ultimate victory in the Civil War and the defeat of the Confederacy. Historians have long marveled at the absence of any mention of the Union, the Confederacy, or emancipation in the Gettysburg Address. It is surely true that Lincoln omitted these subjects because he aimed for higher, more universal truths, ones that transcended the immediate events and meanings of the war itself. But to have mentioned any of these matters would also have implied a finite ending to the conflict, an ending to the death and dying, and that was something Lincoln could not yet see. Tying the Gettysburg dead to either the Union or the Confederacy carried with it the implicit suggestion that when one side or the other triumphed, the dying would end. Tying the dead to emancipation likewise carried with it the underlying suggestion that the war's death toll might decline once emancipation was fully achieved.[48]

Tying the dead to any of this placed them within Lincoln's purview as the president; it placed death more firmly in his control than he actually felt. By the fall of 1863, there were hopeful signs, but signs only, of an eventual Union victory. This would not translate into a reduction of the casualties anytime soon. Fresh from his deep disappointment with Meade, Lincoln could from Gettysburg see no end to the war or its death toll.

He was far too astute a politician to admit this openly. But we know—again, from that private rumination on the war and divine will in the fall of 1862—that he had begun to see the war's death toll as serving a purpose beyond his presidency. And if the Gettysburg Address was in many ways a statement of hope and purpose, it carried within it a subtle bleaker undercurrent of understanding that the dying would not and could not yet end, that there was much "unfinished work" ahead. He could promise the nation at Gettysburg that it was all for a high and noble cause. He could not promise them when or how it would all end. Only God knew that.

When he admitted as much—when by the time of Gettysburg he had begun to admit both privately and publicly that he possessed no real control over the war's dead—he was finding a means by which to end, or at least ameliorate, his writhing in the agony of his lonely "worse place than hell." He reacted to the Gettysburg victory in a calmer, more measured way. He sounded a tone of restrained thanks; he maintained an even emotional keel in the public eye, even as he privately felt disappointment over the battle's aftermath. He chose not to send Meade that angry message.

He needed to find a relatively calm place within himself, a place where he could direct the war and pursue his presidential duty without being tortured by its enormous human cost. Perhaps paradoxically, he did so by letting go, in a sense—by releasing control of the killing and the dying to a higher plane. It was a form of surrender, but surrender that gave him a small degree of private peace. More men would die every time he pushed his commanders to do battle. He had come to accept this.

It had taken him a while to get to this point; it was a process. Through the end of 1862, he had done almost nothing to address death's meaning in the war's context, and he directly spoke very little to the suffering caused by the war's many dead soldiers. He allowed a vacuum to form, and it was filled in ways not at all to his liking or in his best interests, with the stories of his supposed indifference to the battlefield dead and the implausible tales of his preoccupation with ghosts and séances. His enemies were busily defining the meaning of the war's dead. They were filling that vacuum and in ways damaging to his presidency.

The weaknesses of the presidency itself, an office that had not yet developed sophisticated mechanisms for shaping public perception, were to blame. But perhaps there was also a certain personal preoccupation at work, with the deaths of Willie, Edward Baker, and Colonel Ellsworth occurring so early in Lincoln's White House tenure. Even as the first battles of the war were ratcheting up the casualties, Lincoln found himself repeatedly immersed in his own suffering and the private turmoil of his wife. Both he and Mary were able to effectively keep their anguish from the public's prying eyes, but it was never easy, and if either the president or the First Lady occasionally allowed their personal losses to predominate, at the expense of paying more attention to how they might guide the nation as a whole through its ordeal of mourning, no one could blame them.

This is not to suggest that Lincoln was indifferent to public perception—quite the contrary. He was always keenly aware of public opinion and its importance, and he believed in the power of political leaders like himself to accurately perceive, mold, and direct it. "Our government rests in public opinion," he once observed, and "whoever can change public opinion, can change the government."[49] But the relationship between death and public opinion was different. Throughout his life, Lincoln was quite careful to observe the proprieties of funeral rituals and mourning, knowing how seriously these matters were taken in nineteenth-century America. Before the war, in matters of death, public opinion had always shaped him, not the other way around.

Now, as president, he was a public figure, shaping the way millions of Americans related to the deaths of their loved ones. He set the rules for national mourning; he explained what the war's deaths were all about and why they mattered. Lincoln was a bit slow to understand this, and in any event, he had never been one to ruminate at length about the meaning of death. Death had always been a great, mysterious thing to Lincoln, since his earlier days when it had swooped in and taken his mother, his sister, Ann Rutledge, and Eddy. In each case when death touched him so personally, he responded not with any assurance that he knew what death was about, but rather with a sense that death was an inexplicable, uncontrollable mystery.

They were all deaths he could not control, from Willie's inadvertent ingestion of tainted water to the soldiers' corpses lying on the fields of Gettysburg. No president had ever before been required to lead the nation through this sort of bloodletting, and occasionally he slipped, as at Antietam and in the aftermath of Fredericksburg. But Lincoln was finding his way, groping slowly but steadily toward a place where he could stand and direct the nation with reasonable calm and at least an understanding—if not a controlling influence—regarding the war's dead.

9. DUTY

Johanna Connor's death began with a flash and a bang, followed by searing flames and blinding smoke, all of which engulfed her in a few seconds. The smoke and fire were accompanied by a withering hail of bullets, creating a crescendo of lethality so terrible that afterward no one was entirely certain what killed her—the smoke, the fire, or the hot chunks of lead. She was twenty years old.

Johanna was one of thousands of Northern women employed by the Union war effort to field its million-man army and navy. On the morning of June 17, 1864, Johanna and thirty other young women were seated on benches in a long, low brick building at the Washington Arsenal, a mammoth military complex located in the nation's capital. Their job was to assemble, or "choke," musket cartridges. Sweltering in the hot midsummer heat, they opened the windows for fresh air. Shortly after noon, a shower of sparks puffed through one of the windows—probably from pans of chemicals used to make "star shells" that had been placed nearby and were cooked by the sun's rays—and detonated one of a number of gunpowder containers sitting near the girls.

The containers of black powder exploded, one after the other, creating an enormous concussive force that was contained and magnified by the building's thick walls. Johanna must not have been killed initially, for her corpse was largely intact, if charred and burned beyond nearly all recognition by the fires that raged through the building. Her head was so badly mangled that her brains were partially exposed, suggesting she may have been maimed by flying bullets and debris. She was placed in a straw-lined box; her brother-in-law managed to identify her by a swatch of her dress he recognized, clinging to what was left of her body. "This is Johanna Connor," read a placard on her corpse, along with the shattered remains of twenty of her coworkers.[1]

Lincoln attended the massive funeral, held two days after the explosion. He was a silent participant, giving no speech during the ceremony at the arsenal nor at the cemetery where the women were laid to rest. He rode in a carriage with Secretary Stanton—along with nearly 150 other carriages— down Pennsylvania Avenue, one among a city of mourners. "The streets were literally crowded with people along the lines of the procession," noted a reporter, "and housetops along the avenue were also thronged. . . . No such demonstration of popular sympathy has ever been expressed in Washington before as by this immense outpouring of people."[2]

It was Lincoln's first funeral in a long time. He had not attended a funeral since the death of Secretary of War Edwin Stanton's young son in the summer of 1862. This no doubt reflected his extremely hectic schedule; he was a busy man and becoming ever busier.[3] But that aside, his understated presence at the Washington Arsenal funeral was entirely in character with how he approached the war dead by 1864. He was now well settled into a relentless, determined mindset. He would see the thing through to the end, come what may—even his own demise. Hyperbolic expressions of his mortality crept into his writing and speeches. "I expect to maintain this contest until successful, or till I die, or am conquered, or my term expires, or Congress or the country forsakes me," he wrote to Seward. When he met with a group of border state Unionists, many of whom were ambivalent regarding black freedom, Lincoln was pointedly determined not to yield, telling them "he would rather die than take back a word of the Proclamation of Freedom."[4]

His generals were now equally grim and serious: Ulysses S. Grant, William Tecumseh Sherman, Philip Sheridan, men who withstood the war's casualties with a steely eyed, no-nonsense calm. Grant told Sheridan to execute his campaign in Virginia's Shenandoah Valley in such a manner as to transform the valley into "a barren waste." He later wrote to another

Union general that Sheridan had performed the job so well that "crows flying over it for the balance of this season will have to carry their provender with them." Grant also approved the campaign waged by Sherman in Georgia and the Carolinas, which achieved a lasting legacy as the embodiment of Sherman's famous dictum to "make Georgia howl."[5]

This was not "total war" in the modern sense. While Union commanders like Grant, Sheridan, and Sherman talked a menacing talk, in practice they did not truly want to kill large numbers of people. Nor did their commander in chief. But Lincoln and his generals knew that their central effort must be the killing of Confederate soldiers. Men on the battlefield must die for the war to end.

Lincoln had long since arrived at that conclusion, and now he had in place generals who agreed. "I have seen your despatch in which you say 'I want Sheridan put in command of all the troops in the field, with instructions to put himself South of the enemy, and follow him to the death,'" Lincoln wrote to Grant. "This, I think, is exactly right, as to how our forces should move."[6]

He wanted a grinding, unremitting campaign against Confederate soldiers in the field, and during the spring and summer of 1864, Grant gave it to him. His major push into the area of Virginia known as the Wilderness turned into yet another parade of casualty lists and graves, as the Army of the Potomac grappled with Lee's Army of Northern Virginia in a series of murderous battles in and around Richmond. And yet the Confederacy's capital city was not the primary target, as it had been for George McClellan and other early Union generals. The primary target was Lee's army—"wherever Lee goes, there you will also go," Grant ordered his subordinate commanders—and what this meant, in practical terms, was killing and wounding enough soldiers in the Army of Northern Virginia to effectively end its usefulness as a military force and thus substantially end the war.[7]

Grant was as good as his word, as he hammered ceaselessly away at Lee. The horrors of the Wilderness met or exceeded anything the president or the nation had previously experienced: close to thirty thousand dead and wounded men on both sides during three hard days of fighting. Burial details overwhelmed by the task of disposing of all the bodies were by now a familiar sight. But the gloomy setting of the Wilderness and some of its more peculiar horrors—men burned to death by forest fires raging out of control in the deep underbrush; soldiers grappling hand to hand in hastily dug, mud-filled pits; an area known as the "Bloody Angle," in which men threw bayoneted muskets at one another like spears—created particularly awful images. "Hundreds of Confederates, dead or dying, lay piled over one another in those pits," wrote a journalist who helped bury the bodies near the Bloody Angle. "The fallen lay three or four feet deep in some places, and, with but few exceptions, they were shot in or about the head. . . . The trenches were nearly full of muddy water. It was the most horrible sight I had ever witnessed."[8]

Grant remained unperturbed. "Our losses have been heavy," he admitted to Stanton in May, but "I think the loss of the enemy must be greater. . . . I propose to fight it out on this line if it takes all summer." Lincoln heartily approved. "I have seen your despatch expressing your unwillingness to break your hold where you are," he telegraphed Grant. "Neither am I willing. Hold on with a bull-dog gripe, and chew and choke, as much as possible."[9]

He visited Grant in mid-June, traveling with Tad by steamer to the army's sprawling central supply depot at a previously obscure little cotton port village, incongruously named City Point. With the Union army's arrival, it was now indeed a city, the wharves crowded with equipment, warehouses, and hastily constructed wooden buildings, along with a veritable sea of white tents. City Point also grew hospital beds like mushrooms: first six thousand, then ten thousand, and eventually fifteen thousand beds were housed in the hospital facility.

There were also graves. Each hospital created its own makeshift cemetery, burying the dead as quickly and with as much decency as circumstances allowed. After the war, many of the bodies would be reinterred in a massive single area, City Point National Cemetery, wherein lay the remains of nearly seven thousand soldiers. In the summer of 1864, however, these bodies lay scattered in clusters of graves here and there, peppering the place with wooden headboards or whatever could be found to mark a man's final resting place.[10]

Lincoln must have seen at least some of these gravesites as he toured the City Point facilities, including the hospitals—no doubt a somber sight. But unlike his visits to McClellan earlier, on this occasion there was little tension, Lincoln evincing a trust in Grant and his staff that he never felt with Little Mac. "The President was in very good spirits at the Cabinet [meeting]," Welles wrote. "His journey has done him good, physically, and strengthened him mentally in confidence in the Genl. and army."[11]

Still, the president was occasionally nervous, particularly when he knew the army was directly engaged in battle. He slept little during the three days of the Wilderness Campaign. One congressman found him pacing nervously up and down in his office in the White House. Welles recorded in his diary that the president visited him and discussed what little he had heard regarding the campaign. "I have been very anxious for some days in regard to our armies in the field," Lincoln admitted. Overriding Stanton's objections, Lincoln allowed a New York reporter to use the military telegraph system to wire his editor a story on the campaign, on the condition that the reporter would immediately tell the president all he knew of the battle's progress. Lincoln even sent a special train to fetch the reporter to the White House, where the president queried him at some length regarding what he had seen.[12]

But for all his anxiety, Lincoln spent relatively little time in the telegraph office reading dispatches, largely because Grant deliberately cut himself off from communications with the capital as he engaged Lee in battle. It was a decision Lincoln approved. "Not expecting to see you again before the Spring campaign opens," he wrote to Grant right before the Wilderness battles commenced. "The particulars of your plans I neither know, or seek to know." This was a measure of the president's trust in Grant. "You are vigilant and self-reliant," he assured his commanding general, "and, pleased with this, I wish not to obtrude any constraints or restraints upon you."[13]

There was no despair over the long casualty lists, no exclamations of "my God, what will the country say?" and no talk of being in a "worse place than hell." As the Wilderness Campaign settled itself into a siege affair before the town of Petersburg, Virginia, Lincoln responded with a low-key note of optimism, releasing a brief statement on May 9 asking the nation to offer a prayer of gratitude to God. That same evening, in response to a serenade from well-wishers at the White House, he declared, "I am, indeed, very grateful to the brave men who have been struggling with the enemy in the field," but he said nothing directly regarding the many dead soldiers lying in the Wilderness fields.[14]

In the wake of the savagery of the Wilderness Campaign and the grueling siege operations that had Lee pinned down in Petersburg, the Confederate high command in July launched a diversionary assault on Washington, a relatively small force of approximately ten thousand to fifteen thousand men under the dyspeptic Confederate general Jubal Early, whom Lee affectionately dubbed his "bad old man." Early personified what the war had become, in its callousness and almost casual acceptance of mayhem. On the way to Washington, cavalry under Early burned the town of Chambersburg, Pennsylvania, when its citizens refused to pay a ransom of $100,000 in gold, targeting in particular the homes of known Republicans, African Americans (one of whom was shot when he tried to save his house from the fire), and those who were known to have assisted them. Early later claimed that he had ordered the burning by way of retaliation for Union atrocities in the South, his ransom demand being "compensation for the destruction" and an attempt to "open the eyes of the people of the other towns at the North, to the necessity of urging upon their government the adoption of a different policy."[15]

The assault was more of a large-scale raid; Early had no hope of capturing the capital city, ringed as it was with a series of forts well stocked with heavy artillery and soldiers. But he did better than anyone had a right to expect, making his way to within sight of the Capitol dome and bringing the city's outer works under fire. "I can see a couple of columns of smoke just north of the White House," Hay recorded in his diary. Early cut telegraph wires leading into the city, adding to a general uneasy feeling of being besieged, particularly since, as Orville Browning noted, "the sound of the guns [was] occasionally heard." One reporter characterized the city's mood as "gloomy," with "much apprehension among the people."[16]

Lincoln betrayed no outward emotion, even as Washington was threatened by an enemy force for the first time in nearly two years. "The loss of the capital he regarded as a disaster that would probably be fatal," remembered one observer who saw him at this time, yet he did not "exhibit any evidence of excitement or apprehension." He also came—for the first and last time in the war—under direct enemy fire. On July 11, he rode out to Fort Stevens on the city's outskirts, as Early's men were engaged in bringing the fort under their guns. "He was in the Fort when it was first attacked, standing on the parapet," Hay wrote. "A soldier roughly ordered him to get down or he would have his head knocked off."[17]

Early later exulted that although his raid ended in a retreat back to Virginia, at least he "scared Abe Lincoln like hell." In fact, he had done nothing of the kind. People who saw Lincoln at this time remarked on his unruffled disposition. "The President is in very good feather this evening," Hay remarked on July 11. "He seems not in the least concerned about the safety of Washington." He returned to Fort Stevens the next day and again observed the enemy's fire as Early began his retreat south; according to legend, he

was again told by a soldier standing nearby to get down, the soldier supposedly being none other than future Supreme Court justice Oliver Wen-
dell Holmes Jr. An army surgeon standing nearby caught a bullet in his leg;
Lincoln remained unperturbed, "pleasant and in confident humor." When
Welles visited Fort Stevens later that day, he found Lincoln calmly "sitting
in the shade—his back against the parapet toward the enemy."[18]

During the summer and into the fall, he maintained that same steady,
grim determination. He sometimes grew despondent about his prospects
for reelection—needlessly, as it turned out—and he had his share of political headaches. But he did not waver in his confidence in Grant or in his
belief that his "chew and choke" approach would ultimately bring victory.
Always he urged his commanders to run the enemy to the ground, with no
outward expressions of doubt regarding casualties, and he was invariably
disappointed if he felt they had not done their utmost. "Met the President
between the War Department and White House," Browning recorded in
his diary on July 15. "Said he was in the dumps—that the rebels who had
besieged us were all escaped."[19]

Not everyone approved or shared this grinding, killing vision of the war.
Mary Lincoln felt that her husband had misplaced confidence in Grant.
She told him that Grant had "no regard for life. . . . [He] is an obstinate fool
and a butcher." The epithet stuck, especially among antiwar Northerners
and McClellan's supporters during the 1864 campaign, when the general
was nominated by the Democratic Party for the presidency. At one New
York campaign rally for McClellan, the crowd audibly groaned when Grant's
name was mentioned, followed by chants of "the butcher!" and "Grant the
butcher!" Lincoln ignored them all.[20]

By now a death needed to be truly extraordinary to grab his attention.
The Washington Arsenal fire certainly did so, as the national headlines and
immense crowds attested. Ever attuned to the nuances of politics and public opinion, Lincoln would have understood the value of appearing at the
victims' funeral, by way of openly demonstrating his compassion and coun-
teracting the charges leveled by his enemies that he was a callous man—"the
great violator of the Constitution, and still greater butcher of men . . . who
remains unmoved in the face of the greatest misery," according to one critic.
And perhaps it was no coincidence that he chose to attend the funeral just
as the old Antietam song episode was receiving renewed attention from the
opposition press.[21]

He had become reserved in death's presence, choosing his words carefully and sparingly—or saying nothing at all, communicating with his simple presence at the funeral a quiet commiseration with the deceased and their families. Death was now so commonplace, so normal for both himself and the country that he was not given to many public pronouncements or open displays of grief.

But it could still move him, even in that time of countless graves. Perhaps on some level he needed death not to become *too* normal, needed himself not to become too accepting and too benumbed. Some deaths still needed to be unusual and required reflection. Death needed a degree of unaccept-ability; it needed to retain at least some horror, like the horror when young women were "blown to atoms." For what would it say about a president and a nation that failed to stop and reflect when such a tragedy occurred? This was so even in a time when scores of soldiers had been similarly blown to atoms on countless battlefields, or died in their own filth from dysentery or other diseases in camp hospitals, or were the victims of any of the war's other obscenities, none of which prompted mourners to line the streets. Johanna's death, and those of her coworkers, called for at least a brief pause, bowed heads, and quiet mourning, and thus Lincoln attended his first funeral in nearly two years.

This need for death to be both ordinary and extraordinary was also the context of that famous letter Lincoln sent to Lydia Bixby, written six months after the arsenal funeral:

> I have been shown in the files of the War Department a statement of the Adjutant General of Massachusetts, that you are the mother of five sons who have died gloriously on the field of battle. I feel how weak and fruitless must be any words of mine which should attempt to beguile you from the grief of a loss so overwhelming. But I cannot refrain from tendering to you the consolation that may be found in the thanks of the Republic they died to save. I pray that our Heavenly Father may assuage the anguish of your bereavement, and leave you only the cher-ished memory of the loved and lost, and the solemn pride that must be yours, to have laid so costly a sacrifice upon the altar of Freedom.[22]

The Bixby letter was not what it seemed. Mrs. Bixby had actually lost two sons, not five, and at least one (possibly two) deserted, though the president did not know any of this. She was believed by those who knew her to be a

Southern sympathizer with no very kind opinion of Abraham Lincoln. It is also highly likely that Lincoln did not write the letter and that John Hay composed it for the president's signature. This being the case, it is not altogether fruitful to do a close textual analysis of the letter's contents, since the exact words are probably Hay's and not Lincoln's. Indeed, given what we know of the president's hectic routine—with piles and piles of paper daily crossing his desk—it may well be that he did little more than glance at his secretary's work, affixed his signature, and moved on.[23]

A transcript made its way into print, first appearing in a Boston newspaper four days after it was written, and then receiving wide coverage in Northern newspapers.[24] A few political opponents chose to denigrate it; a Philadelphia anti-Lincoln organ dismissed the Bixby letter as "cheap sympathy" and wondered at the "hypocrisy" of the president, who "is thus ostentatiously shedding his tears over the remains of Mrs. Bixby's sons, [and who] has two sons who are old enough to be laid upon 'the altar' but whom he keeps at home in luxury." (Tad was in fact only eleven years old, and Robert would soon join General Grant's staff.) But most seemed to agree with the assessment of an editor in faraway Denver who reprinted the letter and opined, "If Mr. Lincoln is sometimes the author of rough English—as one who saws a board without plaining it—he also occasionally turns out a piece of finished work, showing a master hand."[25]

Even if he did not write the letter, and even if Mrs. Bixby did not actually lose five sons, it nonetheless served as an effective public relations tool, and it is in this sense that the letter is revealing of Lincoln's late-war approach to the war's high human cost. Like his attendance at the arsenal victims' funeral, it was quiet and understated but nonetheless powerful, all the more so because it was ostensibly a private letter of condolence, rather than a speech or some other public pronouncement intended for political effect. The president was genuinely "tender and sympathetic," one Massachusetts paper put it. Many newspapers reprinted the letter's text with no additional comment, aside from an occasional characterization of the language as "touching" and "noble," albeit some ventured a bit further in their praise; "as an heir loom in the [Bixby] family, it will be worth more than gold," suggested a Boston newspaper, "and will serve to comfort thousands of others in their loss of husbands and sons."[26]

Lincoln did not contact many bereaved parents and loved ones in this way. After he wrote Elmer Ellsworth's parents to express his dismay at their son's death, he wrote only one other such letter, a brief note to a young woman named Fanny McCullough, whose father, Lieutenant Colonel William Mc-Cullough, had been killed in battle in December 1862. In that letter, he gives a glimpse of his own personal mechanism for grieving, honed after coping with the deaths of his sons and others close to him. "Perfect relief is not possible, except with time," he counseled Fanny. "You can not now realize that you will ever feel better. Is not this so? And yet it is a mistake. You are sure to be happy again. To know this, which is certainly true, will make you some less miserable now. I have had experience enough to know what I say; and you need only to believe it, to feel better at once. The memory of your dear Father, instead of an agony, will yet be a sad sweet feeling in your heart, of a purer, and holier sort than you have known before."[27]

It was a rare moment, this confluence of Lincoln's private mourning with that of a mourning nation. As with the arsenal fire victims, a death needed to be of an unusual nature to capture the president's attention. In Fanny McCullough's case, both she and her father were from Illinois, and Colonel McCullough had been in command of a cavalry regiment from Lincoln's home state when he was killed. He had been a court clerk in one of the counties where Lincoln practiced law before the war, so the president knew the man and his family from earlier days.[28]

Otherwise, Lincoln was not inclined to send a written condolence, even as a form letter or certificate, to the family of a deceased soldier, as would later wartime presidents (Franklin Roosevelt, for example, whose signature appeared on letters of condolence mailed to many of the families of soldiers killed during World War II, along with immediate notification via Western Union telegram and a death certificate). The Lincoln administration produced no such system, for several reasons. The sheer numbers of the dead would have made even a brief pro forma note almost impossible to produce and distribute in adequate quantities. The mistakes regarding Lydia Bixby's situation illuminate another difficulty: the lack of certainty regarding whether a given soldier had actually been killed. Many families were given no definitive information regarding the fate of their loved ones, learning of their loss only when letters stopped arriving from the front.[29]

If Lincoln wanted to offer comfort to the bereaved, he was compelled by circumstances to do so only in the most general terms. Possibly the Bixby letter was intended by the president as more than a personal communique to Mrs. Bixby; it may have been one of those private letters for public consumption that he sometimes wrote during the war, knowing the letter would eventually find its way into print. We have no way of knowing whether this was Lincoln's intent, but he surely did find fortuitous the Bixby letter's widespread publication and generally favorable reception.

He had begun to speak more of soldiers' battlefield sacrifices. Gratitude to the dead formed a subtle, unstated subtext in his Gettysburg Address, a sentiment that he expressed more openly during the ensuing months. In his annual message to Congress in December 1863, he closed by noting that he and Congress "do also honorably recognize the gallant men . . . to whom, more than to others, the world must stand indebted for the home of freedom disenthralled, regenerated, enlarged, and perpetuated." When he accepted renomination for the presidency six months later, he included in his formal letter to Republican Party leaders his approval of their formal statement of thanks to the country's fallen soldiers. "I am especially gratified that the soldier and the seaman were not forgotten by the convention, as they forever must and will be remembered by the grateful country for whose salvation they devote their lives," he wrote. He sounded a similar note in his public speeches. "I am, indeed, very grateful to the brave men who have been struggling with the enemy in the field," he told a group of well-wishers who gathered at the White House in May 1864.[30]

His sense of gratitude was no doubt genuine. He knew, perhaps better than anyone else, just how much had been sacrificed by the many thousands of dead young men scattered in battlefield graves throughout the nation. It was at this time that he gave his speech to the Sanitary Fair in Philadelphia, speaking of the heavens being "hung in black."[31]

But there is also a discordant element in Lincoln's expressions of gratitude toward the soldiers who fell in the war's terrible storm, because the idea of gratitude carries with it the corollary of choice. We are grateful for an act because we understand implicitly that the act did not have to occur. The person to whom we are grateful might have chosen otherwise. Yet most of the men who died at Gettysburg and elsewhere did not truly have much of a choice. They were compelled to follow orders into battle, as they followed orders when they first entered the army. Volunteerism had long since ceased to provide an adequate foundation for the armed forces. Both the Union and the Confederacy resorted to conscription, and both sides used harsh means—imprisonment, floggings and other corporal punishment, and sometimes even executions—to put and keep men in the ranks.

Lincoln did what he could to avoid executing men for desertion. He routinely reviewed soldiers' death sentences—what he sardonically referred to as "butcher-day"—and commented to his friend Leonard Swett, "I must go through these papers and see if I can find *some excuse* to let these poor fellows off." It was a matter of importance to Lincoln, this effort to ease the strain of war. When one Union officer tried to persuade Lincoln to reinstate the executions of twenty deserters, the president refused, and with a good deal of emotion. "General, there are too many weeping widows in the United States now," he retorted. "For God's sake don't ask me to add to the number; for, I tell you plainly, *I won't do it!*"[32]

Word soon spread about the president's largesse, and he developed a reputation in army ranks as a kind man, "Father Abraham," who avoided meting out harsh punishments to ordinary men when he could. Some errant soldiers even showed up at the White House, begging forgiveness for their transgressions, which they often received. "The bearer, William Henry Craft, a corporal in Co. C. in the 82nd. N.Y. Volunteers, comes to me voluntarily, under apprehension that he may be arrested, convicted, and punished as a deserter," Lincoln wrote on a scrap of paper in December 1863. Just what the corporal had done to run this risk is unknown, but the president was willing to overlook it, provided Craft return to his post: "I hereby direct him to report forthwith to his regiment for duty, and, upon condition that he does this, and faithfully serves out his term, or until he shall be honorably discharged for any cause, he is fully pardoned for any supposed desertion heretofore committed."[33]

There were many similar examples of the president's compassion. He both annoyed military officials who were attempting to enforce military law and discipline and endeared himself to rank-and-file soldiers who saw the president as a fair-minded man, loath to inflict capital punishment on them for their transgressions. Others simply chuckled over what they perceived as Lincoln's soft-heartedness. "I was amused at the eagerness with which the President caught any fact which would justify him in saving the life of a condemned soldier," Hay wrote in his diary. "Cases of cowardice he was especially averse to punishing with death. He said it would frighten the poor devils too terribly to shoot them."[34]

Lincoln's reluctance to have men shot harks back to his days growing up in Indiana and his dislike of hunting or anything that smacked of violence or cruelty. But this reluctance can be exaggerated. He did allow some men to be executed. Not every soldier sentenced to death for cowardice or desertion received presidential clemency, and it often boiled down to the content of a man's character. "He was only merciless in cases where meanness or cruelty were shown," Hay wrote.[35]

Lincoln did not see himself as merely a butcher, sending men to their death without pity or reason. The war was an "experiment" in democracy, as he described it, and part of the experiment was learning whether men would choose to die for their country. There was an implied decision in the citizenship of a free man in a democracy, a decision to repay what was owed for the price of freedom by a willingness to offer up the "last full measure" and take the chance of ending up a corpse on a battlefield.

Lincoln tasked Southerners for just this reason. He always thought average white Southerners, especially nonslaveholders, did not really have their hearts in secession or the war. He did not believe the Confederacy was dedicated to any sort of "proposition" other than human bondage—certainly it was not dedicated to the liberty of white Southerners, in his estimation, and therefore the calculus of men fighting and dying in Confederate uniforms was different. He replied to New York governor Horatio Seymour's request that the administration wait for a judge's ruling on the conscription laws by writing, "We are contending with an enemy who, as I understand, drives every able bodied man he can reach, into his ranks, very much as a butcher drives bullocks into a slaughter-pen. No time is wasted, no argument is used. . . . It produces an army with a rapidity not to be matched on our side, if we first waste time to re-experiment with the volunteer system, already deemed by congress, and palpably, in fact, so far exhausted, as to be inadequate; and then more time, to obtain a court decision, as to whether a law is constitutional."[36]

Well might a white Southerner have said much the same of Lincoln. His letter to Seymour made its way into the opposition press, and the reaction was predictable. "We have little hesitation in saying that we think the letter of Mr. Lincoln callous and brutal," argued one anti-administration editor in Maine, who lamented that "a great many people will be stupid enough not to see the difference between the drivers of the Southern bullocks and the Northern bullocks. . . . We think this allegorical simile however classic in Illinois it might be considered, exceedingly unfortunate in view of the present exigencies and happenings."[37]

Yet Lincoln was not being disingenuous or hypocritical. The Union was, in Lincoln's estimation, a society of freemen, either to that status born or having acquired it after emigrating from abroad. Other men had died on the battlefields of the Revolution to afford the Americans in Lincoln's day this privilege. It was a debt owed by all Americans to the Founding Fathers, a debt that might require repayment: the last full measure. And if repayment of that debt in turn required a draft—which Lincoln believed was constitutional under the war powers vested in him and Congress—then this was acceptable, because the men drafted had made a decision to live in a free and democratic society. Having made that decision, they owed a debt, like everyone else. Unlike the Confederacy, his soldiers were free men fighting to make other men free; or, as he put it so eloquently in his 1862 annual message to Congress, "In *giving* freedom to the *slave*, we *assure* freedom to the *free*—honorable alike in what we give, and what we preserve."[38]

His clemency was often balanced by an expectation that the reprieved soldier would make good on his debt with a willingness to go back and face death in battle, to balance the scales and compensate for earlier failures. "On the case of a soldier who had once deserted and reenlisted he endorsed, 'Let him fight instead of shooting him,'" Hay recalled. "Col. Thomas C. Devin represents that Robert Gill, now of Co. D. 6th. N.Y. Cavalry . . . is under sentence of death for desertion," Lincoln wrote in a typical letter to Stanton, "and that since his desertion, he has fought at Gettysburg and in several other battles, and has otherwise behaved well; and he asks that said Gill may be pardoned and sent to his Regiment. Let it be done." In another, addressed "to whom it may concern," he provided a reprieve for Private John Thornton, who was fearful he might be punished as a deserter, saying that the private would be "fully pardoned for any supposed desertion heretofor committed," provided he return to his regiment and "faithfully serves out his term." Having been approached with many such cases, he finally in February 1864 issued blanket authority to commanders in the field to "restore to duty deserters under sentence, when in their judgment the service will be thereby benefited."[39]

He had not really thought this way before the war, never really connecting a willingness to face death with civic life and the responsibilities of American citizenship. There had been no need then, but now that need was acute. Gratitude must be appropriately counterbalanced with expectation. Choice must be counterbalanced with duty. "I present you sincere thanks for myself and the country," he told an Ohio regiment in August 1864. "I almost always feel inclined, when I happen to say anything to soldiers, to impress upon them in a few brief remarks the importance of success in this contest."

Their service and, by extension, the sacrifices of their fallen comrades were ultimately worth it; men were dying for a cause that transcended themselves and their times. "It is not merely for to-day, but for all time to come that we should perpetuate for our children's children this great and free government, which we have enjoyed all our lives. . . . It is for this the struggle should be maintained, that we may not lose our birthright."[40]

There was a somber tone to this little speech, an intimation that his men were engaged in suffering for a higher cause—worthy suffering, but suffering nonetheless. He no longer offered "congratulations" to soldiers for results in the field, as he had in his unfortunate pronouncement following Fredericksburg. Nor was he much inclined to speak of a soldier winning "glory" on the field of battle, a word connoting the pursuit of public renown or the trappings of military honor and fame.[41]

Instead, he referenced a soldier's responsibility. Soldiering was not the seeking of medals, rank, or headlines. It was a job, and a grim one at that; a necessary requirement of patriotic citizenship that entailed sacrifice, sometimes the ultimate sacrifice. In September 1864, he issued an order of thanks to a unit from Ohio, "one hundred day troops" who had lent their services to the army during the previous summer's campaigns and come to the aid of Washington during the Early raid. Lincoln acknowledged both their value and the fact that they had participated in the important (and dangerous) campaigns in the Shenandoah Valley and the siege trenches around Petersburg. In doing so, he indulged in no gaudy language of victories won or battlefield plaudits; instead, he quietly tendered his and the nation's gratitude for the Ohio men who "performed with alacrity the duty of patriotic volunteers."[42]

"Duty" was, fundamentally, a debt, and black men as well as white now owed that debt. The Emancipation Proclamation brought African Americans into the arc of American duty. They were now, in Lincoln's eyes, part of that same basic equation. It was their willingness to die that, in Lincoln's eyes, sealed their status as bona fide American citizens.

Early in the war, he had been unsure, as were many other white Americans, about the black man's resolve. While on the more enlightened side of the racial spectrum, he was a product of his times. The white supremacy endemic to those times had its effect, and he worried that black men armed as soldiers would, when the moment came, fail in their duty to face death in combat; that they would throw down their guns and run away. "I am not sure we could do much with the blacks," he told a delegation of antislavery men in September 1862. "If we were to arm them I fear that in a few weeks the arms would be in the hands of the rebels."[43]

But like so many other white Americans, Lincoln received a lesson in the mettle of black soldiers during the summer of 1863, when one of the first African American units of the war, the 54th Massachusetts Volunteer Infantry, mounted a valiant (if ultimately fruitless) assault on Fort Wagner, a Confederate stronghold guarding the mouth of Charleston Harbor. The fort was a formidable redoubt, and the men of the 54th and supporting white units were compelled by geography to assault the place head-on, hurling themselves directly into the teeth of murderous Confederate fire. Nearly three hundred black men and their white officers (including the 54th's colonel, Robert Gould Shaw) were killed, wounded, or captured, with many of those taken prisoner slain by their Confederate captors. "It is impossible to see how our troops could have shown more devotion and daring," noted a Massachusetts newspaper.[44]

While Lincoln did not directly speak to the Fort Wagner assault, over-shadowed as it was by the nearly simultaneous Union victories at Gettysburg and Vicksburg, thereafter any small doubts he may have entertained about black men as soldiers disappeared entirely. They had proven their worth by risking and in many cases suffering death in combat. They had done their duty. "Peace does not appear so distant as it did. I hope it will come soon, and come to stay," he wrote nearly two months after the Fort Wagner assault. "It will then have been proved that, among free men, there can be no successful appeal from the ballot to the bullet; and that they who take such appeal are sure to lose their case, and pay the cost. And then, there will be some black men who can remember that, with silent tongue, and clenched teeth, and steady eye, and well-poised bayonet, they have helped mankind on to this great consummation."[45]

"Silent tongue, and clenched teeth, and steady eye": it was classic bit of Lincolnian prose, an apt and almost lyrical invocation of what he as president at once admired and was grateful for in his soldiers, and also expected from them. He would tolerate no bigoted criticism of black men in blue uniforms. "You say you will not fight to free negroes," he wrote to critics of emancipation, with the icy rejoinder that "some of them seem willing to fight for you." Just as he had seen the willingness to die for democracy and freedom as the sine qua non of the white soldier's bargain, the choice that distinguished between free men and "bullocks," so too had the black men lying on the beach before Fort Wagner made their choice and paid their debt. "Negroes, like other people, act upon motives. Why should they do any thing for us, if we will do nothing for them? If they stake their lives for us, they must be prompted by the strongest motive—even the promise of freedom. And the promise being made, must be kept."[46]

By performing their duty, black soldiers had entered into that same circle of protection Lincoln afforded the rest of the men in Union uniform when he commuted their sentences and the like, and he would not tolerate mistreatment of black soldiers. At the end of July 1863, in the wake of rumors that the Confederates defending Fort Wagner had murdered black soldiers trying to surrender, and after the Confederate congress passed a law threatening to sell black prisoners of war into slavery, Lincoln issued his own Order of Retaliation, proclaiming that "for every soldier of the United States killed in violation of the laws of war, a rebel soldier shall be executed; and for every one enslaved by the enemy or sold into slavery, a rebel soldier shall be placed at hard labor on the public works and continued at such labor until the other shall be released and receive the treatment due to a prisoner of war." He did not mince words. "The law of nations and the usages and customs of war as carried on by civilized powers, permit no distinction as to color in the treatment of prisoners of war as public enemies," he stated, and "to sell or enslave any captured person, on account of his color, and for no offence against the laws of war, is a relapse into barbarism and a crime against the civilization of the age."[47]

Lincoln would have black men die for their country; he would not have them murdered. That was not part of their duty, any more than it was Johanna Connor's duty to die or the duty of widows like Lydia Bixby to give over so many sons to the cause. These things sometimes did happen, but they were not expected; they were not the normal price exacted by duty. When the unexpected occurred, he might still sometimes attend a funeral or write a letter, quietly acknowledging that, in some instances at least, the price had been too high, the debt more than repaid.

As 1864 waned, Lincoln increasingly concentrated his energies on what would come after the war: issues of reconstruction, integrating the freedmen into American public life, and the many difficult legal and political problems involved in bringing the rebellious states and their conquered white population back into the Union. He was looking to a future fraught with what he admitted were "great difficulties." He would begin his second term of office expecting four more years of serious challenges in trying to put the country together, and his concerns were understandably far more with the living than the dead.

Still, the war's cost in human lives was an underlying theme when he delivered his second inaugural address in March 1865. He strongly echoed the themes he had first pondered on that scrap of paper more than two years previously. Referencing the North's and the South's religiosity, he observed that "each looked for an easier triumph, and a result less fundamental and astounding. Both read the same Bible, and pray to the same God; and each invokes His aid against the other. It may seem strange that any men should dare to ask a just God's assistance in wringing their bread from the sweat of other men's faces; but let us judge not that we be not judged. The prayers of both could not be answered; that of neither has been answered fully. The Almighty has His own purposes."

Then he came to the point regarding the war's many dead. "Fondly do we hope—fervently do we pray—that this mighty scourge of war may speedily pass away," he declared. "Yet, if God wills that it continue, until the wealth piled by the bond-man's two hundred and fifty years of unrequited toil shall be sunk, and until every drop of blood drawn with the lash, shall be paid by another drawn with the sword, as was said three thousand years ago, so still it must be said 'the judgments of the Lord, are true and righteous altogether.'"[48]

At Gettysburg, he had told the nation that the war's death toll was beyond his control and that both he and the war functioned in the service of a higher cause, the end of which end he could not foresee. Now he could see more clearly both the cause and the end. The cause was a mighty reckoning, a balancing of justice's scales and a giving of lives in repayment for the taking of so many slaves' lives. This was the only way he could truly make sense of it all. If individual soldiers had a duty to repay their debt to their country by risking and sometimes suffering death, then the country as a whole had a similar duty to repay the debt it owed for the terrible national sin of slavery.

Here was a Lincoln with a clearer vision of what the dying truly meant. It was a new theme, this idea of a reckoning, of a national debt repaid. He had never spoken this way before, certainly not in the service of understanding death and its purpose. Throughout his life, he had eschewed the very idea that he could somehow comprehend the meaning of death. His mother, his sister, Ann Rutledge, his two young boys—they had perished in the name of an unknown and unknowable fate, willed by a God whose plans he never pretended to understand.

But now, at the very end of that ruinous war, he began to comprehend the point of the dying, and if his understanding looked backward to the war's uncountable graves, it also looked forward to the looming project of national reconciliation and reconstruction. What Lincoln wanted, with his use of the dead to balance the scales, was a reconstruction pursued without a national sense of guilt or the endless recriminations he knew were a very real risk in a war that had often brought out the worst in his countrymen. He wanted no eye-for-an-eye approach to reconstruction. He wanted instead a clean slate, a beginning for national reconciliation on a level field.

This was not a pernicious species of moral relativism; Lincoln made it quite clear in his address that one side, the Confederacy, intended to preserve the evil of human bondage. "To strengthen, perpetuate, and extend this interest was the object for which the insurgents would rend the Union, even by war," he said, "while the government claimed no right to do more than to restrict the territorial enlargement of it." But Lincoln's moral clarity regarding the right and the wrong of the war did not extend to a perpetuation of the hatreds wrought by battle. He very much wanted "malice towards none," and with the balancing of the scales, the war dead provided that clean beginning.[49]

Too often the Second Inaugural Address has been read by subsequent generations of Americans as closure, a sublime and grand culmination to Lincoln's presidency and his life that would soon end. But it may also be read as a start; Lincoln did not know he would soon die, and he believed he was now embarking on the challenging project of restoring the American Union. He was looking for a way to start that process, and his answer was to press the war's dead into its service. So many Americans, black and white, had fulfilled their duty in war; now, their deaths would be pressed into service to fulfill the needs of peace.

CONCLUSION

Lincoln's death began with the report of a very small pistol, a single-shot derringer that easily fit into the palm of a man's hand. A sudden loud bang, a puff of blue-white smoke, and then . . . silence.

He probably heard and felt nothing after John Wilkes Booth's bullet plowed through his brain and lodged just behind his right eye. Mary's hysterical screams; the swirl of confusion as Booth made good his escape by first severely wounding with a knife Henry Rathbone, a Union officer who with his fiancée had accompanied the Lincolns to Ford's Theatre that evening, and then sliding over the balustrade to make his escape; Mary now trying to hold Lincoln's limp head up as he slumped forward in his chair—none of this registered on the unconscious president's senses.[1]

He lived for another nine hours. Theater-goers gingerly carried him across the street to a tiny room in a boardinghouse, laying him out diagonally on a bed too short for his six-foot-four frame. Throughout the evening, his breathing periodically quickened, his pulse fading and becoming uneven, his limbs shaking; one of the attending physicians would then stick his finger inside the bullet wound and free the clot that had formed, as the clot caused pressure on the brain to increase and hence the labored breathing. Removing the clot relieved the pressure, and soon thereafter the process began again, the pillow under the president's head growing slowly more bloodstained. He never awoke.

His pulse grew noticeably fainter as dawn approached, his breathing shallower; finally, at 7:22 A.M., it stopped entirely. After the initial violence of the gunshot, it was a remarkably quiet passing for a man who had witnessed throughout his life his share of prolonged and agonizing deaths: his mother's wretched seven-day ordeal in the Indiana woods, Willie's weeks-long up-and-down battle with typhoid, the nearly infinite varieties of violent and gruesome deaths caused by the war.[2]

Death had tugged at his elbow until the end. He paid his final visit to the Army of the Potomac in late March 1865, just three weeks before his assassination. During the visit, he rode to a portion of the Petersburg battlefield where the two sides had engaged in recent battle, one of many such encounters up and down the trench lines. By this point in the war, big self-contained battles were relatively unusual, replaced by a steady drip of violent little episodes that killed soldiers nearly every day.

The president and his party rode to a high portion of the ground behind the lines. Here he saw the actual disposal of dead bodies. "We passed through the spot where the fighting had been most severe, and where great numbers of dead were still lying, with burial parties at their dreadful work," recalled an officer who accompanied the president. "Mr. Lincoln was quiet and observant, making few comments. . . . [He] looked worn and haggard. He remarked that he had seen enough of the horrors of war, that he hoped this was the beginning of the end, and that there would be no more bloodshed or ruin of homes." The officer then related a story in which he had recently come upon a red-headed young Confederate boy on the battlefield, clad in butternut and mortally wounded by a bullet that had passed through his head; the officer gave him some water, and the boy died in his arms. "Mr. Lincoln's eyes filled with tears and his voice choked with emotion, and he repeated the well-known expression about 'robbing the cradle and the grave.'"[3]

He remained with the army several more days. On March 31, Grant mounted a general assault on the Confederate defenses, probing for a weak point. Lincoln knew this larger operation was impending, and perhaps still haunted by the sight of all those dead bodies a few days previously, he struck those around him as downcast. "The knowledge of the loss of life that must follow hung about him until he could think of nothing else," believed the president's bodyguard, William Crook. Toward evening, with the battle still raging and cannon fire reverberating nearby, Lincoln retired to the vessel that had carried him from Washington. "Mr. Lincoln would not go to his room," Crook remembered. "Almost all night he walked up and down the deck, pausing now and then to listen or look out into the darkness to see if he could see anything. I have never seen such suffering in the face of any man." The following morning, Lincoln rode along a portion of the battle-field, again strewn with the dead from both sides, between forts nicknamed "Fort Hell" and "Fort Damnation" by the men. As they rode, they passed the body of a man shot directly through the forehead and another whose arms were missing. "The president's face settled into its old lines of sadness," Crook observed.[4]

He also continued to be haunted by deaths closer to home. During a carriage ride with Mary the morning of his assassination, he told her, "We must both be more cheerful in the future; between the war and the loss of our darling Willie, we have been very miserable." They spoke of a trip to Europe after his second presidential term ended.[5]

Mary never fully recovered from her husband's death. As he lay in that boardinghouse across from Ford's Theatre, she periodically threw herself onto his prostrate body, shrieking with grief and begging for last words from her dying husband. "She implored him to speak to her," recalled Lincoln's secretary of the interior Usher Linder, one of the many men present, and "after indulging in dreadful incoherences for some time was finally persuaded to leave." She spent the rest of the evening and early morning until Lincoln's passing sobbing in an adjoining room.[6]

She was thereafter a haunted and pitiable soul, isolated for weeks in her room and "completely prostrated with grief," according to Elizabeth Keckly. When she finally left the White House, young Tad in tow, she began a lonely, peripatetic existence that would see her eventually confined to an insane asylum by her worried oldest son, Robert—worried, among other things, about his mother's increased vulnerability to charlatans who took her money in exchange for false promises of contacting Abraham's ghost. "My poor husband!" she sobbed to Keckly one day. "Had he never been President, he might be living to-day! Alas! All is over with me!"[7]

History has not been kind to Mary for her behavior in the wake of Abraham's death, and yet it does Mary a disservice to suggest that she had always reacted to death in such an unstable fashion. When Eddy died, she behaved with propriety according to the standards of the time, and even during Willie's death and mourning, she remained publicly stable and outwardly appropriate in her grief. But the cracks were beginning to appear in that facade, with her private hysterics that were hidden from public view but all too visible to Abraham, Elizabeth Keckly, and Mary's family. After the assassination, the facade fell away completely, and there were intimations nationwide that she was broken and mentally unstable. Mary died in her sister Elizabeth's Springfield home in 1882, a lonely and deeply wounded woman, "weighed down by woe," as one obituary observed.[8]

So was much of America. The extensive period of national mourning that followed Lincoln's assassination was a grand display of national bereavement, a funeral among funerals. A large service was held in Washington, D.C., after which Lincoln's body was transported by train for services and viewings in eleven other cities before arriving in Springfield for interment in a specially constructed mausoleum at Oak Ridge Cemetery. Hundreds of thousands gathered to pass the coffin or line the tracks, heads bare, as the train rumbled by; historians estimate that an astonishing one in four Americans saw Lincoln or his funeral car.[9]

What would Lincoln have made of it all? He probably would have been taken aback by the sheer scale of his own funeral, perhaps even a bit amused by the whiff of pretension in the grandeur, with each city vying to outdo the others in the size of its crowds, the height of its funeral arch, the lyricism of its funeral music, the pathos of its orations. "If [he] had known how big a funeral he would have had, he would have died years ago," Lincoln once joked about a deceased colleague in the Illinois legislature. Some similar sentiment would likely have come to his mind.[10]

Most of all, he probably would have felt that same perplexity, that sense of mystery and ultimate unknowability, that had so often permeated his thinking about death and its meaning. "With firmness in the right, as God gives us to see the right, let us strive on to finish the work we are in," he told his audience in his Second Inaugural Address. "As God gives us to see the right"—that was an important qualifier. He knew the heavens were hung in black; he was never so arrogant as to believe he fully understood the reasons why.

NOTES

BIBLIOGRAPHY

INDEX

NOTES

INTRODUCTION: PHILADELPHIA, JUNE 16, 1864

1. *Albany (NY) Evening Journal*, June 17, 1864; *Philadelphia Press*, June 17, 1864. For a general discussion of the Sanitary Commission, see Margaret Humphreys, *Marrow of Tragedy: The Health Crisis of the American Civil War* (Baltimore: Johns Hopkins University Press, 2013), 142–45; and Judith Ann Giesberg, *Civil War Sisterhood: The U.S. Sanitary Commission and Women's Politics in Transition* (Boston: Northeastern University Press, 2000).

2. *San Francisco Bulletin*, July 22, 1864.

3. Duane Hamilton Hurd, *History of Essex County, Massachusetts* (Philadelphia: J. W. Lewis, 1888), 1:915; Samuel P. Bates, *History of Pennsylvania Volunteers, 1861–5* (Harrisburg, PA: B. Singerly, 1869), 2:198.

4. Abraham Lincoln, "Speech at the Great Sanitary Fair," June 16, 1864, in *The Collected Works of Abraham Lincoln*, ed. Roy P. Basler (New Brunswick, NJ: Rutgers University Press, 1953) 7:394 (hereafter cited as *CW*).

5. "The First Part of King Henry the Sixth," *The Complete Works of William Shakespeare*, accessed February 10, 2017, http://shakespeare.mit.edu/1henryvi/full.html. There is no evidence that Lincoln read *Henry VI*, but the phrase had also entered the American vernacular.

1. GOOD DEATH

1. John Hanks, interview with John Miles, May 25, 1865, in Douglas L. Wilson and Rodney O. Davis, eds., *Herndon's Informants: Letters, Interviews, and Statements about Abraham Lincoln* (Urbana: University of Illinois Press, 1998), 5 (hereafter cited as *HI*).

2. Dennis Hanks, interview with William H. Herndon, June 13, 1865, *HI*, 36; A. H. Chapman, written statement, September 8, 1865, *HI*, 96.

3. Lincoln, "Autobiography Written for John L. Scripps," c. June 1860, *CW* 4:61; Nathaniel Grigsby, interview with William H. Herndon, September 12, 1865, *HI*, 111.

4. For physical descriptions of Lincoln's parents, see Nathaniel Grigsby, interview with William H. Herndon, September 12, 1865, *HI*, 111; A. H. Chapman to William H. Herndon, September 8, 1865, *HI*, 97; Dennis F. Hanks to William H. Herndon, c. December 1865, *HI*, 149.

5. Lincoln to Jesse W. Fell, enclosing autobiography, December 20, 1859, *CW* 3:511.

6. E. Tucker, *History of Randolph County, Indiana* (Chicago: A. L. Klingman, 1852), 97; William Monroe Cockrum, *Pioneer History of Indiana* (Oakland City, IN: Press of the Oakland City Journal, 1907), 504.

7. Lincoln, "The Bear Hunt," c. September 6, 1846, *CW* 1:386.

8. See generally Roderick Nash, *Wilderness and the American Mind*, 5th ed. (New Haven, CT: Yale University Press, 2014), esp. chap. 4.

9. Dennis F. Hanks, interview with William H. Herndon, June 13, 1865, *HI*, 39–40.

10. Charles Blanchard, *Counties of Morgan, Monroe, and Brown, Indiana* (Chicago: F. A. Battey, 1884), 165–66.

11. Cockrum, *Pioneer History of Indiana*, 503; the authors from which I have quoted here and elsewhere commit occasional minor errors of spelling, punctuation, and grammar. Rather than correct each error with [*sic*], I have allowed the errors to remain in their original form.

12. Lincoln, "The Bear Hunt," c. September 6, 1846, *CW* 1:388.

13. Dennis F. Hanks, interview with William H. Herndon, June 13, 1865, *HI*, 39.

14. Lincoln, autobiography for John L. Scripps, c. June 1860, *CW* 4:62.

15. Nathaniel Grigsby to William H. Herndon, September 4, 1865, *HI*, 94; Matilda Johnston Moore, interview with William H. Herndon, September 8, 1865, *HI*, 109.

16. At least one neighbor seems to have thought the Sparrows were in fact Nancy's biological parents; see William Wood, interview with William H. Herndon, September 18, 1865, *HI*, 123.

17. D. Jesse Wagstaff, *International Poisonous Plants Checklist: An Evidence-Based Reference* (New York: Taylor and Francis, 2008), 12.

18. Walter H. Lewis and Memory P. F. Elvin-Lewis, *Medical Botany: Plants Affecting Human Health*, 2nd ed. (Hoboken, NJ: John Wiley and Sons, 2003), 90.

19. It seems unlikely that the cow was owned by the Lincolns, given that milk sickness was first detected in the Brooner and Sparrow families. On the Brooner family, see *History of Warrick, Spencer, and Perry Counties* (Chicago: Goodspeed and Co., 1885), 557.

20. Lewis and Elvin-Lewis, *Medical Botany*, 90.

21. Augustus Chapman, written statement, September 8, 1865, *HI*, 98.

22. Dennis F. Hanks, interview with William H. Herndon, June 13, 1865, *HI*, 41.

23. William Wood, interview with William H. Herndon, September 18, 1865, *HI*, 123.

24. Dennis F. Hanks, interview with William H. Herndon, June 13, 1865, *HI*, 40.

25. Drew Gilpin Faust, *This Republic of Suffering: Death and the American Civil War* (New York: Alfred A. Knopf, 2007), 7–28; Thomas Fuller and William Pickering, *Good Thoughts in Bad Times* (London: Pickering, 1841), 340.

26. Faust, *Republic of Suffering*, 7–11.

27. Dennis Hanks, interview with William H. Herndon, June 13, 1865, *HI*, 40.

28. See generally J. William Worden, *Children and Grief: When a Parent Dies* (London: Guildford Press, 2001), which has much useful information on modern research into this subject, esp. chaps. 1 and 4, though it is designed primarily for present-day child psychologists and clinicians; also helpful is Suzanne Sjöqvist, ed., *Still Here with Me: Teenagers and Children on Losing a Parent*, trans. Margaret Myers (London: Jessica Kingsley, 2007).

29. Alexander K. McClure, *Abraham Lincoln and Men of War Times*, 4th ed. (1892; repr., Lincoln: University of Nebraska Press, 1996), 78.

30. William Wood, interview with William H. Herndon, September 15, 1865, *HI*, 123.

31. Ibid., 124; Dennis Hanks, interview with William H. Herndon, June 13, 1865, *HI*, 40; Henry B. Rankin, *Personal Recollections of Abraham Lincoln* (New York: Putnam and Sons, 1916), 320; Michael Burlingame, "Lincoln's Depressions: 'Melancholy Dripped from Him as He Walked,'" in *The Inner World of Abraham Lincoln* (Urbana: University of Illinois Press, 1994), 94.

32. On Thomas's faith, see Dennis F. Hanks, interview with Erastus Wright, June 8, 1865, *HI*, 28; and A. H. Chapman, written statement, September 8, 1865, *HI*, 97. Also see generally Allen C. Guelzo, *Abraham Lincoln as a Man of Ideas* (Carbondale: Southern Illinois University Press, 2009), 33–34; and Guelzo's earlier, excellent biography centered around Lincoln's religiosity, *Abraham Lincoln: Redeemer President* (Grand Rapids, MI: William B. Eerdman's, 1999), 36–40, though I would somewhat disagree with Guelzo's suggestion that Abraham broke so profoundly with his father on religious matters, since he seemed to retain the Hardshell Baptist's fatalism.

33. John F. Cady, "The Religious Environment of Lincoln's Youth," *Indiana Magazine of History* 37 (March 1941), 16–19; William E. Bartelt, *"There I Grew Up": Remembering Abraham Lincoln's Indiana Youth* (Indianapolis: Indianapolis Historical Society, 2008), 135–36.

34. Lincoln later remembered that Elkin preached the funeral sermon in the Lincoln home "several months after her death"; see Rankin, *Personal Recollections*, 320. However, Lincoln did not mention the contents of the sermon or the reason for the delay. See also A. H. Chapman, written statement, September 8, 1865, *HI*, 97–98; and Jonathan Todd Hobson, *Footprints of Abraham Lincoln* (Dayton, OH: Otterbein Press, 1909), 18, 20, who states that Lincoln wrote to Elkin, asking him to preach the sermon, but the source for this assertion is unclear. Also see Philip D. Jordan, "The Death of Nancy Hanks Lincoln," *Indiana Magazine of History* 40 (June 1944), 103–10.

35. At least one early biography furnishes details about Nancy's funeral regarding the sermon, hymns, and Abraham's behavior, but the sources for this information are unclear and may well simply be a fanciful imagining of these events; see James Baldwin, *Abraham Lincoln: A True Life* (New York: American Book Co., 1904), 52.

36. Lincoln to Andrew Johnston, April 18, 1846, *CW* 1:378; autobiography written for John L. Scripps, c. June 1860, *CW* 4:62. He did also mention Nancy in a letter to Mrs. Orville Browning, April 1, 1838, *CW* 1:118, but the circumstances of this letter suggest he may have been writing more as parody than an actual reference to memories of Nancy.

37. Nathaniel Grigsby, interview with William H. Herndon, September 12, 1865, *HI*, 113; David Turnham, interview with William H. Herndon, September 15, 1865, *HI*, 122; John Hanks, interview with William H. Herndon, c. 1865–66, *HI*, 456.

38. Hobson, *Footprints of Lincoln*, 21–22; Nathaniel Grigsby to William H. Herndon, September 4, 1865, *HI*, 94. That the child was born deceased was affirmed by Augustus Chapman, a neighbor; see Chapman, written statement, September 8, 1865, *HI*, 100.

39. Francis Marion Van Natter, *Lincoln's Boyhood: A Chronicle of His Indiana Years* (New York: Public Affairs Press, 1963), 52, contends that "apparently" no midwife was present, but the account of Mrs. Lamar (see Hobson, *Footprints of Lincoln*, 22) directly contradicts this, and it would have been contrary to the commonly accepted practice of having a midwife present, even in frontier areas.

40. Hobson, *Footprints of Lincoln*, 22. On understanding the various causes of stillbirths, I relied on Fabio Facchinetti, Gustaaf A. Dekker, Dante Baronciani, and George Saade, eds., *Stillbirth: Understanding and Management* (Boca Raton, FL: CRC Press, 2010), esp. 109–14.

41. A. H. Chapman, written statement, September 8, 1865, *HI*, 100; *Chicago Times Herald*, December 22, 1895; Samuel E. Kercheval to Jesse W. Weik, December 2, 1887, *HI*, 645.

42. Lincoln, autobiography written for John L. Scripps, c. June 1860, *CW* 4:65.

43. James Short to William H. Herndon, July 7, 1865, *HI*, 73; Lynn McNulty Greene to William H. Herndon, July 30, 1865, *HI*, 80; John McNamar to William H. Herndon, January 20, 1867, *HI*, 545–46.

44. James Short to William H. Herndon, July 7, 1865, *HI*, 73; Lynn McNulty Greene to William H. Herndon, July 30, 1865, *HI*, 80; Robert B. Rutledge to William H. Herndon, November 1, 1866, *HI*, 383; George U. Miles to William H. Herndon, March 23, 1866, *HI*, 236–37; John Y. Simon, "Abraham Lincoln and Ann Rutledge," *Journal of the Abraham Lincoln Association* 11 (1990): 13–33.

45. Robert B. Rutledge to William H. Herndon, November 1, 1866, *HI*, 383; William G. Greene, interview with William H. Herndon, May 30, 1865, *HI*, 21; John Hill to William H. Herndon, June 6, 1865, *HI*, 23–25; Hardin Bale, interview with William H. Herndon, May 29, 1865, *HI*, 13.

46. John Hill to William H. Herndon (enclosed clipping from Menard Axis), February 15, 1862, *HI*, 25; Isaac Cogdal, interview with William H. Herndon, c. 1865–66, *HI*, 440.

47. See the excellent historiographic overview in Simon, "Lincoln and Ann Rutledge," 13–18. For critics of Mary Lincoln (William Herndon, for example), the alleged romance with Rutledge proved a useful contrivance to argue that Lincoln never really loved his wife, a claim that has appeared in numerous biographies; see, e.g., Carrie Douglas Wright, *Lincoln's First Love: A True Story* (Chicago: A. C. McClurg and Co., 1901).

48. William G. Greene, interview with William H. Herndon, May 30, 1865, *HI*, 21; Robert B. Rutledge to William H. Herndon, November 18, 1866, *HI*, 402.

49. William G. Greene, interview with William H. Herndon, May 30, 1865, *HI*, 21; James Smith to William H. Herndon, December 24, 1867, *HI*, 547.

50. On the pathology and symptoms of typhoid, see Donald Emmeluth, *Typhoid Fever* (Philadelphia: Chelsea House, 2004).

51. William G. Greene, interview with William H. Herndon, May 30, 1865, *HI*, 21; John Jones, written statement enclosed in letter from Robert Rutledge to William H. Herndon, October 22, 1866, *HI*, 387.

52. Oliver Carruthers and R. Gerald McMurtry, *Lincoln's Other Mary* (Chicago: Ziff-Davis, 1946), 201.

53. Jesse William Weik, *The Real Lincoln: A Portrait* (Boston: Houghton Mifflin, 1922), 395; Simon, "Lincoln and Ann Rutledge," 28.

54. Lincoln to C. U. Schlater, January 5, 1849, *CW* 2:19.

2. EDDY

1. On the history of the Lincoln home, see the useful and detailed description in Alan Manning, *Father Lincoln: The Untold Story of Abraham Lincoln and His Boys—Robert, Eddy, Willie, and Tad* (Guilford, CT: Lyons Press, 2016), 28–29.

2. Robert Rutledge to William H. Herndon, November 21, 1866, *HI*, 409.

3. On Mary's background, see Catherine Clinton, *Mrs. Lincoln: A Life* (New York: HarperCollins, 2009), 9−47. There are many excellent accounts of their courtship; see Clinton, *Mrs. Lincoln*, 48−77, and esp. Douglas L. Wilson, *Honor's Voice: The Transformation of Abraham Lincoln* (New York: Alfred A. Knopf, 1998), 195−232.

4. Bonnie E. Paull and Richard E. Hart, *Lincoln's Springfield Neighborhood* (Charleston, SC: History Press, 2015), 39−45; Richard Lawrence Miller, "Life at Eighth and Jackson," in Frank J. Williams and Michael Burkhimer, eds., *The Mary Lincoln Enigma: Historians on America's Most Controversial First Lady* (Carbondale: Southern Illinois University Press, 2012), 66; Katherine Helm, *The True Story of Mary, Wife of Lincoln* (New York: Harper, 1928), 98.

5. Mary Todd Lincoln to Abraham Lincoln, May 1848, in Justin G. Turner and Linda Levitt Turner, eds., *Mary Todd Lincoln: Her Life and Letters* (New York: Alfred A. Knopf, 1972), 37. For general observations about Eddy's "sickly" health, see Jean H. Baker, *Mary Todd Lincoln: A Biography* (New York: W. W. Norton, 1989), 105; Glenna R. Schroeder-Lein, *Lincoln and Medicine* (Carbondale: Southern Illinois University Press, 2012), 11; and David Herbert Donald, *Lincoln* (New York: Simon and Schuster, 1995), 107. On the New England tour, see Paul Finkelman and Martin J. Hershock, eds., *The Political Lincoln: An Encyclopedia* (Washington, DC: CQ Press, 2008), 418; and Stacy Pratt McDermott, *Mary Lincoln: Southern Girl, Northern Woman* (New York: Routledge, 2015), 69.

6. John C. Gunn, *Gunn's Domestic Medicine, or The Poor Man's Friend* (Pittsburgh: Edwards and Newman, 1839), 501; Ben H. McClary, "Introducing a Classic: 'Gunn's Domestic Medicine,'" *Tennessee Historical Quarterly* 45 (Fall 1986): 210−16. On the various possible home treatments for sick children in this era, see Charles E. Rosenberg, *Right Living: An Anglo-American Tradition of Self-Help Medicine and Hygiene* (Baltimore: Johns Hopkins University Press, 2003), 3−4; Florence W. Asher, "Women, Wealth, and Power: New York City, 1860−1900," PhD diss., City University of New York, 2006, 203−4; Mary Ellen Jones, *Daily Life on the Nineteenth Century American Frontier* (Westport, CT: Greenwood Press, 1998), 200; and Baker, *Mary Todd Lincoln*, 125−26, who also lists some possible home remedies. For the cough pills advertisement, see *Illinois Journal*, January 1, 1850.

7. On tuberculosis as "constitutional," see John Duffy, "Social Impact of Disease in the Late Nineteenth Century," in Judith Walzer Leavitt and Ronald L. Numbers, *Sickness and Health in America: Readings in the History of Medicine and Public Health* (Madison: University of Wisconsin Press, 1978), 419.

8. Benjamin Marten, *A New Theory of Consumptions* (London: R. Knapock, 1720), chaps. 1, 3. Some sources state definitively that Eddy died from diphtheria, but the sourcing for this is suspect; see Carol A. Dyer, *Biographies of Disease:*

Tuberculosis (Santa Clara, CA: Greenwood Press, 2010), 15–17, and the close analysis in Schroeder-Lein, *Lincoln and Medicine*, 11. One interesting theory holds that Eddy died from thyroid cancer, reflecting a family genetic predisposition toward a rare disorder called MEN2B; see an exhaustive discussion of this possibility in John G. Sotos, *The Physical Lincoln* (Mt. Vernon, VA: Mt. Vernon Book Systems, 2008); and Schroeder-Lein, *Lincoln and Medicine*, 11–12. Most historians have accepted the tuberculosis theory; Eddy's symptoms fit the disease, and tuberculosis was responsible for the deaths of large numbers of children (and adults) during this time period; see the useful discussion of this in McDermott, *Mary Lincoln*, 69.

9. *Sangamo (IL) Journal*, January 2, 1850.

10. Samuel P. Wheeler, "Solving a Lincoln Literary Mystery: 'Little Eddie,'" *Journal of the Abraham Lincoln Association* 33 (Summer 2012), 34, writes that doctors at first diagnosed Eddy with diphtheria, but it is unclear which doctors he is referring to or which sources support this assertion. Baker, *Mary Todd Lincoln*, 124, makes a similar assertion, as do several other works, suggesting either an early misdiagnosis of diphtheria from unnamed local doctors or that Eddy simply died of diphtheria outright. See McDermott, *Mary Lincoln*, 69; Sandra L. Quinn and Sanford Kantor, *American Royalty: All the President's Children* (Westport: Greenwood Press, 1995), 95; and Stephen Mansfield, *Lincoln's Battle with God: A President's Struggle with Faith and What It Meant for America* (Nashville: Thomas Nelson, 2012), 83. However, the exact primary sources for any of these assertions are unclear; I have not located any definitive, reliable primary source suggesting either a misdiagnosis or a death from diphtheria for Eddy by a doctor (or anyone else).

11. On Wallace's background, see John Carroll Power, *History of the Early Settlers of Sangamon County, Illinois* (Springfield, IL: Edwin A. Wilson and Co., 1876), 748. On medicine during this period, see M. Monir Madkour, *Tuberculosis* (New York: Springer, 2004), 25; Jan-Willem Gerritsen, *The Control of Fuddle and Flash: A Sociological History of the Regulation of Alcohol and Opiates* (Leiden, Netherlands: Koninklijke, 2000), 117–19.

12. Dyer, *Biographies of Disease*, 15–17.

13. See Paull and Hart, *Lincoln's Springfield Neighborhood*, esp. chap. 4. I qualify my statements here because census records for 1850 do show an Irish girl named Catherine Gordon living in the Lincoln home, but it is not clear exactly when in 1850 she did so. It is also possible that a Portuguese woman named Frances Affonsa, who is identified as a laundress working for the Lincolns from November 1849 to February 1861, may have been present, but it is not clear whether she lived with the Lincolns during all or part of this span. Also, Mrs. John Todd Stuart, who visited the Lincoln home after Eddy's death and provides the only extant eyewitness account of Mary's mourning, mentions the presence of a servant in the home,

but it is not clear from her description exactly when Mrs. Stuart's visit occurred; it may well have been after April, when we know Lincoln had hired Vance; see interview with Mrs. John Todd Stuart, *Chicago Tribune*, February 12, 1900, 14.

14. See Flurin Condrau, "Beyond the Total Institution: Towards a Reinterpretation of the Tuberculosis Sanatorium," in Flurin Condrau and Michael Worboys, eds., *Tuberculosis Then and Now: Perspectives on the History of an Infectious Disease* (Montreal: McGill-Queen's University Press, 2010), 72–75.

15. James Gourley, interview with William H. Herndon, c. 1865–66, *HI*, 453; see also Paull and Hart, *Lincoln's Springfield Neighborhood*, 28, 146.

16. Lincoln quote in Elizabeth Todd Edwards, interview with William H. Herndon, c. 1865–66, *HI*, 444–45. On Mary's relationship to Elizabeth, see generally Stephen Berry, *House of Abraham: Lincoln and the Todds, a Family Divorced by War* (New York: Mariner Books, 2009), 25–30, 47. None of the Todd sisters remarked directly on Eddy's illness, but Frances identified herself as a generally regular visitor to the Lincoln home; see Frances Todd Wallace, interview with William H. Herndon, c. 1865–66, *HI*, 485.

17. Lloyd Ostendorf and Walter Oleksy, eds., *Lincoln's Unknown Private Life: An Oral History by His Black Housekeeper Mariah Vance, 1850–1860* (Mamaroneck, NY: Hastings House, 1995), 69.

18. "Domestic man" quote from Frances Todd Wallace, interview with William H. Herndon, c. 1865–66, *HI*, 485; see also James Gourley, interview with William H. Herndon, c. 1865–66, *HI*, 452–53; and John B. Weber, interview with William H. Herndon, November 1, 1866, *HI*, 389.

19. On the shawl, see Francis Fisher Browne, *The Every-day Life of Abraham Lincoln* (Chicago: Browne and Howell, 1914), 125.

20. Lincoln to John D. Johnston, January 12, 1851, *CW* 2:96–97. On service at state Whig convention, see *Illinois Journal*, December 24, 1851; and Martha L. Benner and Cullom Davis et al., eds., *The Law Practice of Abraham Lincoln: Complete Documentary Edition*, 2nd ed. (Springfield: Illinois Historic Preservation Agency, 2009), http://www.lawpracticeofabrahamlincoln.org (hereafter cited as *LPAL*).

21. Interview with Mrs. John Todd Stuart, *Chicago Tribune*, February 12, 1900, 14.

22. Search results for "undertaker" in the Springfield, Illinois, City Directory for 1855 on Ancestry.com, accessed June 18, 2015. I have located little evidence of a direct connection between Lincoln and any of these individuals. In 1840, Lincoln did litigate a debt-related case that had a defendant named Francis, but it is unclear from the rather sparse records whether this as the same J. Francis mentioned above; see *Maxwell v. Francis, et al.* (1840), *LPAL*.

23. Robert Haberstein and William Lamer, *The History of American Funeral Directing*, 5th ed. (New York: National Funeral Directors Assoc., 2001), 18; Vanderlyn

R. Pine, *Caretaker of the Dead: The American Funeral Director* (New York: Irvington, 1975), 15–16.

24. See John Todd Stuart to J. A. Reed, in Helm, *True Story of Mary*, 117. Exactly when this visit occurred is unclear from the letter, and some historians have assumed that Smith did not actually meet Lincoln until right after Eddy died; see, e.g., Ronald C. White Jr., *A. Lincoln: A Biography* (New York: Random House, 2009), 180. But an account by a Lincoln friend named Thomas Lewis states that Lincoln sent for Smith to talk with him right after he returned from his visit with the Todd family in Kentucky, suggesting that Lincoln had at least met Smith prior to Eddy's illness; see Rufus Rockwell Wilson, ed., *Intimate Memories of Lincoln* (Elmira, NY: Primavera Press, 1945), 129–30.

25. *Springfield Illinois Journal*, January 1, 1850; see also Penny Colman, *Corpses, Coffins, and Crypts: A History of Burial* (New York: Henry Holt and Co., 1997), 79–82.

26. Edward J. Russo and Curtis R. Mann, *Oak Ridge Cemetery* (Charleston, SC: Arcadia, 2009), 10–11. In 1855, the city would begin laying plans to establish Oak Ridge Cemetery as the city's primary cemetery. Also see Carl Volkmann and Roberta Volkmann, *Springfield's Sculptures, Monuments, and Plaques* (Charleston, SC: Arcadia, 2008), 97.

27. Colman, *Corpses, Coffins, and Crypts*, 90–94.

28. Matt. 19:14 (King James Version). Flood is identified as a stonecutter in the 1855 city directory, per search results for "stone" in the Springfield, Illinois, City Directory for 1855 on Ancestry.com, accessed July 2, 2015. See also Megan E. Springate, *Coffin Hardware in Nineteenth-Century America* (Walnut Creek, CA: Left Coast Press, 2015), 69; Karen Sanchez-Eppler, *Dependent States: The Child's Part in Nineteenth-Century American Culture* (Chicago: University of Chicago Press, 2005), chap. 3.

29. See Dana Luciano, *Arranging Grief: Sacred Time and the Body in Nineteenth-Century America* (New York: New York University Press, 2007), 5–8; and James J. Farrell, *Inventing the American Way of Death, 1830–1920* (Philadelphia: Temple University Press, 1980), chaps. 1–3.

30. On Swedenborg's ideas, see http://www.swedenborg.com/emanuel-swedenborg/writings, accessed July 26, 2017.

31. Lincoln, "Handbill Replying to Charges of Infidelity," July 31, 1846, *CW* 1:382.

32. *Springfield Illinois Journal*, February 2, 1850; Lincoln to John D. Johnston, February 23, 1850, *CW* 2:77. On the custom of an overnight vigil, see Jason Emerson, *Giant in the Shadows: The Life of Robert T. Lincoln* (Carbondale: Southern Illinois University Press, 2012), 22.

33. The poem was titled "The Lock of Hair," written by Lydia M. Sigourney; see Julie Aronson and Marjorie E. Weiseman, *Perfect Likeness: European and*

American Portrait Miniatures from the Cincinnati Art Museum (New Haven, CT: Yale University Press, 2006), 66.

34. See Jacqueline S. Thursby, *Funeral Festivals in America: Rituals for the Living* (Lexington: University Press of Kentucky, 2006), 89–90; Farrell, *American Way of Death*, 157–58; and Margaret Coffin, *Death in Early America: The History and Folklore of Customs and Superstitions of Early Medicine, Funerals, Burials, and Mourning* (Nashville: Thomas Nelson, 1976), 78.

35. See, e.g., Anne E. Beidler, *The Addiction of Mary Todd Lincoln* (New York: Coffeetown Press, 2009), 134. On the practice of women not attending funerals, see Susan Smart, *A Better Place: Death and Burial in Nineteenth-Century Ontario* (Toronto: Dundurn Press, 2011), 58; and Marian Gouverneur, *As I Remember: Recollections of American Society during the Nineteenth Century* (New York: D. Appleton and Co., 1911), 28.

36. Farrell, *American Way of Death*, 40. See also Ferenc Morton Szasz and Margaret Connell Szasz, *Lincoln and Religion* (Carbondale: Southern Illinois University Press, 2014), 26; Wheeler, "Solving a Lincoln Literary Mystery," 35.

37. Lou Taylor, *Mourning Dress: A Costume and Social History* (New York: Routledge, 1983), 14.

38. Thursby, *Funeral Festivals in America*, 90; Karen Halttunen, *Confidence Men and Painted Women: A Study of Middle-Class Culture in America, 1830–1870* (New Haven, CT: Yale University Press, 1982), 147; Robert de Valcourt, *The Illustrated Manners Book: A Manual of Good Behavior and Polite Accomplishment* (New York: T. C. Leland, 1855), 157.

39. On hearses, see Smart, *Better Place*, 52; and James K. Crissman, *Death and Dying in Central Appalachia: Changing Attitudes and Practices* (Urbana: University of Illinois Press, 1994), 102. On the etiquette for the cortege, see *How to Behave: A Pocket Manual of Republican Etiquette, and Guide to Correct Personal Habits* (New York: Fowler and Wells, 1857), 99.

40. See "Indenture for Cemetery Plot," December 2, 1851, *CW* 2:162. Later, Eddy's body would be moved again to Oak Ridge Cemetery and reinterred next to his father.

41. Clifton D. Bryant, ed., *Handbook of Death and Dying* (Thousand Oaks, CA: Sage, 2003), 1:832.

42. Jeffrey Steele, "The Gender and Racial Politics of Mourning," in Peter N. Stearns and Jan Lewis, eds., *An Emotional History of the United States* (New York: New York University Press, 1998), 93–95.

43. William H. Herndon and Jesse W. Weik, *Herndon's Lincoln* (1889; repr., Urbana: University of Illinois Press, 2006), 473; Smith quoted in William E. Barton, *The Soul of Abraham Lincoln* (1920; repr., Urbana: University of Illinois Press, 2005), 47.

44. Lincoln to John D. Johnston, February 23, 1850, *CW* 2:76–77; see also Joshua Lawrence Schenk, *Lincoln's Melancholy: How Depression Challenged a President and Fueled His Greatness* (New York: Houghton Mifflin, 2005), 107.

45. Schenk, *Lincoln's Melancholy*, 95–98; see also Mary McCartin Wearn, *Negotiating Motherhood in Nineteenth-Century American Literature* (New York: Routledge, 2008), 30–31.

46. *Springfield Illinois Journal*, January 1, 1850; Walter Raleigh Houghton, *American Etiquette and Rules of Politeness* (Chicago: Rand McNally and Co., 1889), 270–73. See also Kate Sweeny, *American Afterlife: Encounters in the Customs of Mourning* (Athens: University of Georgia Press, 2014), 17–20; and Jill Condra, ed., *The Greenwood Encyclopedia of Clothing through World History* (Westport, CT: Greenwood Press, 2008), 3:83; on the differing standards regarding periods of mourning, see Taylor, *Mourning Dress*, 101.

47. "Mourning and Funeral Usages," *Harper's Bazaar*, April 17, 1886.

48. See interview with Mrs. John Todd Stuart, *Chicago Tribune*, February 12, 1900, 14.

49. See, e.g., Larry D. Mansch, *Abraham Lincoln, President-Elect: The Four Critical Months from Election to Inauguration* (New York: McFarland, 2007), 36; Jason Emerson, *The Madness of Mary Lincoln* (Carbondale: Southern Illinois University Press, 2007), 12; and Turner and Turner, *Mary Todd Lincoln*, 40, whose assertions of Mary's collapse and uncontrolled weeping have no visible basis in primary source evidence. Others cite Mrs. John Todd Stuart's interview, *Chicago Tribune*, February 12, 1900, 14, as proof of Mary's desolate emotional state, but a careful reading of this interview shows that Mrs. Stuart did not describe Mary as doing anything other than refusing to eat a meal. Some historians also cite the reminiscences of Mary Edwards Brown to the effect that Mary was entirely unhinged in her grief for Eddy; see Dorothy Meserve Kunhardt, "An Old Lady's Lincoln Memories," *Life*, February 9, 1959, 57, but again, a close reading of this source indicates only that Mary refused a meal. Some might have been confused by a statement earlier in this article to the effect that Mary was "hysterical with grief," but it is not clear exactly who made this assertion (57); possibly it was former Lincoln neighbor Mary Black Remann, but a careful reading suggests that the assertion was actually made by the author of the *Life* magazine article, Kunhardt, and is supported by no apparent primary source evidence.

3. THE IDEAS OF DEATH

1. Dennis F. Hanks, interview with William H. Herndon, June 13, 1865, *HI*, 37; Sarah Bush Lincoln, interview with William H. Herndon, September 8, 1865, *HI*, 107.

2. On the relationship between Abraham and Thomas, see Brian R. Dirck, *Lincoln in Indiana* (Carbondale: Southern Illinois University Press, 2017), 55–68.

3. Lincoln to John D. Johnston, January 12, 1851, *CW* 2:97.

4. See Harold Holzer, *Lincoln and the Power of the Press: The War for Public Opinion* (New York: Simon and Schuster, 2014), 42, 82, 162.

5. *Illinois Daily Journal*, February 7, 1850.

6. Wheeler, "Solving a Lincoln Literary Mystery," 34–46.

7. Michael Burlingame, "Lincoln's Depressions," in *Inner World of Abraham Lincoln*, 103.

8. The text of "Mortality" is available in many places; I used http://www.abraham lincolnonline.org/lincoln/education/knox.htm, accessed August 17, 2015. See also Robert V. Bruce, "The Riddle of Death," in *The Lincoln Enigma: The Changing Faces of an American Icon*, ed. Gabor Boritt (New York: Oxford University Press, 2001), 134–35.

9. Lincoln, "My Childhood-Home I See Again," c. February 25, 1846, *CW* 1:367–70.

10. Lincoln to Andrew Johnston, September 6, 1846, *CW* 1:386.

11. Lincoln to Joshua F. Speed, February 3, 1842, *CW* 1:267; see also Bruce, "Riddle of Death," 136–39.

12. Thomas Bowdler, ed., *The Family Shakespeare in Ten Volumes* (London: Longman, Hurst, Rees, Orme, Browne, and Green, 1825), 10:242.

13. Lincoln to James H. Hackett, August 17, 1863, *CW* 6:392; Bowdler, *Family Shakespeare*, 6:61.

14. Bowdler, *Family Shakespeare*, 6:61

15. Bruce makes this point with particular (and convincing) force in his essay "Riddle of Death," 137–39; Mark S. Schantz, *Awaiting the Heavenly Country: The Civil War and America's Culture of Death* (Ithaca, NY: Cornell University Press, 2008), 44; Isaac Cogdal, interview with William H. Herndon, c. 1865–66, *HI*, 441.

16. On his close study of Blackstone, see Robert B. Rutledge to William H. Herndon, November 30, 1866, *HI*, 426; and Brian R. Dirck, *Lincoln the Lawyer* (Urbana: University of Illinois Press, 2007), chap. 1.

17. William Blackstone, *Commentaries on the Laws of England* (1765; repr., Chicago: University of Chicago Press, 1979), 1:132, 301, 348, 416.

18. Ibid., 1:422.

19. Dirck, *Lincoln the Lawyer*, 54–75.

20. See George R. Dekle Sr.'s excellent overview of these cases in *Prairie Defender: The Murder Trials of Abraham Lincoln* (Carbondale: Southern Illinois University Press, 2017).

21. *People v. Armstrong* (1858), *LPAL*; also Dirck, *Lincoln the Lawyer*, 115–16.

22. Dirck, *Lincoln the Lawyer*, 118; also William Walker to William H. Herndon, June 3, 1865, *HI*, 22.

23. Dirck, *Lincoln the Lawyer*, 22.

24. *Baker v. Addington, et al.* (June 1840), *LPAL*; *Bond v. Barrett, et al.* (August 1850), *LPAL*; *People v. House* (April 1857), *LPAL*; *McLean County Bank and Gridley v. Chicago and Mississippi Railroad* (June 1856), *LPAL*.

25. Lincoln to Jesse W. Fell, Enclosing Autobiography, December 20, 1859, *CW* 3:512.

26. Edward Everett, *Eulogy on Thomas Dowse, of Cambridgeport* (Boston: John Wilson and Son, 1859), 44, 46.

27. Thomas Sewall, *An Eulogy on Dr. Godman, Being an Introductory Lecture, Delivered November 1, 1830* (Washington, DC: W. M. Greer, 1830), 8.

28. Joseph Leonard Tillinghast, *Eulogy Pronounced in Providence, July 17, 1826, upon the Characters of John Adams and Thomas Jefferson* (Providence, RI: Miller and Grattan, 1826), 8.

29. On Lincoln and the Adams funeral, see Lincoln to Henry Slicer, June 1, 1848, *CW* 1:475.

30. Power, *Early Settlers of Sangamon County*, 537; Newton Bateman and Paul Selby, eds., *Historical Encyclopedia of Illinois and History of Sangamon County* (Chicago: Munsell, 1912), 2:613; Lincoln to Joshua F. Speed, February 3, 1842, *CW* 1:268; Lincoln, "Eulogy on Benjamin Ferguson," February 8, 1842, *CW* 1:268–69. Lincoln's reference to Ferguson's role in arbitrating his neighbors' disputes may refer to Ferguson's role as an arbitrator in a court in which Lincoln was involved; see *Hough v. Thomas*, March 1841, *LPAL*.

31. Roy P. Basler, the editor of *The Collected Works of Abraham Lincoln*, noted these errors; see Lincoln, "Eulogy on Zachary Taylor," July 25, 1850, *CW* 2:83–90.

32. *Sangamon Journal*, July 9, 1852.

33. Lincoln, "Eulogy on Henry Clay," July 6, 1852, *CW* 2:122, 126, 130.

34. Lincoln, "Remarks at Closing of the Sanitary Fair, Washington, DC," March 18, 1864, *CW* 7:254.

35. Lincoln, "Speech in Springfield, Illinois," July 17, 1858, *CW* 2:519; see also Robert W. Johannsen, *Stephen A. Douglas* (Urbana: University of Illinois Press, 1997), 655.

36. Lincoln, "Speech in Lewistown, Illinois," August 17, 1858, *CW* 2:547.

37. Lincoln, "Speech in Philadelphia, Pennsylvania," February 22, 1861, *CW* 4:240.

38. Text of Melville's poem, "The Portent," at https://www.poetryfoundation. org/poems-and-poets/poems/detail/45903, accessed August 1, 2016.

39. Ted A. Smith, *Weird John Brown: Divine Violence and the Limits of Ethics* (Stanford, CA: Stanford University Press, 2015), 166; David S. Reynolds, *John Brown, Abolitionist: The Man Who Killed Slavery, Sparked the Civil War, and Seeded Civil Rights* (New York: Alfred A. Knopf, 2005), 108, 130.

40. Reynolds, *John Brown*, 282.

41. Ibid., 322–29.

42. The text of Brown's interview is from http://law2.umkc.edu/faculty/projects /ftrials/johnbrown/browninterview.html, accessed August 4, 2016.

43. Brown indeed consciously laid the groundwork for his own future martyrdom, a point well made by Paul Finkelman in his excellent essay "Manufacturing Martyrdom: The Antislavery Response to John Brown's Raid," in Finkelman, ed., *His Soul Goes Marching On: Responses to John Brown and the Harpers Ferry Raid* (Charlottesville: University of Virginia Press, 1995), 43.

44. Louis DeCaro Jr., ed., *John Brown Speaks: Letters and Statements from Charlestown* (London: Rowman and Littlefield, 2015), 105.

45. Oscar W. Firkins, *Ralph Waldo Emerson* (Mineola, NY: Dover, 2000), 139.

46. J. T. Lloyd, *Henry Ward Beecher: His Life and Work* (London: Walter Scott, 1887), 259; text of Natick resolutions from https://archive.org/details/10928042 .4856.emory.edu, accessed August 5, 2016.

47. On these issues, see the thoughtful nuanced analysis of Brown's martyrdom in Eyal Naveh, "John Brown and the Legacy of Martyrdom," in Peggy A. Russo and Paul Finkelman, eds., *Terrible Swift Sword: The Legacy of John Brown* (Athens: Ohio University Press, 2005), 77–90.

48. Lincoln, "Speech at Elwood, Kansas," November 30 or December 1, 1859, *CW* 3:496.

49. Lincoln, "Speeches at Leavenworth, Kansas," December 3, 1859, *CW* 3:502–3.

50. Lincoln, "Speech at Cooper's Institute," February 27, 1860, *CW* 3:538, 541.

4. ELMER

1. *New York Times*, May 25, 1861; John Hay, "A Young Hero: Personal Reminiscences of Colonel E. E. Ellsworth," *McClure's Magazine* 6 (December 1895–May 1896), 354.

2. Ruth Painter Randall, *Colonel Elmer Ellsworth* (Boston: Little, Brown and Co., 1960), 8–40; Charles A. Ingraham, "Colonel Elmer E. Ellsworth: First Hero of the Civil War," *Wisconsin Magazine of History* 1 (June 1918), 7–9.

3. On Lincoln's mentoring and fatherlike persona to younger men, see Michael Burlingame's perceptive essay "Surrogate Father Abraham," in his *Inner World of Abraham Lincoln*, 73–91, and his observations regarding Lincoln's self-identification with Ellsworth in *Abraham Lincoln: A Life* (Baltimore: Johns Hopkins University Press, 2008), 2:177.

4. Michael Burlingame, ed., *At Lincoln's Side: John Hay's Civil War Correspondence and Selected Writings* (Carbondale: Southern Illinois University Press,

2000), 149; Lincoln to Ephraim D. and Phoebe Ellsworth, May 25, 1861, *CW* 4:385; Randall, *Ellsworth*, 155–56, 210.

5. Hay to William H. Herndon, September 5, 1866, in Burlingame, *At Lincoln's Side*, 123; Ingraham, "Elmer E. Ellsworth," 20; Michael S. Greene, *Lincoln and the Election of 1860* (Carbondale: Southern Illinois University Press, 2011), 102.

6. Ingraham, "Elmer E. Ellsworth," 13–14.

7. Hay, "Young Hero," 356.

8. Herndon and Weik, *Herndon's Lincoln*, 199.

9. Henry A. Buckingham, *Harry Burnham, the Young Continental, or Memoirs of an American Officer during the Campaigns of the Revolution* (New York: Burgess and Garrett, 1851), 255.

10. Lincoln, "Speech before the U.S. House of Representatives," July 27, 1848, *CW* 1:510; autobiography for Jesse N. Fell, December 20, 1859, *CW* 3:512. For a good brief overall discussion of Lincoln's Black Hawk War experiences, see Wilson, *Honor's Voice*, 89–91.

11. Lincoln, "Seventh Debate with Stephen Douglas," October 15, 1858, *CW* 3:316.

12. On Cameron's fitness for the job, or lack thereof, see Paul Kahan, *Amiable Scoundrel: Simon Cameron, Lincoln's Scandalous Secretary of War* (Lincoln: University of Nebraska Press, 2016), 153–55.

13. Lincoln, "Speech in Springfield, Illinois," November 20, 1860, *CW* 4:142–43.

14. Harold Holzer, ed., *Dear Mr. Lincoln: Letters to the President* (Reading, MA: Addison-Wesley, 1993), 341; R. A. Hunt to Lincoln, January 18, 1861, Abraham Lincoln Papers, Library of Congress, Washington, DC; Henry Clay Whitney, *Lincoln the President* (New York: Current Literature, 1909), 319.

15. Only James K. Polk, Millard Fillmore, and Franklin Pierce were younger than Lincoln on the day of their inauguration.

16. Ward Hill Lamon, *Recollections of Abraham Lincoln* (1895; repr., Lincoln: University of Nebraska Press, 1994), 47.

17. Lincoln, "Springfield Farewell Address," February 11, 1861, *CW* 4:190.

18. "A young creole" to Abraham Lincoln, c. 1861, in Holzer, *Dear Mr. Lincoln*, 342; Daniel Stashower, *The Hour of Peril: The Secret Plot to Murder Lincoln before the Civil War* (New York: Minotaur Books, 2013), 56; William H. Herndon to Jesse W. Weik, November 14, 1865, in Douglas L. Wilson and Rodney O. Davis, eds., *Herndon on Lincoln: Letters* (Urbana: University of Illinois Press, 2016), 165.

19. *New York Times*, July 9, 1860.

20. Randall, *Ellsworth*, 214–15.

21. *Exercises Connected with the Unveiling of the Ellsworth Monument, at Mechanicville, May 27, 1874* (Albany, NY: Joel Munsell, 1875), 36.

22. Randall, *Ellsworth*, 148.

23. Michael R. Burlingame and John R. Turner Ettlinger, eds., *Inside Lincoln's White House: The Complete Civil War Diary of John Hay* (Carbondale: Southern Illinois University Press, 1997), 16–17.

24. Ibid., 17; *New York Times*, July 9, 1860; Randall, *Ellsworth*, 237–39.

25. Burlingame and Ettlinger, *Inside Lincoln's White House*, 5; Randall, *Ellsworth*, 237.

26. Robert Colby to Abraham Lincoln, May 18, 1861, Lincoln Papers.

27. Tyler Dennett, ed., *Lincoln and the Civil War in the Diaries and Letters of John Hay* (New York: DaCapo Press, 1988), 8; Burlingame and Ettlinger, *Inside Lincoln's White House*, 12.

28. Lincoln to Elmer Ellsworth, April 15, 1861, *CW* 4:333; Randall, *Ellsworth*, 227; Lincoln, "Draft of Proposed Order Establishing a Military Bureau," March 18, 1861, *CW* 4:291; Lincoln to Simon Cameron, March 5, 1861, *CW* 4: 273; Burlingame, *At Lincoln's Side*, 149.

29. Lincoln to Elmer Ellsworth, April 15, 1861, *CW* 4:333.

30. See Brownell's account in Evert A. Duyckinck, *History of the War for the Union* (New York: Johnson, Fry and Co., 1862), 198–99.

31. Noah Brooks, *Abraham Lincoln: And the Downfall of American Slavery* (New York: G. P. Putnam's, 1896), 274.

32. Ibid., 198–99; *New York Times*, May 27, 1861.

33. *New York Herald*, May 25, 1861.

34. *Life of James W. Jackson, the Alexandria Hero, the Slayer of Ellsworth, the First Martyr in the Cause of Southern Independence* (Richmond, VA: West and Johnson, 1862), 33–34; *New York Herald*, May 25, 1861.

35. *New York Herald*, May 25, 1861.

36. Homer Bates, *Lincoln in the Telegraph Office* (New York: Century Co., 1907), 29; *New York Herald*, May 25, 1861.

37. *New York Times*, May 27, 1861; Margaret Leech, *Reveille in Washington* (New York: NYRB Classics, 2011), 94.

38. On the use of the East Room for state funerals, see Michael Nelson, ed., *Guide to the Presidency* (New York: Routledge Press, 2012), 937. See also Charles A. Church, *Past and Present in the City of Rockford and Winnebago County, Illinois* (Chicago: S. J. Clarke, 1905), 89.

39. Julia Taft Bayne, *Tad Lincoln's Father* (1931; repr., Lincoln: University of Nebraska Press, 2001), 15.

40. Ashley M. Bycock, "Embalming in Memory: Mourning, Narrativity, and Historiography in the Nineteenth-Century United States," PhD diss., Northwestern University, 2008, 178.

41. *New York Times*, May 27, 1861; John Strausbaugh, *City of Sedition: The History of New York City during the Civil War* (New York: Hachette Books, 2010), ii; Leech, *Reveille in Washington*, 94–95.

42. Lincoln to Ephraim D. and Phoebe Ellsworth, May 25, 1861, *CW* 4:385.

43. Harry E. Pratt, *Concerning Mr. Lincoln* (Springfield, IL: Abraham Lincoln Association, 1944), 81.

44. Michael Burlingame, ed., *Lincoln's Journalist: John Hay's Anonymous Writings for the Press, 1860–1864* (Carbondale: Southern Illinois University Press, 1998), 70; Bayne, *Tad Lincoln's Father*, 15; Randall, *Ellsworth*, 264.

45. Lincoln to Ephraim D. and Phoebe Ellsworth, May 25, 1861, *CW* 4:386.

46. Burlingame, *Lincoln's Journalist*, 70; Joseph Medill to Abraham Lincoln, May 25, 1861, Lincoln Papers.

47. *New York Times*, May 25, 1861.

48. *Fremont (OH) Daily Journal*, May 25, 1861. See also "One of Your People" to Abraham Lincoln, May 28, 1861, Lincoln Papers, which characterized Ellsworth's demise as essentially a noncombat death.

49. "Death of Elmer Ellsworth," *Jewish Life in Mr. Lincoln's City*, accessed August 11, 2016, http://www.jhsgw.org/exhibitions/online/lincolns-city/items/show/245; "Secessionist Prisoner Captured at Alexandria, the Marshall House at Alexandria, the Murder of Colonel Ellsworth," *Harper's Weekly*, June 15, 1861.

50. *Life of James W. Jackson*, 9.

51. Randall, *Ellsworth*, 272. On Ellsworth's effect on Northern popular opinion, see generally Adam Stauffer, "'The Fall of a Sparrow': The (Un)timely Death of Elmer Ellsworth and the Coming of the Civil War," *Gettysburg College Journal of the Civil War Era* 1 (2010), 51.

52. Lincoln, "Message to Congress in Special Session," July 4, 1861, *CW* 4:441.

5. WILLIE

1. Bayne, *Tad Lincoln's Father*, 40. Correspondent Noah Brooks wrote a similar tale of Tad waving a "captured Rebel flag" from a White House window in April 1865; one wonders if this was the Ellsworth flag, removed from the drawer yet again. See Michael Burlingame, ed., *Lincoln Observed: Civil War Dispatches of Noah Brooks* (Baltimore: Johns Hopkins University Press, 1998), 182.

2. Elizabeth Keckley, *Behind the Scenes, or Thirty Years a Slave, and Four Years in the Lincoln White House* (New York: G. W. Carleton, 1868), 41. I have chosen throughout this work to spell her last name "Keckly," following the analysis of this issue by Jennifer Fleischner in *Mrs. Lincoln and Mrs. Keckly: The Remarkable Story of the Friendship between a First Lady and a Former Slave* (New York: Broadway Books, 2004). However, her name is spelled "Keckley" in the book she

authored, *Behind the Scenes*, so the citations will use the spelling under which the book was published.

3. Burlingame, *At Lincoln's Side*, 135.

4. Keckley, *Behind the Scenes*, 46; Bayne, *Tad Lincoln's Father*, 107.

5. Bayne, *Tad Lincoln's Father*, 128–29, 132–33.

6. See generally James Marten, *The Children's Civil War* (Chapel Hill: University of North Carolina Press, 1998), esp. chaps. 1, 4.

7. Matthew Pinsker, *Lincoln's Sanctuary: Abraham Lincoln and the Soldiers' Home* (New York: Oxford University Press, 2003), 4–5; P. D. Gurley, "Extracts from an Unpublished Manuscript," in *Lincoln in His Own Time: A Biographical Chronicle of His Life, Drawn from Recollections, Interviews, and Memoirs by Family, Friends, and Associates*, ed. Harold K. Bush (Iowa City: University of Iowa Press, 2011), 65.

8. William H. Herndon to Isaac N. Arnold, October 24, 1883, in Wilson, *Herndon on Lincoln*, 154.

9. Burlingame, *At Lincoln's Side*, 165; Joseph Wallace, *The Life and Public Services of Edward D. Baker, United States Senator from Oregon* (Springfield, IL: Journal Co., 1870), 109–10; *New York World*, October 25, 1861. The counting of nine bullets in his body is related in the *Washington, DC, Daily Republican*, October 24, 1861.

10. Burlingame, *Lincoln Observed*, 215; *New York Tribune*, October 23, 1861.

11. *New York Tribune*, October 23, 1861; also Martin Crawford, ed., *William Howard Russell's Civil War: Private Diary and Letters, 1861–1862* (Athens: University of Georgia Press, 1992), 159.

12. *New York Commercial Advertiser*, October 24 and 31, 1861. The embalming procedure attracted the attention of those "curious to witness the process."

13. Burlingame and Ettlinger, *Inside Lincoln's White House*, 27; J. D. Baltz, *Hon. Edward D. Bates, Senator from Oregon* (Lancaster, PA: Baltz, 1888), 22; Betty Bolles Ellison, *The True Mary Todd Lincoln: A Biography* (Jefferson, NC: McFarland, 2014), 143; Daniel Mark Epstein, *The Lincolns: Portrait of a Marriage* (New York: Ballantine Books, 2008), 244–45.

14. Crawford, *William Howard Russell's Civil War*, 159; Clinton, *Mrs. Lincoln*, 152; Epstein, *Lincolns*, 52. Mary mentions Baker as among the leading luminaries in their social-political circle in her letter to Francis Bicknell Carpenter, December 8, 1865, in Turner and Turner, *Mary Todd Lincoln*, 298.

15. Michael Burlingame, "The Lincolns' Marriage: A Fountain of Misery, of a Quality Absolutely Infernal,'" in *Inner World of Abraham Lincoln*, 220; Epstein, *Lincolns*, 345; H. Donald Winkle, *Lincoln's Ladies: The Women in the Life of the Sixteenth President* (Nashville: Cumberland House, 2004), 149–50.

16. E.g., *New York Commercial Advertiser*, October 24, 1861; *New York Herald*, October 24, 1861; *Washington, DC, Daily National Intelligencer*, October 24 and 25, 1861.

17. Harry C. Blair and Rebecca Tarshis, *The Life of Colonel Edward D. Baker, Lincoln's Constant Ally* (Portland: Oregon Historical Society, 1960), 157. Willie's poem and letter to the *National Republican* are reproduced in Keckley, *Behind the Scenes*, 41–42.

18. Charles Sumner, *An Oration Delivered by Charles Sumner, November 27, 1861* (New York: Young Men's Republican Union, 1861), 5. See also S. U. Deverett to Abraham Lincoln, December 11, 1861, Lincoln Papers.

19. *Salem (MA) Register*, February 27, 1862.

20. I am here following Glenna R. Schroeder-Lein's convincing analysis in *Lincoln and Medicine*, 22–24, which makes a good case for their having contracted typhoid via the basement.

21. Emmeluth, *Typhoid Fever*, 18–30.

22. Ibid., 8–11.

23. Lincoln to Anson G. Henry, July 4, 1860, *CW* 4:82.

24. Keckley, *Behind the Scenes*, 43.

25. *Salem (MA) Register*, February 27, 1862; *Philadelphia Press*, February 21, 1862.

26. For the typhoid treatments common in that era, see Magnus Huss, *Statistics and Treatment of Typhus and Typhoid Fever* (London: Longman, Brown, Green, and Longmans, 1855), esp. 96–180.

27. Some sources suggest that Willie was the first of the two brothers to be taken ill. The first public mention of this illness was in the *New York Tribune*, February 11, 1862, which names only Willie as being sick.

28. Gurley, "Extracts from an Unpublished Manuscript," 63; Bayne, *Tad Lincoln's Father*, 199–200.

29. *New York Evening Post*, February 22, 1862; *Washington, DC, Evening Star*, February 14, 1862; John Nicolay, journal entry for February 18, 1862, in Michael Burlingame, ed., *With Lincoln in the White House: Letters, Memoranda, and Other Writings of John G. Nicolay, 1860–1865* (Carbondale: Southern Illinois University Press, 2006), 182.

30. *Washington, DC, Evening Star*, February 6, 1862; Keckley, *Behind the Scenes*, 42–43.

31. *Washington, DC, Evening Star*, February 19, 1862; Erika Holst, "'One of the Best Women I Ever Knew': Abraham Lincoln and Rebecca Pomeroy," *Journal of the Abraham Lincoln Association* 31 (Summer 2010), 12–16. While Lincoln seems to have been caught off guard by Willie's passing, others saw it coming; see John Nicolay

to Therena Bates, February 21, 1862, in Burlingame, *With Lincoln in the White House*, 71, who wrote that Willie's death had been seen as inevitable for several days.

32. Bayne, *Tad Lincoln's Father*, 199.

33. *Salem (MA) Register*, February 27, 1862; *Providence (RI) Evening Press*, February 12, 1862; *Sandusky (OH) Register*, February 26, 1862; Keckley, *Behind the Scenes*, 43; Nicolay, journal entry for February 20, 1862, in Burlingame, *With Lincoln in the White House*, 71.

34. C. Edwards Lester, *The Light and Dark of the Rebellion* (Philadelphia: George W. Childs, 1863), 144. A good explanation of this "French process" (also later used to preserve Lincoln's body) can be found in E. Lawrence Abel, *A Finger in Lincoln's Brain: What Modern Science Reveals about Lincoln, His Assassination, and Its Aftermath* (Santa Barbara, CA: Praeger, 2015), 117; and Pascale Trompette and Melanie Lemonnier, "Funeral Embalming: The Transformation of a Medical Innovation," *Science Studies* 22 (2009), 12.

35. *Philadelphia Inquirer*, February 24, 1862; *Providence (RI) Evening Press*, February 24, 1862; *Washington, DC, Evening Star*, February 24, 1862; *Newark (NJ) Sentinel of Freedom*, February 25, 1862.

36. Keckley, *Behind the Scenes*, 44. Detailed descriptions of the funeral were published and reprinted throughout the North; see, e.g., *New London (CT) Daily Chronicle*, February 28, 1862; *Washington, DC, Evening Star*, February 24, 1862.

37. Guelzo, *Redeemer President*, 321; David R. Barbee, "President Lincoln and Doctor Gurley," *Abraham Lincoln Quarterly* 5 (March, 1948), 3–24; Grant R. Brodrecht, "'Our Country': Northern Evangelicals and the Union during the Civil War and Reconstruction," PhD diss., University of Notre Dame, 2008, 67. The full text of Gurley's eulogy appears at http://www.abrahamlincolnonline.org/lincoln/education/williedeath.htm, accessed October 2, 2016; and in Gurley, "Extracts from an Unpublished Manuscript," 62–64.

38. *Washington, DC, Evening Star*, February 24, 1862.

39. *Springfield (MA) Republican*, February 28, 1862.

40. Bayne, *Tad Lincoln's Father*, 199.

41. Burlingame, *At Lincoln's Side*, 135; Nathaniel Parker Willis, "Sketch on the Funeral for Willie Lincoln (1862)," in Bush, *Lincoln in His Own Time*, 72.

42. *Springfield (MA) Republican*, February 22 and 28, 1862.

43. Ibid., February 28, 1862.

44. Ibid., February 15, 1862.

45. *New York Evening Post*, February 22, 1862.

46. Mary Lincoln to William A. Newell, December 16, 1862, Turner and Turner, *Mary Todd Lincoln*, 143; Mary Lincoln to James Smith, June 8, 1870, ibid., 568; Mary Lincoln to Mrs. Charles Eames, July 26, 1862, ibid., 131; Mary Lincoln to Hannah Shearer, November 20, 1864, ibid., 189.

47. "Monarch" quote in Anna L. Boyden, *Echoes from Hospital and White House* (Boston: M. A. Lothrop, 1884), 85; Burlingame, *At Lincoln's Side*, 111.

48. Bayne, *Tad Lincoln's Father*, 200; Burlingame, *At Lincoln's Side*, 112; see also Michael Burlingame, "Lincoln and His Sons," in *Inner World of Abraham Lincoln*, 67; Clinton, *Mrs. Lincoln*, 177.

49. Keckley, *Behind the Scenes*, 51; Clinton, *Mrs. Lincoln*, 176.

50. *New York Evening Post*, March 24, 1862; Burlingame and Ettlinger, *Inside Lincoln's White House*, 35.

51. *Springfield (MA) Republican*, February 28, 1862.

52. *Washington, DC, Evening Star*, March 20, 1862; *Portsmouth (NH) Journal of Literature and Politics*, March 22, 1862; *Lowell (MA) Daily Citizen and News*, March 24, 1862.

53. E.g., *Charleston Mercury*, April 2, 1862; *Augusta (GA) Chronicle*, April 5, 1862; *Boston Liberator*, March 17, 1862.

54. *Salem (MA) Register*, June 16, 1862.

55. Mary Lincoln to Ruth Harris, May 17, 1862, Turner and Turner, *Mary Todd Lincoln*, 125–26; *San Francisco Bulletin*, March 8, 1862.

56. Walter Lowenfels, ed., *Walt Whitman's Civil War* (New York: DaCapo Press, 1961), 258. This description of Mary in full black mourning is somewhat at odds with accounts in newspapers in the spring of 1862 that Mary had ordered an expensive bonnet that was constructed for what would have been called "half-mourning," with white and gray trim; *Wisconsin Patriot*, May 10, 1862.

57. The Englishman's description was reprinted in several contemporary newspapers, e.g., *Columbian Register*, June 21, 1862, and also Harold Holzer, ed., *Lincoln as I Knew Him* (Chapel Hill: Algonquin Books, 1999), 120. An extensive analysis of the hat, now in possession of the Smithsonian Institute, appears at http://american history.si.edu/blog/closer-look-president-lincolns-silk-hat, accessed October 27, 2016.

58. *Washington, DC, National Republican*, April 7, 1862; Lincoln to Dorothea Dix, May 4, 1862, *CW* 10:132.

59. Keckley, *Behind the Scenes*, 43.

60. Ibid., 49; *Boston Advertiser*, February 28, 1862.

61. Helm, *True Story of Mary*, 198–99.

62. Keckley, *Behind the Scenes*, 44.

63. Anna Caroline Gentry, interview with William H. Herndon, September 17, 1865, *HI*, 131.

64. Michael Burlingame discussed this in his essay "Lincoln's Attitude toward Women," in *Inner World of Abraham Lincoln*, 131.

65. McDermott, *Mary Lincoln*, 107; for a scanned facsimile, see http://www .shapell.org/manuscript/abraham-lincoln-mary-lincoln-son-willie-dies-white

-house-typhoid, accessed October 25, 2016; Elizabeth Todd Edwards, interview with William H. Herndon, ca. 1865–66, *HI*, 444–45.

66. Howard Glyndon [Laura Catherine Redding Searing], "The Truth about Mrs. Lincoln," *Independent* 1758 (August 10, 1882), 85.

6. GHOSTS

1. Burlingame and Ettlinger, *Inside Lincoln's White House*, 128. See also Lincoln to Major General Burbridge, August 8, 1864, *CW* 7:484–85; Berry, *House of Abraham*, 149–51.

2. Helm, *True Story of Mary*, 225–27.

3. Francis B. Carpenter, *The Inner Life of Abraham Lincoln: Six Months in the White House* (1866; repr., Lincoln: University of Nebraska Press, 1995), 116.

4. Robert Wesley McBride, *Lincoln's Bodyguard, the Union Light Guard of Ohio* (Indianapolis: Edward J. Hecker, 1911), 26–27.

5. *Boston Christian Era*, February 28, 1862.

6. Boyden, *Echoes from Hospital and White House*, 69–70.

7. J. S. Hastings to Abraham Lincoln, August 9, 1861, Lincoln Papers; Lydia Smith to Abraham Lincoln, October 4, 1862, Lincoln Papers; "G.A.A. Wide Awake" to Abraham Lincoln, December 11, 1860, Lincoln Papers; John W. Edmonds to Abraham Lincoln, June 1, 1863, Lincoln Papers.

8. I. B. Conklin to Abraham Lincoln, December 28, 1861, Lincoln Papers.

9. R. A. Beck to Abraham Lincoln, November 30, 1864, Lincoln Papers.

10. Drew Gilpin Faust discusses this surging interest in *This Republic of Suffering*, esp. chap. 6.

11. Beecher's letter reprinted in the *Chicago Independent*, March 20, 1856; *Rockford (IL) Rock River Democrat*, February 7, 1854.

12. "Free love bagnios" quote in *New York Herald*, November 11, 1861; "Millerism" quote from a speech given by a Copperhead in England, reprinted in *New Hampshire Sentinel*, February 24, 1864; comments in a similar vein in *Philadelphia Democratic Leader*, January 10, 1863; "indiscriminately" quote in *Springfield (IL) Daily Illinois State Dealer*, January 21, 1858. For an excellent overview of the relationship between Spiritualism and radical politics, see Mark A. Lause, *Free Spirits: Spiritualism, Republicanism, and Radicalism in the Civil War Era* (Urbana: University of Illinois Press, 2016), esp. chaps. 1–2.

13. Herndon, *Herndon's Lincoln*, 263.

14. *Springfield (IL) Daily Illinois State Register*, December 24, 1858; *Springfield (IL) Daily Illinois State Journal*, March 2, 1858.

15. Susan B. Martinez cites this document, but with no corroboration, in *The Psychic Life of Abraham Lincoln* (Franklin Lakes, NY: Career Press, 2007), 126.

16. Lause, *Free Spirits,* 70–71; Eliab W. Capron, *Modern Spiritualism: Its Facts and Fanaticisms, Its Consistencies and Contradictions* (Boston: Bela Marsh, 1855), 335.

17. The story of the New York medium in *Cleveland Plain Dealer,* February 18, 1861; the endorsement of the Spiritualist Convention in *New York Evening Post,* August 11, 1864; the rumors of Lincoln's Spiritualism in, e.g., *Springfield (MA) Republican,* February 27, 1861; *Portland (ME) Daily Eastern Argus,* September 17, 1863.

18. Joshua Speed to Abraham Lincoln, October 26, 1863, Lincoln Papers.

19. *New York World,* May 25, 1863. See also the September 13, 1863, issue, in which the *World* composed an extended and surely apocryphal story of Lincoln asking Robert Owen for Spiritualist political advice.

20. "A Citizen of Ohio" [David Quinn], *Interior Causes of the War: The Nation Demonized, and Its President a Spirit-Rapper* (New York: M. Doolady, 1863); *New York Semi-Weekly Press,* September 8, 1863. See also *Camden (NJ) Democrat,* March 21, 1863; *Louisville (KY) Daily Democrat,* March 11, 1863.

21. *Philadelphia Illustrated New Age,* August 19, 1864.

22. Nettie Colburn Maynard, *Was Abraham Lincoln a Spiritualist?* (Philadelphia: Rufus C. Hartranft, 1891), 63, 70–74.

23. Lause, *Free Spirits,* 77, argues that Speed may not have known about Colburn's earlier visits to the White House, not having been in Washington for over a year, an "irregular visitor." Perhaps, but if he wrote the letter at Colborn's behest, which seems likely, why then would she not have at least mentioned those earlier encounters to Speed? This surely would have made the letter stronger and more likely to gain her the president's attention.

24. See Lause, *Free Spirits,* 70–72, which takes a more sympathetic view of Colborn and the material she presents in her book.

25. The *Boston Gazette* account was reprinted in, among other places, the *New York Herald,* May 30, 1863; *Portland (ME) Daily Argus,* June 1, 1863; *Manchester (NH) Weekly Union,* June 2, 1863.

26. *New Haven (CT) Columbian Register,* June 13, 1863; *Manchester (NH) Weekly Union,* June 2, 1863. A virulent anti-Lincoln newspaper did use this story to compose an extended indictment of the president; see *Belfast (ME) Republican Journal,* August 21, 1863.

27. William Herndon expressed an ambivalent opinion on this matter, writing to a religious journal in 1885 that he may have "grounds" of the "probability of the fact" that Lincoln attended séances while living in Springfield, but Herndon is so uncharacteristically vague on this matter—admitting that he had no "personal knowledge"—that I am inclined to discount this source entirely; see William

H. Herndon, "Letter from Lincoln's Old Partner," *Religio-Philosophical Journal,* December 12, 1885, 118.

28. *Decatur (IL) Daily Republican,* October 24, 1891.

29. Theodore C. Pease and James G. Randall, eds., *The Diary of Orville Hickman Browning* (Springfield: Illinois State Historical Society, 1925), 1:608.

30. *United States v. Colchester,* 2 Int. Rev. Rec. 70 (1865), https://law.resource. org/pub/us/case/reporter/F.Cas/0025.f.cas/0025.f.cas.0492.pdf, accessed November 9, 2016; *New York Times,* August 27, 1865.

31. Noah Brooks, "Glimpses of Lincoln in Wartime," *Century Magazine* 49 (January, 1895), 462–63.

32. Lamon, *Recollections,* 121; Don E. Fehrenbacher and Virginia Fehrenbacher, eds., *Recollected Words of Abraham Lincoln* (Stanford, CA: Stanford University Press, 1996), 191; Ervin Chapman, *Latest Light on Lincoln and Wartime Memories* (New York: Fleming H. Revell, 1917), 2:505. In 1885, a man named Jack Laurie wrote in a letter to a Spiritualist publication that the president was a frequent visitor to his parents' Washington home and that Lincoln often attended their séances; the story possesses a small whiff of credibility, since Mary did visit the Lauries for Spiritual advice, as documented by Orville Hickman Browning (Pease and Randall, *Diary of Orville Hickman Browning,* 1:608), but as is always the case, there is no corroborating evidence for Abraham having done so, and it is mentioned by no other reliable non-Spiritualist sources. For the text of this letter, see http:// www.iapsop.com/spirithistory/unlocking_the_mystery_of_a_lincoln_relic.html, accessed November 30, 2016.

7. BATTLEFIELDS

1. "Hell" quote in Theodore Poilpot, ed., *A Comprehensive Sketch of the Battle of Manassas* (Washington, DC: Manassas Panorama, 1886), 22; breakfast description in Benson John Lossing, *The Pictorial Field Book of the United States in the Civil War* (Hartford, CT: T. Belknap, 1874), 1:541; William W. Bennett, *A Narrative of the Great Revival Which Prevailed in the Southern Armies* (Philadelphia: Claxton, Pemsro and Haffelfinger, 1878), 125; horse description in Marilyn Seguin, *Dogs of War and Stories of Other Beasts of Battle in the Civil War* (Boston: Branden, 1998), 119.

2. Frank Moore, ed., *The Civil War in Song and Story, 1860–1865* (New York: Peter Fenton Collier, 1865), 65.

3. Robert Hunter Rhodes, ed., *All for the Union: The Civil War Diary and Letters of Elisha Hunt Rhodes* (New York: Random House, 1985), 76.

4. George Washington Herr, *Episodes of the Civil War: Nine Campaigns in Nine States* (San Francisco: Bancroft Co., 1890), 78.

5. Browne, *Every-day Life of Abraham Lincoln,* 105.

6. Charles Carlton Coffin, "Antietam Scenes," *Century Illustrated Monthly Magazine*, 32 (May–October 1886), 318.

7. Cecil D. Eby Jr., ed., *A Virginia Yankee in the Civil War: The Diaries of David Hunter Strother* (Chapel Hill: University of North Carolina Press, 1961), 112–13.

8. *St. Albans (VT) St. Albans Daily Messenger*, August 2, 1861.

9. Letter printed in *Pittsfield (MA) Sun*, October 16, 1862. See also Faust, *This Republic of Suffering*, 14–18.

10. *Worcester Massachusetts Spy*, August 7, 1861.

11. *New York Tribune*, August 31, 1861; *Springfield (IL) Daily Illinois State Journal*, August 8, 1861.

12. *Cincinnati Commercial Tribune*, August 3, 1861.

13. *Concord (NH) Independent Democrat*, August 8, 1861; *Portland (ME) Daily Eastern Argus*, June 1, 1863.

14. Lincoln, "Annual Address to Congress," December 3, 1861, *CW* 5:36; "Message to Congress in Special Session," July 4, 1861, *CW* 4:421–41.

15. Lincoln, "Proclamation of a National Fast Day," August 12, 1861, *CW* 4:482.

16. *New York Herald*, July 25, 1861.

17. Lincoln to General Don Carlos Buell, January 13, 1862, *CW* 5:98.

18. On his denials, William E. Gienapp and Erica L. Gienapp, eds., *The Diary of Gideon Welles, Lincoln's Secretary of the Navy* (Urbana: University of Illinois Press, 2014), 35 and 35n18; Stephen W. Sears, *George B. McClellan: The Young Napoleon* (New York: Ticknor and Fields, 1988), 117–18.

19. Stephen W. Sears, *Landscape Turned Red: The Battle of Antietam* (New Haven, CT: Ticknor and Fields, 1983), 20.

20. George B. McClellan to Mary Ellen McClellan, June 2, 1862, and June 23, 1862, in Stephen W. Sears, ed., *The Civil War Papers of George B. McClellan: Selected Correspondence, 1860–1865* (New York: DaCapo Press, 1992), 287, 306–7.

21. For a detailed rendering of the story, see L. E. Chittenden, *Recollections of President Lincoln and His Administration* (New York: Harper and Bros., 1891), 266–73.

22. Stephen R. Riggs to Abraham Lincoln, November 17, 1862, Lincoln Papers.

23. Donald, *Lincoln*, 365.

24. Lincoln, "Address on Colonization to a Deputation of Negroes," August 4, 1862, *CW* 5:372.

25. Gienapp and Gienapp, *Diary of Gideon Welles*, 65.

26. I have here been aided in reconstructing Lincoln's visit by a most helpful article, Richard E. Clem, "Stories Conflict over Lincoln's Visit to Antietam," *Washington Times*, September 19, 2003, http://www.washingtontimes.com/news/2003/sep/19/20030919-075636-6787r, accessed December 27, 2016.

27. John G. Nicolay and John Hay, "Abraham Lincoln: A History" (New York: Century, 1890), 7:546.

28. Allan Nevins, ed., *A Diary of Battle: The Personal Journals of Colonel Charles S. Wainwright, 1861–1865* (New York: DaCapo Press, 1998), 118.

29. Lamon, *Recollections*, 148.

30. Nevins, *Diary of Battle*, 118.

31. Lamon, *Recollections*, 144. "Manhattan's" account was reprinted in numerous papers, e.g., *Madison (WI) Weekly Wisconsin Patriot*, February 7, 1863; *Macon (GA) Macon Telegraph*, March 10, 1863; *Manchester (NH) Weekly Union*, February 17, 1863; *New York World*, January 27, 1863.

32. *Manchester (NH) Weekly Union*, February 17, 1863. The *New York Sunday Times* piece is reprinted in the *Camden (NJ) Camden Democrat*, January 10, 1863; *San Francisco Bulletin*, February 27, 1863. This may actually be a somewhat mangled reference to an African American musician named John "Picayune" Butler, who enjoyed a measure of popularity during this time, especially for a song called "Picayune Butler's Come to Town"; see Cecelia Conway, *African Banjos in Appalachia: A Study of Folk Traditions* (Knoxville: University of Tennessee Press, 1995), 101.

33. D. M. Demarest to John Hay, August 2, 1864, Lincoln Papers.

34. *Cleveland Plain Dealer*, September 10, 1864; *New Haven (CT) Columbian Register*, October 15, 1864.

35. *Philadelphia Illustrated New Age*, October 22, 1864; *Cincinnati Daily Inquirer*, July 12, 1864; *Madison (WI) Daily Patriot*, November 1, 1864; *Columbus (OH) Daily Ohio Statesman*, October 6, 1864.

36. Samuel Wilkeson to John G. Nicolay, September, 1864, Lincoln Papers.

37. *Philadelphia Illustrated New Age*, November 8, 1864.

38. *Manchester (NH) Weekly Union*, October 11, 1864.

39. Lamon, *Recollections*, 145; *Cincinnati Daily Inquirer*, September 22, 1864.

40. Lincoln, "Memorandum concerning Ward Hill Lamon and the Antietam Episode," September 2, 864, *CW* 7:548–49.

41. Lamon, *Recollections*, 149.

8. CONTROL

1. Lincoln to Thomas H. Clay, October 8, 1862, *CW* 5:452.

2. Lincoln to Simon Cameron, January 10, 1862, *CW* 5:95.

3. Lincoln to George B. McClellan, October 24, 1862, *CW* 5:474.

4. Gienapp and Gienapp, *Diary of Gideon Welles*, 96.

5. W. Roy Mason, "Notes of a Confederate Staff Officer," in Johnson, *Battles and Leaders*, 3:101.

6. *St. Albans (VT) Messenger*, December 25, 1862; *Pittsfield (MA) Sun*, December 25, 1862. See U.S. Congress, *Report of the Joint Committee on the Conduct of the War*, Senate Report No. 71, 37th Cong., 3rd sess. (Washington, DC: Government Printing Office, 1863), 1:2–6; Bruce Tap, *Over Lincoln's Shoulder: The Committee on the Conduct of the War* (Lawrence: University Press of Kansas, 1998), 144–47.

7. *New York World*, December 17, 1862; *Salt Lake City Deseret News*, January 21, 1863; *New York Journal of Commerce*, commentary reprinted in *Boston Post*, December 18, 1862.

8. *Manchester (NH) Weekly Guardian*, December 22, 1862, reprinting an editorial from the *New York World*; *Concord New Hampshire Patriot and State Gazette*, December 31, 1862.

9. *Belfast (ME) Republican Journal*, January 2, 1863.

10. *Springfield (IL) Daily Illinois State Register*, January 8, 1863.

11. *New York World*, December 17, 1862.

12. Lincoln, "Congratulations to the Army of the Potomac," December 22, 1862, *CW* 6:13.

13. *Philadelphia Democratic Leader*, January 3, 1863.

14. *Boston Daily Advertiser*, December 30, 1862.

15. Bates, *Lincoln in the Telegraph Office*, 189.

16. Gienapp and Gienapp, *Diary of Gideon Welles*, 110; Burlingame, *At Lincoln's Side*, 27.

17. *New York Journal of Commerce*, commentary reprinted in *Boston Post*, December 18, 1862.

18. Lincoln, "Annual Message to Congress," December 1, 1862, *CW* 5:537.

19. Lincoln, "Address on Colonization to a Deputation of Negroes," August 14, 1862, *CW* 5:372.

20. Lincoln, "Response to a Serenade," February 1, 1865, *CW* 8:254.

21. *Portland (ME) Daily Advertiser*, September 27, 1862.

22. The "500,000 sons" cartoon at http://452758903693057864.weebly.com/anti-lincoln-cartoons.html, accessed January 11, 2017; bloody sword illustration at http://www.lib.niu.edu/2001/iht820129.html, accessed January 11, 2017; depiction of Lincoln on a field of dead and dying men at http://www.abraham lincolnsclassroom.org/cartoon-corner/president-lincoln/the-commander-in-chief -conciliating-the-soldiers-votes-on-the-battle-field, accessed January 11, 2017.

23. Washington correspondent quoted in *Worcester (MA) National Aegis*, June 13, 1863.

24. *Memphis Avalanche*, editorial reprinted in the *Boston Liberator*, June 14, 1861.

25. Burlingame, *Lincoln Observed*, 13.

26. Lincoln, "Remarks to a Chicago Delegation," September 13, 1862, *CW* 5:420; Lincoln, "Annual Message to Congress," December 1, 1862, *CW* 5:518.

27. Burlingame, *Lincoln: A Life*, 2:446.

28. Lincoln, "Meditation on Divine Will," c. September 1862, *CW* 5:403–4.

29. Lincoln to Cuthbert Bullitt, July 28, 1862, *CW* 5:346.

30. Lincoln, "Proclamation of a National Fast Day," August 12, 1861, *CW* 4:482.

31. Lincoln, "Proclamation Appointing a National Fast Day," March 30, 1863, *CW* 6:155–56.

32. Lincoln to Albert G. Hodges, April 4, 1864, *CW* 7:282.

33. "Eliza W. Farnham: An Unsung Heroine of Gettysburg," https://npsgnmp .wordpress.com/2012/03/02/eliza-w-farnham-an-unsung-heroine-of-gettysburg, accessed January 23, 2017. See also Gregory A. Coco, *A Strange and Blighted Land: Gettysburg, the Aftermath of Battle* (Gettysburg, PA: Thomas, 1995); and Gabor Boritt, *The Gettysburg Gospel: The Lincoln Speech That Nobody Knows* (New York: Simon and Schuster, 2006), 6–10.

34. *New Haven (CT) Palladium*, July 7, 1863.

35. Lincoln, "Response to a Serenade," July 7, 1863, *CW* 6:319–20.

36. Bates, *Lincoln in the Telegraph Office*, 155–56; Gienapp and Gienapp, *Diary of Gideon Welles*, 248.

37. Burlingame and Ettlinger, *Inside Lincoln's White House*, 64–65; Gienapp and Gienapp, *Diary of Gideon Welles*, 295.

38. Lincoln to George Meade, July 14, 1863, *CW* 6:328.

39. Garry Wills, *Lincoln at Gettysburg: The Words That Remade America* (New York: Simon and Schuster, 1992), 20, 55, 89–90.

40. Ibid., 24–27. For a meticulous study of the process by which he wrote the address, see Martin P. Johnson, *Writing the Gettysburg Address* (Lawrence: University Press of Kansas, 2013).

41. James N. Duffy, Gottfried Krueger, and William H. Corbin, *Final Report of the Gettysburg Battle-field Commission of New Jersey* (Trenton, NJ: John L. Murphy, 1890), 6.

42. "Contract for Removing the Dead," *Gettysburg (PA) Adams Sentinel*, http:// www.crossroadsofwar.org/research/newspapers/?id=6934, accessed July 1, 2018; Boritt, *Gettysburg Gospel*, 72–73; Michael Kammen, *Digging Up the Dead: A History of Notable American Reburials* (Chicago: University of Chicago Press, 2010), 102; James M. Paradis, *African Americans and the Gettysburg Campaign* (Lanham, MD: Scarecrow Press, 2005), 57–59; Mark H. Dunkelman, *Gettysburg's Unknown Soldier: The Life, Death, and Celebrity of Amos Humiston* (Westport, CT: Praeger, 1999), 155.

43. Wills, *Lincoln at Gettysburg*, 33, 206–8; *Madison (WI) Weekly Wisconsin Patriot*, November 28, 1863.

44. Boritt, *Gettysburg Gospel*, 91–93.

45. E.g., *New Haven (CT) Palladium*, November 16, 1863; *Philadelphia Illustrated New Age*, November 14, 1863.

46. Lincoln, "Address Delivered at the Dedication of the Ceremony at Gettysburg," November 18, 1863, *CW* 7:18.

47. Ibid., 7:19.

48. As a rule, Lincoln was unwilling to offer any concrete predictions regarding the war's end; see his "Speech to the Philadelphia Sanitary Fair," June 16, 1864, *CW* 7:395.

49. Lincoln, "Speech at a Republican Banquet," December 10, 1856, *CW* 2:385.

9. DUTY

1. *Washington, DC, Daily National Intelligencer*, June 18 and 21, 1864.

2. *Washington, DC, Evening Star*, June 20, 1864; *Springfield (MA) Republican*, June 25, 1864.

3. Gienapp and Gienapp, *Diary of Gideon Welles*, 70.

4. Lincoln to William Seward, June 28, 1862, *CW* 5:292; Lincoln, "Remarks to Union Kentuckians," November 21, 1862, *CW* 5:503.

5. Mark Neely does an excellent job of sorting out the exact context and circumstances of these oft-used quotes; see Neely, *The Civil War and the Limits of Destruction* (Cambridge, MA: Harvard University Press, 2009), 116.

6. Lincoln to Ulysses S. Grant, August 3, 1864, *CW* 7:476.

7. Ulysses S. Grant, *Personal Memoirs of Ulysses S. Grant* (New York: Dover, 1995), 482n.

8. G. Norton Galloway, "Hand to Hand Fighting at Spotsylvania," *Century Magazine* 24 (1887), 307.

9. Ulysses S. Grant to Edwin M. Stanton, May 11, 1864, in John Y. Simon and John F. Marszalek, eds., *The Papers of Ulysses S. Grant* (Carbondale: Southern Illinois University Press, 1982), 10:422; Lincoln to Ulysses S. Grant, August 17, 1864, *CW* 7:499.

10. "City Point National Cemetery, Hopewell, Virginia," *National Park Service*, https://www.nps.gov/nr/travel/national_cemeteries/VIrginia/City_Point_National_Cemetery.html, accessed April 10, 2016.

11. Gienapp and Gienapp, *Diary of Gideon Welles*, 431.

12. Lincoln to Mrs. Sara B. Meconkey, May 9, 1864, *CW* 7:334; Bates, *Lincoln in the Telegraph Office*, 246–47.

13. Lincoln to Ulysses S. Grant, April 30, 1864, *CW* 7:324; Bates, *Lincoln in the Telegraph Office*, 245.

14. Lincoln, "Proclamation to the Friends of Union and Liberty," *CW* 7:333; Lincoln, "Response to a Serenade," May 9, 1864, *CW* 7:334.

15. Jubal A. Early, *A Memoir of the Last Year of the War for Independence* (Philadelphia: R. P. Pryne, 2015), 118.

16. Burlingame and Ettlinger, *Inside Lincoln's White House*, 221; Pease and Randall, *Diary of Orville Hickman Browning*, 675; *Philadelphia Inquirer*, July 14, 1864.

17. Chittenden, *Recollections of President Lincoln*, 428; Burlingame and Ettlinger, *Inside Lincoln's White House*, 221.

18. Burlingame and Ettlinger, *Inside Lincoln's White House*, 222; Gienapp and Gienapp, *Diary of Gideon Welles*, 446.

19. Pease and Randall, *Diary of Orville Hickman Browning*, 676.

20. Keckley, *Behind the Scenes*, 134; *Boston Liberator*, August 26, 1864.

21. *Cincinnati Daily Inquirer*, July 28, 1864.

22. Lincoln to Lydia Bixby, November 21, 1864, *CW* 8:116–17.

23. See Michael Burlingame's analysis of the Bixby letter controversy in his article "New Light on the Bixby Letter," *Journal of the Abraham Lincoln Association* 16 (Winter 1995), 59–71. Burlingame makes a convincing case for Hay as the letter's likely author.

24. E.g., *Boston Liberator*, December 2, 1864; *Hartford (CT) Daily Courant*, November 26, 1864; *Providence (RI) Evening Press*, November 26, 1864; *Worcester (MA) Palladium*, November 30, 1864.

25. *Philadelphia Illustrated New Age*, November 28, 1864; see also *Columbus (OH) Crisis*, December 14, 1864; *Denver (CO) Rocky Mountain News*, December 15, 1864.

26. *Worcester (MA) National Aegis*, December 3, 1864; *Salem (MA) Observer*, December 3, 1864; *Chicago New Covenant*, December 17, 1864; *Boston Recorder*, December 2, 1864. For examples of the minimalist approach of merely reprinting the letter with little additional comment on its contents, see, e.g., in addition to the newspapers cited in the previous note, *Boston Traveler*, November 26, 1864; *Washington (PA) Reporter*, December 7, 1864; *Boston Daily Advertiser*, November 26, 1864; *Frank Leslie's Illustrated Newspaper*, December 24, 1864.

27. Lincoln to Fanny McCullough, December 23, 1862, *CW* 6:16–17.

28. Ibid., 6:17n1.

29. On this point of lack of information regarding dead soldiers, see Faust, *This Republic of Suffering*, esp. chap. 3

30. Lincoln, "Annual Message to Congress," December 8, 1863, *CW* 7:53; Lincoln to William Dennison and Others, June 27, 1864, *CW* 7:411; Lincoln, "Response to Serenade," May 9, 1864, *CW* 7:334.

31. Lincoln, "Speech at Great Central Sanitary Fair," June 16, 1864, *CW* 7:394.

32. Fehrenbacher and Fehrenbacher, *Recollected Words*, 441; Swett to William H. Herndon, January 17, 1866, *HI*, 166.

33. Lincoln, "To Whom It May Concern," December 23, 1863, *CW* 7:89.

34. Burlingame and Ettlinger, *Inside Lincoln's White House*, 64; see also William C. Davis, *Lincoln's Men: How President Lincoln Became Father to an Army and a Nation* (New York: Free Press, 1999), 173–91.

35. Burlingame and Ettlinger, *Inside Lincoln's White House*, 64.

36. Lincoln to Horatio Seymour, August 7, 1863, *CW* 6:370. He also made of this line a bit of a grim joke, telling the story of Confederate conscription agents who "take every man who hasn't been dead more than two days!"; see Paul M. Zall, ed., *Abe Lincoln Laughing: Humorous Anecdotes from Original Sources by and about Abraham Lincoln* (Berkeley: University of California Press, 1982), 112.

37. *Portland (ME) Daily Eastern Argus*, August 26, 1863.

38. Lincoln, "Annual Message to Congress," December 1, 1862, *CW* 5:537.

39. Burlingame and Ettlinger, *Inside Lincoln's White House*, 64; Lincoln to Edwin M. Stanton, January 28, 1864, *CW* 7:158; Lincoln, "To Whom It May Concern," January 18, 1864, *CW* 7:137; Lincoln, "Order Commuting Sentence of Deserters," February 26, 1864, *CW* 7:208.

40. Lincoln, "Speech to One Hundred Sixty-Sixth Ohio," August 22, 1864, *CW* 7:512.

41. He did "congratulate" the 166th Ohio (see ibid.), but his use of the word in this context seems to have been a congratulations that the men had returned home unscathed; in a similar vein, see his "Speech to Forty-Second Massachusetts Regiment," October 31, 1864, *CW* 8:84. His use of "glory" or "glorious" in connection with battlefield sacrifice was likewise very infrequent. He did make a vague reference to recent events "bring[ing] up glorious names" in his "Response to a Serenade" following the Gettysburg and Vicksburg victories, July 7, 1863, *CW* 6:320. He also mentioned the "glorious achievements" of the army in his "Proclamation of Thanksgiving and Prayer," September 3, 1864, *CW* 7:533. But these cases were exceptional. Also, the inclusion of the word *glorious* in the Bixby letter seems to me to reinforce the argument that he did not actually write that letter; Lincoln to Lydia Bixby, November 21, 1864, *CW* 8:117.

42. Lincoln, "Order of Thanks to One Hundred Day Troops from Ohio," September 10, 1864, *CW* 7:547. See also his broader proclamation, "Order of Thanks to One Hundred Day Troops," October 1, 1864, *CW* 8:33.

43. Lincoln, "Reply to Emancipation Memorial," September 13, 1862, *CW* 5:424.

44. *Lowell (MA) Daily Citizen and News*, July 29, 1863.

45. Lincoln to James C. Conkling, August 26, 1863, *CW* 6:410.

46. Ibid., 6:409.

47. Lincoln, "Order of Retaliation," July 30, 1863, *CW* 6:357.

48. Lincoln, "Second Inaugural Address," March 4, 1865, *CW* 8:333.

49. Ibid., 8:332–33.

CONCLUSION

1. For a good description of the wound, see Edward Steers Jr., *Blood on the Moon: The Assassination of Abraham Lincoln* (Lexington: University Press of Kentucky, 2001), 118.

2. Waldo Emerson Reck, *A. Lincoln: His Last 24 Hours* (London: McFarland and Co., 1987), 147–48, 157.

3. John S. Barnes, "With Lincoln from Washington to Richmond in 1865, Part I," *Appleton's Magazine* 9 (May 1907), 519.

4. William H. Crook, "Lincoln's Last Day: New Facts Now Told for the First Time," *Harper's Monthly Magazine* 115 (September 1907): 519.

5. Mary Lincoln to Simon Cameron, April 6, 1866, in Turner and Turner, *Mary Todd Lincoln*, 351–52; Helm, *True Story of Mary*, 225.

6. Reck, *A. Lincoln*, 139. See also Clinton, *Mrs. Lincoln*, 245–47.

7. Keckley, *Behind the Scenes*, 83, 85.

8. *Jackson (MI) Citizen Patriot*, July 19, 1882.

9. Merrill D. Peterson, *Lincoln in American Memory* (New York: Oxford University Press, 1994), 14–22.

10. Zall, *Abe Lincoln Laughing*, 73.

BIBLIOGRAPHY

Abel, E. Lawrence. *A Finger in Lincoln's Brain: What Modern Science Reveals about Lincoln, His Assassination, and Its Aftermath.* Santa Barbara, CA: Praeger, 2015.

Abraham Lincoln Papers. Washington, DC: Library of Congress.

Adams, Michael C. C. *Living Hell: The Dark Side of the Civil War.* Baltimore: Johns Hopkins University Press, 2014.

Aronson, Julie, and Marjorie E. Weiseman. *Perfect Likeness: European and American Portrait Miniatures from the Cincinnati Art Museum.* New Haven, CT: Yale University Press, 2006.

Asher, Florence W. "Women, Wealth, and Power: New York City, 1860–1900." PhD diss., City University of New York, 2006.

Baker, Jean H. *Mary Todd Lincoln: A Biography.* New York: W. W. Norton, 1989.

Baldwin, James. *Abraham Lincoln: A True Life.* New York: American Book Co., 1904.

Baltz, J. D. *Hon. Edward D. Bates, Senator from Oregon.* Lancaster, PA: Baltz, 1888.

Barbee, David R. "President Lincoln and Doctor Gurley." *Abraham Lincoln Quarterly* 5 (March 1948): 3–24.

Baringer, William E. "On Enemy Soil: President Lincoln's Norfolk Campaign." *Abraham Lincoln Quarterly* 7 (March 1952): 4–26.

Barnes, David M. *The Draft Riots in New York, July 1863.* New York: Baker and Godwin, 1863.

Barnes, John S. "With Lincoln from Washington to Richmond in 1865, Part I." *Appleton's Magazine* 9 (May 1907): 519–38.

Bartelt, William E. *"There I Grew Up": Remembering Abraham Lincoln's Indiana Youth.* Indianapolis: Indianapolis Historical Society, 2008.

Barton, William E. *The Soul of Abraham Lincoln*. 1920. Reprint, Urbana: University of Illinois Press, 2005.

Bateman, Newton, and Paul Selby, eds. *Historical Encyclopedia of Illinois and History of Sangamon County*. 2 vols. Chicago: Munsell, 1912.

Bates, Homer. *Lincoln in the Telegraph Office*. New York: Century Co., 1907.

Bates, Samuel P. *History of Pennsylvania Volunteers, 1861–5*. Harrisburg, PA: B. Singerly, 1869.

Bayne, Julia Taft. *Tad Lincoln's Father*. 1931. Reprint, Lincoln: University of Nebraska Press, 2001.

Beidler, Anne E. *The Addiction of Mary Todd Lincoln*. New York: Coffeetown Press, 2009.

Bell, William A. "Games of Boyhood." *Indiana School Teacher* 38 (1893): 555–70.

Benner, Martha L., and Cullom Davis et al., eds. *The Law Practice of Abraham Lincoln: Complete Documentary Edition*. 2nd ed. Springfield: Illinois Historic Preservation Agency, 2009. http://www.lawpracticeofabrahamlincoln.org.

Bennett, William W. *A Narrative of the Great Revival Which Prevailed in the Southern Armies*. Philadelphia: Claxton, Pemsro and Haffelfinger, 1878.

Bergin, Brian. *The Washington Arsenal Explosion: Civil War Disaster in the Capital*. Charleston, SC: History Press, 2012.

Berry, Stephen. *House of Abraham: Lincoln and the Todds, a Family Divorced by War*. New York: Mariner Books, 2009.

Blackstone, William. *Commentaries on the Laws of England*. 4 vols. 1765. Facsimile of the first edition. Chicago: University of Chicago Press, 1979.

Blair, Harry C., and Rebecca Tarshis. *The Life of Colonel Edward D. Baker, Lincoln's Constant Ally*. Portland: Oregon Historical Society, 1960.

Blanchard, Charles. *Counties of Morgan, Monroe, and Brown, Indiana*. Chicago: F. A. Battey, 1884.

Boritt, Gabor. *The Gettysburg Gospel: The Lincoln Speech That Nobody Knows*. New York: Simon and Schuster, 2006.

Bowdler, Thomas, ed. *The Family Shakespeare in Ten Volumes* (London: Longman, Hurst, Rees, Orme, Browne and Green, 1825).

Boyden, Anna L. *Echoes from Hospital and White House*. Boston: M. A. Lothrop, 1884.

Bradley, Chester D. "President Lincoln's Campaign against the Merrimac." *Journal of the Illinois State Historical Society* 51 (Spring 1958): 80–84.

Brodrecht, Grant R. "'Our Country': Northern Evangelicals and the Union during the Civil War and Reconstruction." PhD diss., University of Notre Dame, 2008.

Brooks, Noah. *Abraham Lincoln: And the Downfall of American Slavery*. New York: G. P. Putnam's, 1896.

———. "Glimpses of Lincoln in Wartime." *Century Magazine* 49 (January 1895): 457–67.

———. *Washington in Lincoln's Time*. New York: Century Co., 1895.

Browne, Francis Fisher. *The Every-day Life of Abraham Lincoln*. Chicago: Browne and Howell, 1914.

Bruce, Robert V. "The Riddle of Death." In *The Lincoln Enigma: The Changing Faces of an American Icon*, edited by Gabor Boritt, 130–45. New York: Oxford University Press, 2001.

Bryant, Clifton D., ed. *Handbook of Death and Dying*. 2 vols. Thousand Oaks, CA: Sage, 2003.

Buckingham, Henry A. *Harry Burnham, the Young Continental, or Memoirs of an American Officer during the Campaigns of the Revolution*. New York: Burgess and Garrett, 1851.

Burlingame, Michael. *Abraham Lincoln: A Life*. 2 vols. Baltimore: Johns Hopkins University Press, 2008.

———, ed. *At Lincoln's Side: John Hay's Civil War Correspondence and Selected Writings*. Carbondale: Southern Illinois University Press, 2000.

———. *The Inner World of Abraham Lincoln*. Urbana: University of Illinois Press, 1994.

———, ed. *Lincoln Observed: Civil War Dispatches of Noah Brooks*. Baltimore: Johns Hopkins University Press, 1998.

———, ed. *Lincoln's Journalist: John Hay's Anonymous Writings for the Press, 1860–1864*. Carbondale: Southern Illinois University Press, 1998.

———. "New Light on the Bixby Letter." *Journal of the Abraham Lincoln Association* 16 (Winter 1995): 59–71.

———, ed. *With Lincoln in the White House: Letters, Memoranda, and Other Writings of John G. Nicolay, 1860–1865*. Carbondale: Southern Illinois University Press, 2006.

Burlingame, Michael, and John R. Turner Ettlinger, eds. *Inside Lincoln's White House: The Complete Civil War Diary of John Hay*. Carbondale: Southern Illinois University Press, 1997.

Bush, Harold K., ed. *Lincoln in His Own Time: A Biographical Chronicle of His Life, Drawn from Recollections, Interviews, and Memoirs by Family, Friends, and Associates*. Iowa City: University of Iowa Press, 2011.

Bycock, Ashley M. "Embalming in Memory: Mourning, Narrativity, and Historiography in the Nineteenth-Century United States." PhD diss., Northwestern University, 2008.

Cady, John F. "The Religious Environment of Lincoln's Youth." *Indiana Magazine of History* 37 (March 1941): 16–30.

Capron, Eliab W. *Modern Spiritualism: Its Facts and Fanaticisms, Its Consistencies and Contradictions.* Boston: Bela Marsh, 1855.

Carpenter, Francis B. *The Inner Life of Abraham Lincoln: Six Months in the White House.* 1866. Reprint, Lincoln: University of Nebraska Press, 1995.

Carruthers, Oliver, and R. Gerald McMurtry. *Lincoln's Other Mary.* Chicago: Ziff-Davis, 1946.

Chapman, Ervin. *Latest Light on Abraham Lincoln and War-Time Memories.* 2 vols. New York: Fleming H. Revell, 1917.

Chittenden, L. E. *Recollections of President Lincoln and His Administration.* New York: Harper and Bros., 1891.

Church, Charles A. *History of Rockford and Winnebago County, Illinois.* Rockford, IL: W. P. Lamb, 1900.

———. *Past and Present in the City of Rockford and Winnebago County, Illinois.* Chicago: S. J. Clarke, 1905.

A Citizen of Ohio [David Quinn]. *Interior Causes of the War: The Nation Demonized, and Its President a Spirit-Rapper.* New York: M. Doolady, 1863.

Clem, Richard E. "Stories Conflict over Lincoln's Visit to Antietam." *Washington Times,* September 19, 2003, http://www.washingtontimes.com/news/2003/sep/19/20030919-075636-6787r, accessed December 27, 2016.

Clinton, Catherine. *Mrs. Lincoln: A Life.* New York: HarperCollins, 2009.

Cockrum, William Monroe. *Pioneer History of Indiana.* Oakland City, IN: Press of the Oakland City Journal, 1907.

Coco, Gregory A. *A Strange and Blighted Land: Gettysburg, the Aftermath of Battle.* Gettysburg, PA: Thomas, 1995.

Coffin, Charles Carlton. "Antietam Scenes." *Century Illustrated Monthly Magazine* 32 (May–October 1886): 316–46.

Coffin, Margaret. *Death in Early America: The History and Folklore of Customs and Superstitions of Early Medicine, Funerals, Burials, and Mourning.* Nashville: Thomas Nelson, 1976.

Colman, Penny. *Corpses, Coffins, and Crypts: A History of Burial.* New York: Henry Holt and Co., 1997.

Condra, Jill, ed. *The Greenwood Encyclopedia of Clothing through World History.* Westport, CT: Greenwood Press, 2008.

Condrau, Flurin, and Michael Worboys, eds. *Tuberculosis Then and Now: Perspectives on the History of an Infectious Disease.* Montreal: McGill-Queen's University Press, 2010.

Conway, Cecelia. *African Banjos in Appalachia: A Study of Folk Traditions.* Knoxville: University of Tennessee Press, 1995.

Crawford, Martin, ed. *William Howard Russell's Civil War: Private Diary and Letters, 1861–1862.* Athens: University of Georgia Press, 1992.

Crawford, Mary M., ed. "Mrs. Lydia B. Bacon's Journal, 1811–1812." *Indiana Magazine of History* 40 (December 1944): 367–86.

Crissman, James K. *Death and Dying in Central Appalachia: Changing Attitudes and Practices.* Urbana: University of Illinois Press, 1994.

Crook, William H. "Lincoln's Last Day: New Facts Now Told for the First Time." *Harper's Monthly Magazine* 115 (September 1907): 517–23.

Davis, William C. *Lincoln's Men: How President Lincoln Became Father to an Army and a Nation.* New York: Free Press, 1999.

DeCaro, Louis, Jr., ed. *John Brown Speaks: Letters and Statements from Charlestown.* London: Rowman and Littlefield, 2015.

Dekle, George R., Sr. *Prairie Defender: The Murder Trials of Abraham Lincoln.* Carbondale: Southern Illinois University Press, 2017.

Dennett, Tyler, ed. *Lincoln and the Civil War in the Diaries and Letters of John Hay.* New York: DaCapo Press, 1988.

Dirck, Brian R. *Lincoln in Indiana.* Carbondale: Southern Illinois University Press, 2017.

———. *Lincoln the Lawyer.* Urbana: University of Illinois Press, 2007.

Donald, David Herbert. *Lincoln.* New York: Simon and Schuster, 1995.

Duffy, James N., Gottfried Krueger, and William H. Corbin. *Final Report of the Gettysburg Battle-field Commission of New Jersey.* Trenton, NJ: John L. Murphy, 1890.

Dunkelman, Mark H. *Gettysburg's Unknown Soldier: The Life, Death, and Celebrity of Amos Humiston.* Westport, CT: Praeger, 1999.

Duyckinck, Evert A. *History of the War for the Union.* New York: Johnson, Fry and Co., 1862.

Dyer, Carol A. *Biographies of Disease: Tuberculosis.* Santa Clara, CA: Greenwood Press, 2010.

Early, Jubal A. *A Memoir of the Last Year of the War for Independence.* Philadelphia: R. P. Pryne, 2015.

Eby, Cecil D., Jr., ed. *A Virginia Yankee in the Civil War: The Diaries of David Hunter Strother.* Chapel Hill: University of North Carolina Press, 1961.

Ellison, Betty Bolles. *The True Mary Todd Lincoln: A Biography.* Jefferson, NC: McFarland, 2014.

Emerson, Jason. *Giant in the Shadows: The Life of Robert T. Lincoln.* Carbondale: Southern Illinois University Press, 2012.

———. *The Madness of Mary Lincoln.* Carbondale: Southern Illinois University Press, 2007.

Emmeluth, Donald. *Typhoid Fever.* Philadelphia: Chelsea House, 2004.

Epstein, Daniel Mark. *The Lincolns: Portrait of a Marriage.* New York: Ballantine Books, 2008.

Everett, Edward. *Eulogy on Thomas Dowse, of Cambridgeport.* Boston: John Wilson and Son, 1859.

Exercises Connected with the Unveiling of the Ellsworth Monument, at Mechanicville, May 27, 1874. Albany, NY: Joel Munsell, 1875.

Facchinetti, Fabio, Gustaaf A. Dekker, Dante Baronciani, and George Saade, eds. *Stillbirth: Understanding and Management.* Boca Raton, FL: CRC Press, 2010.

Farrell, James J. *Inventing the American Way of Death, 1830–1920.* Philadelphia: Temple University Press, 1980.

Faust, Drew Gilpin. *This Republic of Suffering: Death and the American Civil War.* New York: Alfred A. Knopf, 2007.

Fehrenbacher, Don E., and Virginia Fehrenbacher, eds. *Recollected Words of Abraham Lincoln.* Stanford, CA: Stanford University Press, 1996.

Finkelman, Paul, ed. *His Soul Goes Marching On: Responses to John Brown and the Harpers Ferry Raid.* Charlottesville: University of Virginia Press, 1995.

Finkelman, Paul, and Martin J. Hershock, eds. *The Political Lincoln: An Encyclopedia.* Washington, DC: CQ Press, 2008.

Finley, James Bradley. *Autobiography of Rev. James B. Finley, or Pioneer Life in the West.* Cincinnati: R. P. Thompson, 1858.

Firkins, Oscar W. *Ralph Waldo Emerson.* Mineola, NY: Dover, 2000.

Fleischner, Jennifer. *Mrs. Lincoln and Mrs. Keckly: The Remarkable Story of the Friendship between a First Lady and a Former Slave.* New York: Broadway Books, 2004.

Flood, Charles Bracelen. *1864: Lincoln at the Gates of History.* New York: Simon and Schuster, 2009.

Fuller, Thomas, and William Pickering. *Good Thoughts in Bad Times.* London: Pickering, 1841.

Galloway, G. Norton. "Hand to Hand Fighting at Spotsylvania." *Century Magazine* 24 (1887): 307–19.

Gerritsen, Jan-Willem. *The Control of Fuddle and Flash: A Sociological History of the Regulation of Alcohol and Opiates.* Leiden, Netherlands: Koninklijke, 2000.

Gienapp, William E., and Erica L. Gienapp, eds. *The Diary of Gideon Welles, Lincoln's Secretary of the Navy.* Urbana: University of Illinois Press, 2014.

Giesberg, Judith Ann. *Civil War Sisterhood: The U.S. Sanitary Commission and Women's Politics in Transition.* Boston: Northeastern University Press, 2000.

Glyndon, Howard [Laura Catherine Redding Searing]. "The Truth about Mrs. Lincoln." *Independent* 1758 (August 10, 1882): 82–87.

Goodspeed, Weston A., and Charles Blanchard. *Counties of Whitley and Noble, Indiana.* Chicago: F. A. Battey, 1882.

Gouverneur, Marian. *As I Remember: Recollections of American Society during the Nineteenth Century.* New York: D. Appleton and Co., 1911.

Grant, Ulysses S. *Personal Memoirs of Ulysses S. Grant.* New York: Dover, 1995.

Greene, Michael S. *Lincoln and the Election of 1860.* Carbondale: Southern Illinois University Press, 2011.

Guelzo, Allen C. *Abraham Lincoln as a Man of Ideas.* Carbondale: Southern Illinois University Press, 2009.

———. *Abraham Lincoln: Redeemer President.* Grand Rapids, MI: William B. Eerdman's, 1999.

Gunn, John C. *Gunn's Domestic Medicine, or The Poor Man's Friend.* Pittsburgh: Edwards and Newman, 1839.

Gurley, P. D. "Extracts from an Unpublished Manuscript." In Bush, *Lincoln in His Own Time*, 62–65.

Haberstein, Robert, and William Lamer. *The History of American Funeral Directing.* 5th ed. New York: National Funeral Directors Assoc., 2001.

Halttunen, Karen. *Confidence Men and Painted Women: A Study of Middle-Class Culture in America, 1830–1870.* New Haven, CT: Yale University Press, 1982.

Harris, William C. *Lincoln's Rise to the Presidency.* Lawrence: University Press of Kansas, 2007.

Harrison, John. *Robert Owen and the Owenites in Britain and America.* New York: Routledge Press, 2010.

Hay, John. "A Young Hero: Personal Reminiscences of Colonel E. E. Ellsworth." *McClure's Magazine* 6 (December 1895–May 1896): 354–61.

Helm, Katherine. *The True Story of Mary, Wife of Lincoln.* New York: Harper, 1928.

Herndon, William H. "Letter from Lincoln's Old Partner." *Religio-Philosophical Journal*, December 12, 1885, 118.

Herndon, William H., and Jesse W. Weik. *Herndon's Lincoln.* 1889. Reprint, Urbana: University of Illinois Press, 2006.

Herr, George Washington. *Episodes of the Civil War: Nine Campaigns in Nine States.* San Francisco: Bancroft Co., 1890.

Hirsch, David, and Dan Van Haften. *Abraham Lincoln and the Structure of Reason.* New York: Savas Beatie, 2010.

History of Greene and Sullivan Counties, State of Indiana, from the Earliest Time to the Present. Chicago: Goodspeed Bros. and Co., 1884.

History of Warrick, Spencer, and Perry Counties. Chicago: Goodspeed and Co., 1885.

Hobson, Jonathan Todd. *Footprints of Abraham Lincoln.* Dayton, OH: Otterbein Press, 1909.

Holst, Erika. "'One of the Best Women I Ever Knew': Abraham Lincoln and Rebecca Pomeroy." *Journal of the Abraham Lincoln Association* 31 (Summer 2010): 12–20.

Holzer, Harold, ed. *Dear Mr. Lincoln: Letters to the President.* Reading, MA: Addison-Wesley, 1993.

———. *Lincoln and the Power of the Press: The War for Public Opinion.* New York: Simon and Schuster, 2014.

———, ed. *Lincoln as I Knew Him.* Chapel Hill: Algonquin Books, 1999.

Houghton, Walter Raleigh. *American Etiquette and Rules of Politeness.* Chicago: Rand McNally and Co., 1889.

Howe, Henry. *Historical Recollections of Ohio.* Cincinnati: Bradley and Anthony, 1850.

Howe, James C., comp. *Official Roster of the Soldiers of the State of Ohio.* Norwalk, OH: Laning Co., 1895.

How to Behave: A Pocket Manual of Republican Etiquette, and Guide to Correct Personal Habits. New York: Fowler and Wells, 1857.

Humphreys, Margaret. *Marrow of Tragedy: The Health Crisis of the American Civil War.* Baltimore: Johns Hopkins University Press, 2013.

Huntington, Tom. *Searching for George Gordon Meade: The Forgotten Victor of Gettysburg.* Mechanicsburg, PA: Stackpole Books, 2013.

Hurd, Duane Hamilton. *History of Essex County, Massachusetts.* Philadelphia: J. W. Lewis, 1888.

Huss, Magnus. *Statistics and Treatment of Typhus and Typhoid Fever.* London: Longman, Brown, Green, and Longmans, 1855.

Hyde, Bill, ed. *The Union Generals Speak: The Meade Hearings on the Battle of Gettysburg.* Baton Rouge: Louisiana State University Press, 2003.

Ingraham, Charles A. "Colonel Elmer E. Ellsworth: First Hero of the Civil War." *Wisconsin Magazine of History* 1 (June 1918): 4–34.

Jackson, Charles O., ed. *Passing: The Vision of Death in America.* Westport, CT: Greenwood Press, 1977.

Johannsen, Robert W. *Stephen A. Douglas.* Urbana: University of Illinois Press, 1997.

Johnson, Don. *Thirteen Months at Manassas/Bull Run.* Jefferson, NC: McFarland and Co., 2013.

Johnson, Martin P. *Writing the Gettysburg Address.* Lawrence: University Press of Kansas, 2013.

Johnson, Robert Underwood, ed. *Battles and Leaders of the Civil War.* 4 vols. New York: Castle Books, 2010.

Jones, Mary Ellen. *Daily Life on the Nineteenth Century American Frontier.* Westport, CT: Greenwood Press, 1998.

Jordan, Philip D. "The Death of Nancy Hanks Lincoln." *Indiana Magazine of History* 40 (June 1944): 103–10.

Kahan, Paul. *Amiable Scoundrel: Simon Cameron, Lincoln's Scandalous Secretary of War.* Lincoln: University of Nebraska Press, 2016.

Kammen, Michael. *Digging Up the Dead: A History of Notable American Reburials.* Chicago: University of Chicago Press, 2010.

Kaufmann, J. E., and H. W. Kaufmann. *Fortress America: The Forts That Defended America, 1600 to the Present.* New York: DaCapo, 2004.

Keckley, Elizabeth. *Behind the Scenes, or Thirty Years a Slave, and Four Years in the Lincoln White House.* New York: G. W. Carleton, 1868.

Kunhardt, Dorothy Meserve. "An Old Lady's Lincoln Memories." *Life,* February 9, 1959, 57–59.

Lamon, Ward Hill. *Recollections of Abraham Lincoln.* 1895. Reprint, Lincoln: University of Nebraska Press, 1994.

Lause, Mark A. *Free Spirits: Spiritualism, Republicanism, and Radicalism in the Civil War Era.* Urbana: University of Illinois Press, 2016.

Lavender, David. *Climax at Bella Vista: The Decisive Battle of the Mexican-American War.* Philadelphia: University of Pennsylvania Press, 1966.

Leavitt, Judith Walzer, and Ronald L. Numbers. *Sickness and Health in America: Readings in the History of Medicine and Public Health.* Madison: University of Wisconsin Press, 1978.

Leech, Margaret. *Reveille in Washington.* New York: NYRB Classics, 2011.

Lester, C. Edwards. *The Light and Dark of the Rebellion.* Philadelphia: George W. Childs, 1863.

Lewis, Walter H., and Memory P. F. Elvin-Lewis. *Medical Botany: Plants Affecting Human Health.* 2nd ed. Hoboken, NJ: John Wiley and Sons, 2003.

Life of James W. Jackson, the Alexandria Hero, the Slayer of Ellsworth, the First Martyr in the Cause of Southern Independence. Richmond, VA: West and Johnson, 1862.

Lincoln, Abraham. *The Collected Works of Abraham Lincoln.* Edited by Roy P. Basler. 9 vols. New Brunswick, NJ: Rutgers University Press, 1953.

Lloyd, J. T. *Henry Ward Beecher: His Life and Work.* London: Walter Scott, 1887.

Lossing, Benson John. *The Pictorial Field Book of the United States in the Civil War.* 3 vols. Hartford, CT: T. Belknap, 1874.

Lowenfels, Walter, ed. *Walt Whitman's Civil War.* New York: DaCapo Press, 1961.

Luciano, Dana. *Arranging Grief: Sacred Time and the Body in Nineteenth-Century America.* New York: New York University Press, 2007.

Madkour, M. Monir. *Tuberculosis.* New York: Springer, 2004.

Manning, Alan. *Father Lincoln: The Untold Story of Abraham Lincoln and His Boys—Robert, Eddy, Willie, and Tad.* Guilford, CT: Lyons Press, 2016.

Mansch, Larry D. *Abraham Lincoln, President-Elect: The Four Critical Months from Election to Inauguration.* New York: McFarland, 2007.

Mansfield, Edward Deering. *The Mexican War.* New York: A. S. Barnes and Co., 1849.

Mansfield, Stephen. *Lincoln's Battle with God: A President's Struggle with Faith and What It Meant for America.* Nashville: Thomas Nelson, 2012.

Marten, Benjamin. *A New Theory of Consumptions*. London: R. Knapock, 1720.

Marten, James. *The Children's Civil War*. Chapel Hill: University of North Carolina Press, 1998.

Martinez, Susan B. *The Psychic Life of Abraham Lincoln*. Franklin Lakes, NY: Career Press, 2007.

Maynard, Nettie Colburn. *Was Abraham Lincoln a Spiritualist?* Philadelphia: Rufus C. Hartranft, 1891.

McBride, Robert Wesley. *Lincoln's Bodyguard, the Union Light Guard of Ohio*. Indianapolis: Edward J. Hecker, 1911.

McClary, Ben H. "Introducing a Classic: 'Gunn's Domestic Medicine,'" *Tennessee Historical Quarterly* 45 (Fall 1986): 210–16.

McClure, Alexander K. *Abraham Lincoln and Men of War Times*. 4th ed. 1892. Reprint, Lincoln: University of Nebraska Press, 1996.

McDermott, Stacy Pratt. *Mary Lincoln: Southern Girl, Northern Woman*. New York: Routledge, 2015.

McPherson, James M. *Tried by War: Abraham Lincoln as Commander in Chief*. New York; Penguin Books, 2008.

The Medical and Surgical History of the Civil War. 12 vols. Wilmington, NC: Broadfoot, 1990–91.

Moore, Frank, ed. *The Civil War in Song and Story, 1860–1865*. New York: Peter Fenton Collier, 1865.

Morton, Joseph W., Jr., ed. *Sparks from the Campfire*. Philadelphia: Keystone, 1893.

Nash, Roderick. *Wilderness and the American Mind*. 5th ed. New Haven, CT: Yale University Press, 2014.

Neely, Mark E. *The Civil War and the Limits of Destruction*. Cambridge, MA: Harvard University Press, 2009.

Nelson, Michael, ed. *Guide to the Presidency*. New York: Routledge Press, 2012.

Nevins, Allan, ed. *A Diary of Battle: The Personal Journals of Colonel Charles S. Wainwright, 1861–1865*. New York: DaCapo Press, 1998.

Nicolay, John G., and John Hay. "Abraham Lincoln: A History." 10 vols. New York: Century, 1890.

North, Thomas. *Five Years in Texas*. Cincinnati: Elm Street Printing, 1871.

Ostendorf, Lloyd and Walter Oleksy, eds. *Lincoln's Unknown Private Life: An Oral History by His Black Housekeeper Mariah Vance, 1850–1860*. Mamaroneck, NY: Hastings House, 1995.

Paradis, James M. *African Americans and the Gettysburg Campaign*. Lanham, MD: Scarecrow Press, 2005.

Paull, Bonnie E., and Richard E. Hart. *Lincoln's Springfield Neighborhood*. Charleston, SC: History Press, 2015.

Pease, Theodore C., and James G. Randall, eds. *The Diary of Orville Hickman Browning.* 2 vols. Springfield: Illinois State Historical Society, 1925.

Peterson, Merrill D. *Lincoln in American Memory.* New York: Oxford University Press, 1994.

Pierson, Arthur Tappan. *Zachariah Chandler: An Outline Sketch of His Life and Public Services.* Detroit: Post and Tribune Co., 1880.

Pine, Vanderlyn R. *Caretaker of the Dead: The American Funeral Director.* New York: Irvington, 1975.

Pinsker, Matthew. *Lincoln's Sanctuary: Abraham Lincoln and the Soldiers' Home.* New York: Oxford University Press, 2003.

Poilpot, Theodore, ed. *A Comprehensive Sketch of the Battle of Manassas.* Washington, DC: Manassas Panorama, 1886.

Porte, Joel, and Saundra Morris, eds. *The Cambridge Companion to Ralph Waldo Emerson.* Cambridge: Cambridge University Press, 1999.

Power, John Carroll. *History of the Early Settlers of Sangamon County, Illinois.* Springfield, IL: Edwin A. Wilson and Co., 1876.

Pratt, Harry E. *Concerning Mr. Lincoln.* Springfield, IL: Abraham Lincoln Association, 1944.

Quinn, Sandra L., and Sanford Kantor. *American Royalty: All the President's Children.* Westport: Greenwood Press, 1995.

Randall, Ruth Painter. *Colonel Elmer Ellsworth.* Boston: Little, Brown and Co., 1960.

Rankin, Henry B. *Personal Recollections of Abraham Lincoln.* New York: Putnam and Sons, 1916.

Reck, Waldo Emerson. *A. Lincoln: His Last 24 Hours.* London: McFarland and Co., 1987.

Reynolds, David S. *John Brown, Abolitionist: The Man Who Killed Slavery, Sparked the Civil War, and Seeded Civil Rights.* New York: Alfred A. Knopf, 2005.

Rhodes, Robert Hunter, ed. *All for the Union: The Civil War Diary and Letters of Elisha Hunt Rhodes.* New York: Random House, 1985.

Rice, Allen Thorndike. *Reminiscences of Abraham Lincoln by Distinguished Men of His Time.* New York: Harper and Bros., 1909.

Rosenberg, Charles E. *Right Living: An Anglo-American Tradition of Self-Help Medicine and Hygiene.* Baltimore: Johns Hopkins University Press, 2003.

Russo, Edward J., and Curtis R. Mann. *Oak Ridge Cemetery.* Charleston, SC: Arcadia, 2009.

Russo, Peggy A., and Paul Finkelman, eds. *Terrible Swift Sword: The Legacy of John Brown.* Athens: Ohio University Press, 2005.

Sanchez-Eppler, Karen. *Dependent States: The Child's Part in Nineteenth-Century American Culture.* Chicago: University of Chicago Press, 2005.

Sandburg, Carl. *Mary Lincoln: Wife and Widow.* 1932. Reprint, Bedford, MA: Applewood Books, 1995.

Schantz, Mark S. *Awaiting the Heavenly Country: The Civil War and America's Culture of Death.* Ithaca, NY: Cornell University Press, 2008.

Schenk, Joshua Lawrence. *Lincoln's Melancholy: How Depression Challenged a President and Fueled His Greatness.* New York: Houghton Mifflin, 2005.

Schroeder-Lein, Glenna R. *Lincoln and Medicine.* Carbondale: Southern Illinois University Press, 2012.

Sears, Stephen W., ed. *The Civil War Papers of George B. McClellan: Selected Correspondence, 1860–1865.* New York: DaCapo Press, 1992.

———. *George B. McClellan: The Young Napoleon.* New York: Ticknor and Fields, 1988.

———. *Landscape Turned Red: The Battle of Antietam.* New Haven, CT: Ticknor and Fields, 1983.

"Secessionist Prisoner Captured at Alexandria, the Marshall House at Alexandria, the Murder of Colonel Ellsworth." *Harper's Weekly,* June 15, 1861.

Seguin, Marilyn. *Dogs of War and Stories of Other Beasts of Battle in the Civil War.* Boston: Branden, 1998.

Sewall, Thomas. *An Eulogy on Dr. Godman, Being an Introductory Lecture, Delivered November 1, 1830.* Washington, DC: W. M. Greer, 1830.

Simon, John Y. "Abraham Lincoln and Ann Rutledge." *Journal of the Abraham Lincoln Association* 11 (1990): 13–33.

Simon, John Y., and John F. Marszalek, eds. *The Papers of Ulysses S. Grant.* 32 vols. Carbondale: Southern Illinois University Press, 1967–present.

Sjöqvist, Suzanne, ed. *Still Here with Me: Teenagers and Children on Losing a Parent.* Translated by Margaret Myers. London: Jessica Kingsley, 2007.

Smart, Susan. *A Better Place: Death and Burial in Nineteenth-Century Ontario.* Toronto: Dundurn Press, 2011.

Smith, Ted A. *Weird John Brown: Divine Violence and the Limits of Ethics.* Stanford, CA: Stanford University Press, 2015.

Sotos, John G. *The Physical Lincoln.* Mt. Vernon, VA: Mt. Vernon Book Systems, 2008.

Springate, Megan E. *Coffin Hardware in Nineteenth-Century America.* Walnut Creek, CA: Left Coast Press, 2015.

Stashower, Daniel. *The Hour of Peril: The Secret Plot to Murder Lincoln before the Civil War.* New York: Minotaur Books, 2013.

Stauffer, Adam. "'The Fall of a Sparrow': The (Un)timely Death of Elmer Ellsworth and the Coming of the Civil War." *Gettysburg College Journal of the Civil War Era* 1 (2010): 44–52.

Stearns, Peter N., and Jan Lewis, eds. *An Emotional History of the United States.* New York: New York University Press, 1998.

Steers, Edward, Jr. *Blood on the Moon: The Assassination of Abraham Lincoln.* Lexington: University Press of Kentucky, 2001.

Strausbaugh, John. *City of Sedition: The History of New York City during the Civil War.* New York: Hachette Books, 2010.

Sumner, Charles. *An Oration Delivered by Charles Sumner, November 27, 1861.* New York: Young Men's Republican Union, 1861.

Sweeny, Kate. *American Afterlife: Encounters in the Customs of Mourning.* Athens: University of Georgia Press, 2014.

Szasz, Ferenc Morton, and Margaret Connell Szasz. *Lincoln and Religion.* Carbondale: Southern Illinois University Press, 2014.

Tap, Bruce. *Over Lincoln's Shoulder: The Committee on the Conduct of the War.* Lawrence: University Press of Kansas, 1998.

Taylor, Lou. *Mourning Dress: A Costume and Social History.* New York: Routledge, 1983.

Thursby, Jacqueline S. *Funeral Festivals in America: Rituals for the Living.* Lexington: University Press of Kentucky, 2006.

Tillinghast, Joseph Leonard. *Eulogy Pronounced in Providence, July 17, 1826, upon the Characters of John Adams and Thomas Jefferson.* Providence, RI: Miller and Grattan, 1826.

Trompette, Pascale, and Melanie Lemonnier. "Funeral Embalming: The Transformation of a Medical Innovation." *Science Studies* 22 (2009): 9–30.

Tucker, E. *History of Randolph County, Indiana.* Chicago: A. L. Klingman, 1852.

Turner, Justin G., and Linda Levitt Turner, eds. *Mary Todd Lincoln: Her Life and Letters.* New York: Alfred A. Knopf, 1972.

U.S. Congress. *Report of the Joint Committee on the Conduct of the War.* Senate Report No. 71, 37th Cong., 3rd sess. Washington, DC: Government Printing Office, 1863, 1:2–6.

Valcourt, Robert de. *The Illustrated Manners Book: A Manual of Good Behavior and Polite Accomplishment.* New York: T. C. Leland, 1855.

Van Natter, Francis Marion. *Lincoln's Boyhood: A Chronicle of His Indiana Years.* New York: Public Affairs Press, 1963.

Volkmann, Carl, and Roberta Volkmann, *Springfield's Sculptures, Monuments, and Plaques.* Charleston, SC: Arcadia, 2008.

Wagstaff, D. Jesse. *International Poisonous Plants Checklist: An Evidence-Based Reference.* New York: Taylor and Francis, 2008.

Wallace, Joseph. *The Life and Public Services of Edward D. Baker, United States Senator from Oregon.* Springfield, IL: Journal Co., 1870.

Wearn, Mary McCartin. *Negotiating Motherhood in Nineteenth-Century American Literature*. New York: Routledge, 2008.

Weik, Jesse William. *The Real Lincoln: A Portrait*. Boston: Houghton Mifflin, 1922.

Wheeler, Samuel P. "Solving a Lincoln Literary Mystery: 'Little Eddie.'" *Journal of the Abraham Lincoln Association* 33 (Summer 2012): 34–46.

White, Ronald C., Jr. *A. Lincoln: A Biography*. New York: Random House, 2009.

Whitney, Henry Clay. *Lincoln the President*. New York: Current Literature, 1909.

Williams, Frank J., and Michael Burkhimer, eds. *The Mary Lincoln Enigma: Historians on America's Most Controversial First Lady*. Carbondale: Southern Illinois University Press, 2012.

Williams, T. Harry. *Lincoln and His Generals*. New York: Alfred A. Knopf, 1952.

Willis, Nathaniel Parker. "Sketch on the Funeral for Willie Lincoln (1862)." In Bush, *Lincoln in His Own Time*, 71–73.

Wills, Garry. *Lincoln at Gettysburg: The Words That Remade America*. New York: Simon and Schuster, 1992.

Wilson, Douglas L. *Honor's Voice: The Transformation of Abraham Lincoln*. New York: Alfred A. Knopf, 1998.

Wilson, Douglas L., and Rodney O. Davis, eds. *Herndon on Lincoln: Letters*. Urbana: University of Illinois Press, 2016.

———, eds. *Herndon's Informants: Letters, Interviews, and Statements about Abraham Lincoln*. Urbana: University of Illinois Press, 1998.

Wilson, Robert. *Mathew Brady: Portraits of a Nation*. New York: Bloomsbury, 2013.

Wilson, Rufus Rockwell, ed. *Intimate Memories of Lincoln*. Elmira, NY: Primavera Press, 1945.

Winkle, H. Donald. *Lincoln's Ladies: The Women in the Life of the Sixteenth President*. Nashville: Cumberland House, 2004.

Worden, J. William. *Children and Grief: When a Parent Dies*. London: Guildford Press, 2001.

Wright, Carrie Douglas. *Lincoln's First Love: A True Story*. Chicago: A. C. McClurg and Co., 1901.

Zall, Paul M., ed. *Abe Lincoln Laughing: Humorous Anecdotes from Original Sources by and about Abraham Lincoln*. Berkeley: University of California Press, 1982.

INDEX

Swedenborg, Emanuel, 30
Swett, Leonard, 162

Taft, Bud, 84–85, 87
Taft, Julia, 71–72, 76, 84–85, 90
Taylor, Zachary, 48, 70
Thirteenth Amendment, 138
Thornton, John, 164
threnody, 39
Tillinghast, Joseph, 47
tremetol, 11
tuberculosis, 24–25
Turner, Nat, 52
typhoid fever, 20, 82–83

undertaking, 28

Vance, Mariah, 25, 35
Vicksburg, Siege of, 143

Wallace, William S., 24–25
Washington, George, 103
Washington Arsenal fire, 151–52, 157

Washington Temperance Society, 48
Webb, James W., 79–80
Webster, Daniel, 102
Webster, Thomas H., 1
Welles, Gideon, 83, 100, 103, 125, 137, 144, 154–55, 157
Welles, Mary Jane, 83, 100, 104
Welsh, John, 1
Whig Party, 27, 48, 50, 83
Whitman, Walt, 91
Whitney, Henry, 62
Wilberforce, Wilbur, 103
Wilderness Campaign, 153–55
Wills, Garry, 145
Wilson, Charles L., 48
Wilson, Henry, 70
Wilson's Creek, Battle of, 115, 120
Wood, William, 12, 15

Yates, T. S., 118

Zouaves, 59, 63–66, 77

BRIAN R. DIRCK is a professor of history at Anderson University in Indiana. He is the author of numerous books and articles on Abraham Lincoln and the Civil War era, including *Lincoln in Indiana*; *Lincoln and Davis: Imagining America, 1809–1865*; *Lincoln the Lawyer*; *Lincoln and the Constitution*; and *Abraham Lincoln and White America*.